BLUE COLLAR WOMEN

Trailblazing Women Take on Men–Only Jobs

BLUE COLLAR WOMEN

Trailblazing Women Take on Men–Only Jobs

Trudie C. Ferguson

with Madeline Sharples

New Horizon Press, Liberty Corner, New Jersey

Requests for permission should be addressed to:
New Horizon Press
P.O. Box 669
Far Hills, NJ 07931

Ferguson, Trudi, with Madeline Sharples.
        Blue Collar Women : Trailblazing women take on men-only jobs

Library of Congress Catalog Card Number: 93-61690

ISBN: 0-88282-092-3 (hc)
ISBN: 0-88282-093-1 (pb)
New Horizon Press

Manufactured in the U.S.A.

1998 1997 1996 1995 1994 / 5 4 3 2 1

(*Photo insert begins after page 127)

CONTENTS

PART I.....Opening The Doors—Again.....1

What's It All About, Rosie?.....6
The Meeting.....18
The Women At Work.....24

PART II.....The Work.....28

What Exactly Do These Women Do?.....30
Requirements.....40
Motivation.....48
Dirty Deals.....67

PART III.....Behind The Scenes.....77

Sexual Harassment And Discrimination.....79
Other Ways To Solve A Harassment Problem.....93

PART IV.....All It Takes Is A Little Attitude.....104

How To Get Around What's Around....108
Jumping Over The HighBar.....119

PART V.....Lifestyles.....132

Where They Come From.....134
Their Families And Their Lives.....147
The Gay Working Life.....158

PART VI.....What We've Learned From These Women.....175

Lessons Learned.....176
Advice.....186

PART VII.....Find And Keep Nontraditional Jobs.....190

The Steps To Getting Involved.....192
The Issues.....197
Some Recent Exapmles.....214

Resources.....239

PART I

OPENING THE DOORS—AGAIN

"This is the only place I know where women with little or no education can earn good money while getting on the job training and a great skill."
Madeline Mixer, Labor Economist, Women's Bureau

This book is about women who work. Not the white collar working women who only earn 75 percent of the salary of their male colleagues or the pink collar working women who barely make living wages. These women work in blue collar "men's" jobs. Not only do they do these jobs and like what they do, they often earn exactly what male workers earn in the same profession. This book is an investigation into the secrets of what they do, how they get along, how they live their lives, and what the rest of us can learn from them.

Here we see brave women, who have interests and life experiences that push and pull them to these jobs. They are the legions of real life Rosie the Riveters in overalls and red bandannas—police, firefighters, plumbers, teamsters, service writers, electricians, ironworkers and welders—who in this book emerge from behind closed doors into the spotlight; so we can squarely look at them. See their faces and what lined them; hear their laughter; learn their inner thoughts, hopes, and difficulties; see their clothes, bodies, and find out about the options and obstacles that other women will face if they want to join them.

Here we learn how some of these women have to struggle against assaults, running the gamut from overt hiring barriers to subtle rejections and discrimination. We find out that many of these women come from nontraditional backgrounds filled with grief, poor educational opportunities, early pregnancies and difficult childhoods. However, we also see that these harsh beginnings sometimes harden the will so that these women have the strength to go outside the boundaries and lead the way. One woman states, "I'm not a trailblazer, not a follower," and that not only doesn't bother her in the least it raises her self esteem.

This is a study of the conditions that foster such courage and boldness, resulting in satisfaction and contribution. We look at what leads to women finding new and fulfilling roles, enabling them to get off welfare, support their children, and be engaged citizens. We also see what leads to others defeat, lack of choice and stifling roles.

Why Are Some Men So Disturbed?

Traditional men don't understand these new women. They aren't used to them. Instead of being their sexual partners, or objects, women who take blue collar jobs are colleagues, and sometimes grimy colleagues, at that. Most working class men have been raised in a macho culture. Behavioral rituals, figures of speech, intricate and unexamined details of work life and ingrained routines are shaken. Having women on the job makes many men examine themselves. That is a hard thing for anybody.

In the 1960s and early 1970s women were deliberately kept out of the trades. The men who already worked in these jobs biggest objections were that there were no separate toilet facilities. Their excuses were many: women want separate facilities, women don't want to get dirty, women don't last, they get pregnant and then how could they do the job?

"It's the men's last bastion," Mixer says. "They had the trades to themselves for 200 years and they are not about to give up easily." Many men tell women anything to keep them out of the trades, and women, especially the less experienced, believe them. We know that a large percentage of men are against women in the trades. So are a large percentage of women.

Since historically the world of work revolved around men, it's easy to understand why. Our information about work has primarily come from the male point of view. In former eras, social standing came from men's occupations. A woman gathered recognition only through her husband and family. Even though society and the family structure have radically changed, many of our male -oriented concepts have not.

However, work is not a static endeavor. Occurring in a larger social context, work is inextricably linked to changing family structures. Work is also linked to the economy in general, to our notions of gender appropriate activities, to how we divide labor duties and to how we portray and educate our children.

Previously, when a large percentage of people lived in traditional families, the definition of men as the breadwinners and women as the homemakers made sense. Now, fewer women have traditional long-term marriages. The meaning of work for these women has fundamentally changed. Work is no longer secondary to childrearing, but has emerged as a centerpiece in their lives. Thus, they look to their work as a means of fulfilling different goals—primary income, meaning, satisfaction, fulfillment. Work has also assumed some of the old functions of the traditional family.

With this radical shift for this percentage of the population comes resounding implications for the rest of us. Nontraditional women are not distinct and cut off from our lives. Their numbers are growing. They are linked tightly to our total social fabric. We must understand and respond in order to maintain the health of our society.

Why Is This Study Significant?

Today there are more and more women in the trades and other women, who have many of the same goals and problems are asking why.

Their reasons vary. For instance "I'm a labor economist, working for the Women's Bureau," says Mixer, "and I don't want to say women are in this for the money—but people, men and women, are in this for the money. How else can many women get off welfare and get apprenticeships that provide good on the job paid training with benefits. They acquire skills they can take anywhere in the country. There are very few requirements. Women who have to work forty hours per week, support children, disabled husbands and elderly parents, who can't go to college and get a graduate degree, can apprentice, hang in there and earn a good living."

Many of the women to whom we talked echoed Mixer's assessment. They felt that money translates into economic freedom which translates into status—and options like, "I can buy my own house," or, "Do I want to go to Europe or buy a boat?" Perhaps dissatisfied women in traditional white collar professions can learn from this. If blue collar women get equal pay for equal work, why don't they?

The other attraction is that many women like blue collar work and the atmosphere. It's a healthy balance of working with the head and hands.

This study also chronicles a social shift. Today's women in the trades challenge commonly held cultural assumptions. They offer healthy models of working on concrete, tangible life-sustaining projects, like buildings and bathtubs and drains. They reject indoor jobs that tie them to desks and computers under fluorescent lights. They offer a new physical image of women, looking more natural, more robust and they expand our definition of women's interests and capabilities. They offer a changing image of family lives not with men at the helm but with women as the primary wage earners.

These pages also reveal stories that don't often get told. Women in nontraditional jobs tell how they got there and why. They talk about their needs and desires. The better lives they have created for themselves and their families, and what they've had to do to fit into their new job atmosphere. For instance, some women in the trades deliberately try to disguise the fact that they are female, because it cuts down on discrimination, harassment and resentment. These women sometimes consciously try to look like men, attempting to have a unisex look instead of being conspicuously female; the only woman on an all-male work crew.

Part of the revolution is also a change of dress. A some traditional women have been taught to preen and doll up to attract men. However, trades women aren't trying to attract men. Self esteem in their jobs is not based on how they look but on whether they do their jobs as well as men do. They sometimes work in places with no bathrooms, let alone mirrors. In construction and other hard-hat jobs as well as laboring jobs like plumbing, becoming dirty or grimy is just part of the job description. It isn't possible to be fastidious about cleanliness on the job in such occupations, because there isn't time to clean up after each task. In these jobs, completing one's scheduled duties on time is the name of the game.

The Secret Is Out!

Good jobs that require no education or experience are out there for women. These jobs, like almost no others, offer women workers the exact same pay as men. In this study we've peeked into the lives and work of uncommon women making uncommon choices. We've seen the emergence of common themes and the appearance of previously unseen options. Like polishing tarnished silver, wiping away the dirt and corrosion, the hard work of careful rubbing reveals a shining precious metal.

ONE

WHAT'S IT ALL ABOUT, ROSIE?

"For all of them, slacks have become the badge of honor."
    Columnist Max Lerner, Fabulous Century:
    1940-50, Time Life Books Inc.Alexandria, VA

It all began during World War II. The men had gone off to war, and suddenly the women were pushed out of the kitchen and into high paying nontraditional professions. A change came over the feminine psyche as the nation began viewing women in another way. In fact, 2.9 million women donned blue collars and went off to their daily jobs in the factories and shipyards. The revolution had begun. Rosie the Riveter was born.

In Creating Rosie the Riveter, Maureen Honey detailed the aggressive campaign to get women into the work force. Conducted by an alliance of big business, government and advertisers hell bent on keeping their good name before the public, the campaign emphasized every woman's patriotic need and duty to take nontraditional jobs. The propaganda, actively contributed to by the government through the Office of War Information and the Magazine Bureau, emphasized that the women had skills for industrial jobs, because they could do such domestic tasks as running an electric mixer in the kitchen.

Women's wartime wages were high, giving them economic power and freedom. This transformation planted the seeds of change. A secret became common knowledge. Women now realized they could work successfully in "men's jobs", once thought to require masculine skills, and still be married with children. Their employers now saw that the women could do these men's jobs competently, causing an eighty percent increase in women in the labor force—from almost eleven million to eighteen million.

However, contrary to popular myth, most of these women had prior work experience. Though three-quarters of them were married, only one-third started out as homemakers. The rest came from lower paying, more traditional women's jobs. War labor shortages were particularly acute in skilled metal trades, aircraft, shipping and small ammunition assembly; all fields that paid higher wages and offered more stimulating work than traditional female occupations.

After the war the women went back into their homes or into low paying, more traditional jobs. No longer were advertisers or employers displaying supportive images of women in traditional male jobs. The propaganda now worked in reverse, enticing them to return home with such images as modern sewing machines adorned with bright chrome trim. Honey suggests that the nature of the war propaganda associated women's war-time work with patriotic duty, rather than with self actualization, and so the ensuing transition of women back into the home and the campaign for consumerism was easy and natural. The new transition was framed in such a way that it conveyed the idea that women did not give up men's jobs that gave them satisfaction and fulfillment, but jobs they had temporarily stepped into, to save their country.

Despite this propaganda, a Women's Bureau 1945 survey of women industrial workers showed that approximately eighty percent wanted to continue working. Nevertheless, while forty-five percent of women production workers had been employed in higher paying durable goods industry in November, 1943, only twenty-five percent of these workers were in such jobs by November, 1946 ("Women's

History Network News," p. 1, October 1991, National Women's History Project).

Honey suggests that the media, particularly magazines, promoted the image of strong, capable women making a contribution to war time, then reverted to images of domestic women content with dish washers and mix masters in their kitchens as soon as the men came marching home. Betty Friedan's *The Feminine Mystique,* published in 1963, pointed out that prior to World War II, heroines from magazine fiction were self-actualizing achievers committed to following a dream, whereas the postwar heroine was devoid of goals for personal growth. She asked, "Was this a desire to return to stability and traditional gender roles? The image of women that emerges is young and frivolous, almost childlike, fluffy and feminine, passive, gaily content in a world of bedroom and kitchen, sex, babies and home."

The following passage from *Wanted: Women in War Industry* by Laura Baker, was written in 1943 in an effort to recruit women to the effort. Difficulties of the experience were framed as an "experiment." Women were praised for "helping Uncle Sam." This is the language that launched women into their first nontraditional jobs—so different than the modern day character assassinations of nontraditional workers:

"It is a revelation to me to observe the way our first group of girls got down to work in one of the plants of the Todd Shipyards Corporation. They were skeptical and so were we. Never before in this country had there been a woman shipyard worker. As a matter of fact, when I toured the Todd Erie Basin Dry Docks in Brooklyn on my first day with the Todd Corporation, I learned I was the first female to set foot on the soil since the yard was opened in 1869.

"But the girls gritted their teeth, rolled up their sleeves and said, 'Let's go!' Every step we took had to be an experiment because there was no experience table to go by, but before long it became clear to us that the scheme would work. With polishing up here and there, we were convinced we'd be able to train enough women to take care of a good part of the vacancies caused by the men being drafted into the armed forces.

"There are women working in most of the Todd shipbuilding and ship repair yards today and they're doing a wonderful job helping Uncle Sam keep the ships sailing. They come to work in the wee hours of the morning dressed in their coveralls and swinging lunch pails. They're not afraid to get their hands and faces covered with grease because they mean business. They're fighting mad now and tackle their jobs as shipfitters, tinsmiths, carpenters, welders, burners, electricians, machinists, firemen and crane operators with a zest that makes your heart beat faster.

"Working conditions are not the pleasantest—it's heavy and dirty work—and the women have to work out in the open in all kinds of weather. But the point is, they're doing it without a complaint and with no flag waving. They know the job must be done and if the rest of our women could get into that spirit, half the fight would be over."

A woman hired by the Vocational Division of the United States Office of Education to see why women quit work shortly after entering employment in the shipyards also wrote:

"Turnover of trained personnel is expensive in peace time but in war time it is inexcusable. Before the war the price of inefficiency could be measured in dollars; today it can be measured only in lives.

"Take this from one who knows, you women who are free to enter war industries and have not yet done so. You have a job to do. The satisfaction you will gain from it is unequaled. One day you will straighten up from your work and look about you, as I did, at your gang, your leadman, your hull, your yard. And as your ship slides gracefully down the skids you will know that it is your war, and that you have had a tangible part in helping to win it."

Who were these women who filled these war year jobs? Where are they? Their secrets are locked away behind wrinkles that belie the important historical role they played. They may seem to have taken on traditional roles easily and happily but their own stories are intricately intertwined with a decaying social experiment. What were their motivations and how do they feel about their jobs and experiences? What did they notice and feel as they participated in what turned out to be the beginning of a fundamental social change?

Most organizations we contacted that so boldly recruited these pioneer women had no independent records of who they were, where they went and if they were still alive. We did not find associations of early tradeswomen or directories of early wartime industrial women workers. No archive or association collectively honors or groups these women. Most remain nameless and faceless, lumped together as a mass representing a social phenomena. Mostly these women are tucked away. They are grandmothers and retirees, hard to identify, without much sense of their own unique place in history. Sadly, many don't realize the importance of the revolutionary role they played in the labor market and in changing male/female, gender and family relationships. They are not consulted for the wisdom they obtained as a result of their unique place in history. They are silenced by anonymity; unable to inform us as we are left to struggle to make sense of the aftermath of that social change.

Through word of mouth and inquiry we were able to identify a few of them. They were surprised we wanted to contact them to learn about their work history. Unassuming and unselfconscious, they had to collect their thoughts about the long ago experience, left to the dusty recesses of their youth. It seemed that almost none had thought about the meaning of that early work experience or elevated it to any special status. Yet, seen in the light of today, we researchers know they had their feet in both worlds: the traditional woman domestic and the manual laborer who was the first of our industrial age to get dirty alongside the men.

We asked those older women we could find a variety of questions. Some of them were: What were their motivations, attitudes and work experiences? How were they treated before, during and after the war? How did they feel about their own experiences? We asked ourselves: Are there lessons we can learn from them about the beginning of a major social shift which just now is awakening from its nearly thirty-year dormancy?

For most of them, we learned, motivation was patriotism, dovetailed with the same driving force we see today—money. Many women needed jobs. Husbands went off to war, maybe never to come back, leaving very young untrained wives alone without support. Young single women whose fathers were itinerant laborers with a lot of children to support simply needed jobs. The war was an incentive—an opportunity—an opening. Women with a variety of motives and attitudes rushed in. They found skepticism, fun, camaraderie, mates and dirty work, somewhat like women entering these blue collar fields find today. However, what was missing was the derision and anger some women find today. The necessity of the war effort made these earlier women welcome. The spirit was different than the displacement we find today in our declining competitive economy where "blue collar women" are often seen as taking the men's jobs and roles. One woman describes how more discrimination crept in more after the war.

Prior to that the general image they communicated was one of innocence. They were young girls giggling, experimenting and participating in an adventure. They were allowed to join and to demonstrate their ability. However, so competently did these first pioneering women do these jobs that the course of our social landscape changed forever.

Lois "Honey" Leen, Industrial Worker During World War II, Seventy-four Years Old

Now working for a modest salary as a historian for the women's movement, she, more than most, has a sense of the value of women's participation in the war effort.

"Actually it was my husband's idea for me to go to trade school. My husband was going to war and he thought he might not come back. I just fell into it. I went to Cogswell Polytechnic in San Francisco. I had only two years in junior college. I was nineteen years old and had never had a job.

"I was one of those women who worked at a nontraditional job during World War II. I worked as a draftsman. It was considered to be a man's job. I worked for Lockheed and Marinship, Sergeant Locks and Hardware which I didn't like so I went to Winchester Repeating Arms in Massachusetts. I followed my husband. Then I worked for Standard Oil and Western Oil.

"It was interesting for me, but the worst was the discrimination. It was better during the war. However, when the men started going back to work, the attitude was, 'we can get back to normal.' They didn't try to fire me because they were aware of my personal situation. I divorced my husband during the war. Besides that, I did good work. They would be hell bent to find anyone to work better than I did. Women had to be better in the first place. But, the attitude after that was you girls get back into the kitchen."

Frances Cuevas, Railroad and Defense Plant Worker During World War II, Seventy-four Years Old

This humble and self effacing grandmother was surprised that anyone would be interested in her experiences working at what she simply thought of as her youthful job.

"We worked for Southern Pacific. We used to ride on the train. A whole bunch of girls came from Mountain View. We commuted on the train which took about an hour. We had to get up real early. We had fun. I was young. Everybody was sociable. I enjoyed work. We swept the floors. All the girls together and the guys. They were really friendly and helpful. At Southern Pacific we just wore slacks and kerchiefs to cover your hair. Then they made me an oiler—a helper—oiling the machinery, using an oil cup. Oh, it was an awful dirty job working where the trains are. There's a lot of machinery in there. We used to climb up and grease the machinery out of the cups.

"At Southern Pacific we were getting eighty-seven cents an hour and then in Sunnyvale about $1.11 at Handy's Defense Plant. We used to wear the coveralls—darn it, I never did take a picture in my uniform. You had to buy your own clothes. We'd wash up real good. At Handy's we had nice overalls, light blue a little darker than power blue. They were nice. Everybody had the same coveralls and caps. It was nice there. They really had the modern machinery. They made airplane parts. I used to have an oil can and I'd go around and oil the machinery. They told us what to do and then we'd go around and remember where all the little holes were. It was a job and I had to work. I couldn't be choosy. We were helping the war, but we were helping ourselves too because we needed the money. We were seven and my father was a laborer—a gardener. He didn't have any kind of job seasonal work. The men were happy to have women working around them—you know how they are. I got to tell you I married one of them. He was a 4F that's why he didn't go to war. He had a problem with his hearing. I was single at the time I was working, but I didn't work when I was married.

"To me it was a just a job and I was happy to be working because so many women were out of a job. Now I'm seventy-four years old. My parents are Spanish. I've had three children and two husbands.

"I worked all my life. Before the war I worked in a cannery after I dropped out of high school. When the war was over I got married, and had children and still worked part time in San Francisco. I worked in the bakery packing cookies, Continental Baking. I was happy with all the jobs. My sister and I started working at about fifteen years old in the cannery. We had to write down we were eighteen years old but they needed the help so bad they didn't care as long as you'd do the work. But, I was tall, 5 feet 5 inches, a big girl, and I was able to do the work."

We wondered if this cheerful attitude, this conviviality and sense of fun reflects Frances' personality or the general atmosphere of social endorsement that existed during the war. One of our early hypotheses was that social backing and girls riding the train together, girls working and "tackling their jobs" in a way that "makes your heart beat faster" might result in a much easier adjustment for women in these jobs today.

Leslie Wake, First Female Dockworker in the Country, Fifty-one Years Old

Leslie is one contemporary woman who had an early foot in the modern world of nontraditional work. She represents the transition from Rosie the Riveter to the women we are profiling in the rest of this book. Her story describes the early experiences of women moving into these fields.

"I'm really historic. I have worked twenty years as a Marine Dockworker. I am the first female in this category in the country. I showed up at my first shift January 11, 1974 at 8:00 a.m. I am a Teamster. I am like a rare animal at the zoo.

"Our job is to load and unload detachable containers. They've recently modernized and mechanized this industry. In the twenty years I've worked as a dock worker there has been increasing refinement in mechanization. I worked a lot harder, personally, in the first five years, than young men coming in today.

"Men gradually accepted me. But I tell them, 'In the old days even you couldn't have done it.' It used to be everything going into a ship had to be loaded into a truck or movable object on wheels, and then thrown on the ground and longshoreman would load it on palettes. Now we do it with forklifts, stuff lashed and swung over the hatch and then a crew of men pick it up and move it into the hole where it had to go. Now it's much easier to drive the container into the nose. You can raise the palette up and then back out. Containers were twenty-five or thirty-five to forty pounds but now we've converted to forty or forty-five pounds. There are more and more regulations, which helps because you don't have to keep adjusting the crane.

"In the old days, loading as I did, you walk in, look back and just see this little light. Unloading, standing in the nose of the container, I have actually turned around and found strange men standing in the container. One guy just said, 'I came to see you. I heard there was a woman doing the work and I drove an extra five miles; and there you are.' The teamster boss, Gunner Hansen, this monster man, called me his little teamster. He'd tell people I could lift 200 pounds over my head, count two, and the men loved me.

"I had a goal for the first time—I cared about money. I had a resolve. I had fallen for the 'okey dokey' and was sure I could do it. I had been close to a B.A. at college and fortunately majored in anthropology, which is the study of different sub cultures. If I hadn't done that I might never have made it. I remember loading cargo and I'd hear men, not talking to me, talking to each other laughing. I would get these flushes. Now I would call it a shame attack. This is the height of egotism. They've known each other for so long. Sometimes I would get angry and feel so alone. I would talk to myself. I had a few women friends through the CLUW—Congress of Labor Union Women. But no other women. Nobody else had this experience.

"There were several stages in which men accepted me and several groups at different times. Now I am part of the groups. I realize now it was difficult for the men. American men were really separated from women at the work place. Blue collar men have a particular language about which they feel ambivalent. They feel pride and would rather say fuck you than excuse me, but at the same time they feel improper and want people to accept them. That's the way they are but then they feel maybe they aren't exactly proper.

"I had lots of counter culture experience. In 1969 I was selected for one of ten worthy student awards in the state. I was the top student. I went to Lewis and Clark, then Montana State University, then Long Beach City College. I was in and out of many different schools, but I had a lot of patience, and I finally finished.

"I was raised in Red Rock Valley in New Mexico on an Indian Reservation. My dad is part Indian. My mom is Anglo. I am the oldest of four girls. We had a dairy farm. I had to work with my dad. We worked hard. I knew that for a fact when I came out of Red Rock Valley and found out people thought women couldn't work that hard. The farms were dependent on women being able to work hard.

They had to help their husbands in the fields. When you own a farm it is like a business and everybody has to do what needs to be done. In glacier country like ours the land is hard. Mom used to say the rocks had babies in the winter. Deep, deep frosts pushed the rocks up. After I left, my dad sold the farm. Then I didn't want to rope another calf, throw another bale of hay from the ground to three feet high on the wagon, or shovel another manure. Mom went to work when I was nine and I helped raise my sisters and brothers. When I got to the dorm in college and I heard women talking about wanting a picket fence, I just thought, *I don't want to change another diaper, starch another underslip, freeze and can another batch of strawberries.* I had done all that.

"I got mad thinking that millions of people are making more money than I was. I wondered, 'What are they doing?' I thought, 'I'm going to find out.' I've tried to encourage women to do this. I say you really can if you just hang on. It's an attitude. Your body will toughen up and you learn how to do things. When I started Jim Kale says it's time women and men work together. He said when he was in Vietnam all he had to work with was women. He learned they didn't do it the way the men did it but they got the jobs done. He said you won't be the strongest or the weakest just get it done. But later he vowed he wasn't going to retire till he fired me. He respected me but had that ambivalent attitude. It was patriarchal, like ownership and pride in me, but when it turned out I had a mind of my own he hated me. When I became a union activist their anger was out of proportion. I think it had to do with the fact that I was a woman standing up to them. That's the level on which sexism is hard to get a hold of.

"My only motivation for this job was money. I was thirty years old feeling I was excessively old not to have a goal. I had a fight with a man in a Safeway checkout line in the ghetto on a hot September day. I'd lived three years in the ghetto because I hated racism. But the conclusion of this fight was a black man telling me of new laws saying they had to hire women at jobs paying $6.35 per hour. I was making $3.00. I'm not afraid of anything for $6.35. Now I earn $17.50 per hour. When a guy showed me dock work and said it was boring I told him, 'I'm thirty-years old. My experience is that the work of the world is boring, so bore me for twice the wage. The teamster guy hiring me said in the interview, to the wall, well I would have thought any women who wants this job is a dyke. He swivels his chair around. I just said I think women are probably a lot more like men. We want to work minimum hours for maximum money.

"Later when I was working this guy called me to say some guys feel the educated words I was using made them feel like I was putting them down. These men have a heart of gold but they are kind of rough. I felt the men didn't ask me to work there. I was going into their work place and their world so I better adjust."

From these few glimpses of these first women's entrance into these nontraditional jobs we see how innocent they were, but we learn their metal and see what the world saw and what their daughters and granddaughters—their husbands, sons and employers saw. From these pioneer women we learned women could do blue collar work well and really enjoy it.

The Transition to the Modern Tradeswomen

The women in nontraditional blue-collar work today are the spiritual daughters and granddaughters of these early pioneers who showed that women could competently do this work. Men saw it, women saw it, employers saw it and daughters saw it. From those pioneers, modern women learned, got a glimpse of self fulfillment and satisfaction coming from higher status and pay and from choosing and doing competently a man's job. Men also got a glimpse of the possibility that their bed mates and house mates could work at blue collar jobs.

However, after the war much of this knowledge was repressed. Then, thirty years later, in the early 1970's, the government reluctantly pushed women again—as a halting outgrowth of their efforts to invoke the Civil Rights Act of 1964 that demanded equal pay and work. The working woman was not originally part of the government's protected class, but nevertheless laws flowing form the Civil Rights Act became vehicles in women's fight for equality.

Women then retrieved the happy, healthy image of Rosie the Riveter from their collective consciousness and began to indentify and apply for these higher paying, equal status jobs. They fought for their rights and as a result of law suits, the mostly unwelcomed compliance laws, the sophisticated massaging of state and federal labor, apprenticeship laws and funding requirements, a few women succeeded.

This time, however, no waving American flags and no honors for selflessness and contribution accompanied them. No posters painted them as pretty smiling girls with red bandannas and overalls. Instead, many were chastised for intrusion, butchiness and bitchiness, and accused of garnering unwarranted protection from President Johnson's overly ambitious "Great Society." Nevertheless, the march begun during the war continued despite the barriers many women in blue collar jobs faced. Insulting job interviews, poor-quality training, demeaning harassment on the job and poor pay commonly associated with "women's work" were slowly being broken down.

TWO

THE MEETING

"At the workshop we had a feeling of belonging that we didn't get working on those crews. Women really were bonding. There was a camaraderie, networking , you made connections and it gave a feeling a community."

Kathy, Preventative Maintenance, United States.

Finally, after years of halting starts beginning with the compliance laws of the early 1970s, the United States West Telephone Company began meeting for support of a group of isolated, lonesome women hired to do physical labor. They had recruited these women because of Federal mandates, but had not educated or integrated the new employees into their male work force. At the meeting, a microcosm of the change that was happening, the small group represented women scattered thinly within a large company. It served to break down some barriers and prove that women were reentering these jobs. However, it took at least ten to fifteen years to get off the ground. Here is what happened:

LouAnn worked for the United States West Telephone Company—not as an operator or service representative like the majority of other women, but out in the field climbing the polls with men. LouAnn was tired of the treatment she was getting; tired of looking at girlie pictures on her colleagues' tool boxes, working in dirty garages and fighting off complaints from wives. She was frustrated by the lack of help, training and civility from her male counterparts in a profession she chose, qualified for and in which she belonged. However, instead of sitting back and taking it, she and the few fellow women craft members agitated and won the chance to get some support—that's really all they wanted—support—a place where they could meet with other women in the profession to share feedback, understanding and help.

LouAnn worked tirelessly to get this idea for a support group accepted by her management and off the ground. She found a sympathetic male officer who agreed to help her put together a vaguely defined training program under the auspices of Equal Employment Opportunity (EEO). They called it "Outside Looking In." LouAnn's idea was launched, and the real work began.

If ever this idea were to become a reality, they had to find other women in other divisions. The first workshop would include telephone company blue collar workers from the whole northern part of the United States between Minneapolis and Montana. A nucleus of very excited and motivated women, including Sheila Danielson, formed a Steering Committee to get out there and search for candidates. Tirelessly they looked up records, managers and checked rumors that would give them clues about where these far-flung women blue collar workers were.

Even with their mounting excitement, the committee members encountered resistance from both men and women who questioned the purpose of such a meeting. Some perceived it as discrimatory—exclusive to a specific group. Yet the group leaders pressed on. After all, they reasoned, this new group would join the multitudes of workshops and training programs for men in management, women in management, women in business ad infinitum. Now it was the turn of the women in blue collar jobs—finally something for them.

Once the list of prospective members was formed and the calls began, the leaders had another hurdle to jump. They had to get permission from lower level managers to release the candidates from work and pay their expenses to come to the workshop. Their sympathetic male mentor helped them with this problem, too. The steering committee was re-energized by their demonstrated power and pleasantly surprised by the activism and efficiency within themselves as individuals and as group leaders.

More committee responsibilities began to emerge as the committee members got into the minute details: party planners discussed menus, negotiators haggled with management over the appropriateness of a company-paid cocktail hour (they didn't win this one), recruiters convinced reluctant women that this would not turn into an ordinary "gossip session," educators working with facilitators designed an appropriate workshop agenda, and public relations people designing the brochure that would entice blue-collar nontraditional women to attend. All the group were nervous and worried that after all the hard work and good intentions, no one would show up.

Finally the big weekend arrived and women began to pour into the hotel—some veterans weathered from outside work, other women pregnant and domestic looking, shy eighteen year olds, older workers talking about their grandchildren, some with tough and masculine demeanors, others glamorous and fashionable. Some had big wads of keys dangling from their pockets, some wore dirty jeans, T-shirts and scruffy boots. Yet, when the sixty plus women all sat down together for the first time, in a large circle that filled the hotel's grand ballroom, they faced each other and gasped in amazement that all of them worked outside in the elements in a "man's" job. The facilitators and outside speakers sensed their enormous strength. The leaders wondered with pride and hope at what they could learn from them and, yes, what the leaders could learn from the prospective members. It turned out, all that had to be done was gather the women into one room. They did the rest.

Friendly introductions set the upbeat tone of the workshop. Divided into groups of six, according to their technical discipline, length of service and marital status, they readily discussed how to cope with families, husbands, pregnancy, child care, colleagues constantly hitting on them and those that thought they were lesbians because, "What other kind of women would do the work they do?" As they became more and more comfortable with each other, it was as though floodgates were released. Stories poured out about dysfunctional families, family dynasties in the phone company, lives of struggle with alcoholism, abusive husbands and the problems of being a single woman trying to support a family. Some told terrible tales of supervisors who punished them simply for being female and who denied them training, time, help, a promotion or the courtesy of a hello. However, all the stories were not negative. They shared stories about pride, determination, perseverance and how in tough times, compassionate friends, colleagues, mates and supervisors came to their rescue.

Faith, one of the women, told of her experience in providing service to a condominium customer. She announced "telephone company" in a low voice, was buzzed in and went upstairs to the opened door of a quite shocked woman, dressed in a scanty negligee, expecting a man. Jeanine, another woman, told of how while working outside in some fields in minus thirty degree weather in the Minneapolis area, she desperately had to go to the bathroom and could see no facilities in sight. Jeanine felt her solution of going into the woods to a clearing and partially taking off her layers and layers of clothes to relieve herself was very inventive, until she found herself the star attraction on the 10th green of a golf course. Beth told the story of a group of dirty women workers who went into a fancy department store during their lunch break to try on mink coats. The scorn on the sale lady's face melted as several dirty women pulled out enough cash to pay for two mink coats in an obvious display that they more than doubled the salary of the clerks who snubbed them. Tears trickled down the cheeks of Alice, one young woman who shared her endless frustration in being the odd woman out. She was only on the telephone utility job three months and thus far felt she had no help, trust, respect or friends. She wasn't even shown how to carry her ladder. Rena, a tough looking older woman said, "If you think it's bad now, you should have been working at this job twenty years ago. There's wasn't this workshop and all of you. Then, we really were alone." Alice said, at the end of that day, "I really feel respect for the older women and appreciate them for beginning to open some doors."

That day there was also a helpful exchange of practical information. One woman, Sue, drove with a dummy sitting beside her as she traveled through bad neighborhoods at night; Carla, another worker, carried a beeper. They told the others where to buy gloves and tools to fit their small hands and how to carry their six-foot ladders. They warned of the consequences of asking and not asking for help. They also identified the good supervisors, gave advice on how to avoid the bad ones, and let the others know what it took to move up to better positions. The first day's business continued with presentations by the facilitators and trainers on assertiveness, conflict resolutions and effective communication. Throughout these candid exchanges, an Equal Employment Opportunity representative recorded everything to take back the next week to their management.

That night the women ate their dinner in the elegant hotel setting, listened to speakers who told of similar struggles of women in other nontraditional professions and basked in the friendships that had already developed from sharing their common experiences. Not wanting to let this mood go, after dinner they stayed up late talking and laughing and crying in small and large groups. These women were enjoying each others' camaraderie, together in a way that none of them had ever experienced before.

Maybe the most significant result was a snowball effect that reshaped the women's self images. They found strength in numbers and through each other saw themselves more clearly, more positively, more realistically. They gained knowledge and feelings of the wonder of their new roles. In addition, they realized, most for the first time, how really brave, free and strong they had been in getting these nontraditional jobs and persevering. The women were able to see through hard work, difficulties and even the insults of their day to day existence and felt liberated and self-affirmed.

This uplifting mood greatly affected the facilitators. Personally, we were captivated by this group of women and inspired by the bravery and challenges of their lives. We were amazed at what these women with little education and training had accomplished against tough odds. We wondered at their strength, and admired the joy and meaning they found in blue collar jobs. They represented unconsidered options and choices that taught us a great deal about counter-cultural thinking and fortitude. Yet, we were saddened at the difficulty of their struggle. We, as women, and members of society, in general, could and should do more to understand these women, these jobs, these problems and these options.

The second day of meetings was filled with Equal Employment Opportunity information, feedback, peer counseling, network building and self scoring personality tests, which both amused and instructed the candidates. The women formed a committee to start a newsletter to keep the momentum going and planned a monthly meeting as a forum for selected speakers and an opportunity to continue their sharing. They also planned to publish a listing of available jobs. As parting gifts, the women received bags containing sweatshirts, pens and cups all marked "Women At Work," but the real gifts were the understanding, knowledge and realizations that they all made possible for each other.

At the end of the conference, the women gathered around the piano and recited, or more accurately, shouted the cheer they had written:

> We like to work with the women outside
> They are rough of hand and thick of hide.
> Their hearts are strong and spirits brave
> They keep us communicating on the air waves.
> So, now when we see a telephone van
> We think of a woman instead of a man.

THREE

THE WOMEN AT WORK

Today's women, marching into nontraditional jobs, when a war effort does not call, are women who choose or accept alternate life work, in order to satisfy their and their families' needs and goals.

These women do physical work that has a rapid, tangible monetary result. Their efforts and labor also result in immediate feedback and gratification. Producing by the sweat of their brow, the results of their work can be seen in our daily lives. Dressed in rough work clothes and uniforms they are not participants in a world of glamorous suits and make-up. Their more utilitarian look includes little make-up, simple hairdos, work clothes and bodies that are firmed daily on the job rather than designed by personal trainers.

"All of us are the same," says Lynn Shaw, an electrician and advocate, after attending a national conference. There she met seven other random tradeswomen from across the country who had been selected to meet with officials in the Department of Labor. Of the seven women sharing their stories, she said, "We're the same women with remarkably similar profiles: Black, White, Asian, from different parts of the country. We all entered the trades in the 1970s when we were about twenty-six or twenty-seven. We all served about four years as a apprentices, had a high school education or a little more." Lynn describes common experiences nontraditional women share.

Although we don't have a clear statistical picture of who these women are, the women interviewed for this book, especially the twenty-two profiled, tell their stories, in their words, lead the way to our better understanding of the identities of the new blue collar women.

The Women	Job	Pay	Marital Status/No. of Children
*Lois "Honey" Lean	Industrial Worker - WWII	$1.20/hour	Divorced
Frances Cuevas	Railroad and Defense Plant Worker - WWII	$0.87-1.11/hour	2 husbands/3 children
*Leslie Wake	Dockworker	$34,600/year	Single/No children
Kathleen Tracy	Plumber	$41,600/year plus medical and retirement benefits	Mate/No children
*Susan Thomas	Meter Reader	$31,200/year	Married/No children
Tanya Richardson	Lifeguard	$14.16/hour	boyfriend/No children
Mary Michels		$45,760/year plus fringes 2.58 annuity double time for overtime after 10 hours	Divorced/Adult children
*Laura Jeffers	Oil Rig Worker	$18.53/hour plus benefits	Divorced/3 children
Yvonne Butler	**Sanitation Worker**	**$35-40,000/year**	**Married/2 children before marrying**
Pam Owens	Ditch Digger	$37,180/year	Divorced/2 children
Wendy Gaston	Auto Alignment Repair	$1,000/month	Single/no children

Betty Kelepecz	Police Detective	$2,493 biweekly (approx)	Married/No children
*Jennifer August	Firefighter	$55,000 per year	Divorced with fiance/Gave up custody of son to ex-husband
Cindy Fraylich	Firefighter	$2,181 biweekly (approx)	Divorced with boyfriend/No children
Silvia Carrillo	Pressroom	$45,760/year	Single/One child
Linda West	Weldor/Artist	$25.00 to 30.00/hour	Divorced with boyfriend/ Pregnant with first child
Lynn Shaw	Electrician	$23.00/hour plus benefits	Married/Stepson
Sylvia Ruize	Undercover Narcotics Agent	$50,000 to $55,000/ year	Married/Pregnant with first child
Kathy Shaughnessy	Preventive Maintenance	$41,000/ year	Single
Brenda Lancaster	Truck Driver	$40,000 to $70,000/year depending on vehicle size and production	Married 3 times/2 children
*Simone Fisher	Ship Captain	$85,000/year	Single/No children
Cheri Wiseman	Mover	$9.00/hour	Divorced, engaged /1 child —Gave 1 up for adoption

Lorie Swenson	Customer Service Technician	$27,000/year + $10/hour overtime	Married/2 children
*Tommie Lee	Auto Repair Service Writer	$45,000/year	Single with boyfriend/No children
Madelyn Elder	Cable Splicer	$35,000/year base; $60,000 to $70,000 with overtime	Gay relationship/No children
*Penny Whistler	Electrician	$45-65,000 per year	Gay relationship
Jeanine Woodson	Sound Electrician	$19.00/hour	Gay/No relationship/1 child
Yolanda Valdez	Painter	$3,400/month	Single/No relationship/ twin daughters
Vivian Price	Apprentice Electrician (Ph.D student)	$25.00/hour plus benefits	**Single/No children**
Margaret Ferguson	**Top secret work in U.S. Navy - WW II**	**$35.00/month (approx)**	**Widowed /No children**
Gail George	**Communication work in U.S. Army - Persian Gulf War**	**$600.00/month**	**Single/No children**

* names indicate alias

Profile Statistics

Education:
57% High School; 43% College
Age at entering nontraditional job:
11% under 20; 57% between 20-30; 32% over 30
Previous background skills in nontraditional Work: 50%
30% Married; 23% Divorced: 46% Children; 13% Gay
Like Work: 86%
Average Age Now: 36

PART II

THE WORK

" *I am in the ditches. If a pipe breaks and there is no tractor I dig a ditch. I lift bathtubs. I've torn my knees up. My body is covered with scars. There are a lot of unpleasant aspects to being in maintenance. I tell my boss, 'Every time you got a stopped up urinal you send me in there.' I'm the only woman plumber. It's a very unpleasant job. But, I have to be able to do this. All the guys do this. It's an honest job. I take a lot of pride in my work A lot of people slide by and take short cuts. I use the proper tools. I don't climb on top of tables instead of using a ladder.* "

Kathleen, Plumber

Look into a truck's cab, peek around a piano strapped to a dolly, or watch construction workers cutting planks or steel workers forging and today you'll probably find women working, sweating hour by hour, day in and day out, and happily earning more money than their counterparts who work 9:00 A.M. to 5:00 P.M. in stores or restaurants. The good looking women who work undercover wired with "heat," or buried underground repairing cable, or lifting freight inside a warehouse look different than most of us, but they also look strong and healthy in their jeans, t-shirts and heavy boots.

For the individuals, working in these jobs their achievements represents the forging of a new frontier. Socially they represent a new reality. There are openings and the economy dictates that many women need to work in order to support themselves and their families. Nontraditional jobs offer well paying careers without much education or training. Even in this tight job market these jobs are available. Even though these employment opportunities are not publicized as being available to women, more women are learning of them. These women are often less sophisticated and articulate than those who, with their higher education, demand equal work, equal pay, and management positions. Yet, they have captured these jobs and that are accompanied by great benefits and good salaries. In fact, while most working women earn about seventy-five percent of what their male counterparts earn in the traditional job market, women in nontraditional jobs earn as much or more than many men. Equal pay is significant to this work.

Women have entered these jobs without much public attention. And, although this work is tough, dirty and physically demanding, they have been successful at them—and often like what they're doing.

However, not all aspects of blue collar work are satisfying and beneficial. While many women love the work they do in spite of the social aspersions, its neglect, and it's dirt, society looks the other way. Women doing this work challenge fundamental beliefs regarding our culture, our femininity and our modern mental emphasis. For most of us who work, computers and machines tie us to desks and cars, such largely mental activities cut us off from physical exertion except in gyms and on Nautilus machines. We get further removed from basic functions such as building and creating as more and more of our efforts become thought processes, resulting in white collar jobs.

On the other hand, women in the trades do physical jobs that result in tangible physical results. Their achievements represent part of our nature that is slipping away in modern society—a strong physical force that results in houses, buildings, phones, food distribution and safety of our communities.

FOUR

WHAT EXACTLY DO THESE WOMEN DO?

"I got a job working in the Prostitute Enforcement Division—posing as a prostitute out on the street in bad areas from 5 P.M. to 1 A.M., basically when the prostitutes are out. You have a body wire and pose on 9th and Alvarado. There is a hotel on the corner. Anything can happen to you, but I'm not really scared. Some of the girls enjoy it—they have fun because you're playing the part of someone else. But sometimes when these men start talking to you dirty, it's like 'You pig' I don't need to hear this from you."
Sylvia, Undercover Narcotics Agent

The work of the blue collar woman is different. The work depends on using physical skills rather than mental ones. Learning technical and vocational skill is, for women never exposed to them before, filled with frustrations and hardships, similar to those experienced by the pioneer women on the prairie. Though so many of them show the weary strain of physical fatigue, they celebrate the triumph of their discovery of these good, rewarding and high paying jobs. In addition, they gain in self esteem because of their physical accomplishments and earning power.

We asked some of them for a description of a typical day on the job.

Tanya, a lifeguard, has learned to be vigilant. "You constantly have to be aware of what's going on. You eat while sitting in the tower. That's where it gets stressful. Your eyes are pretty much constantly concentrating on what's going on. No question it is a long day. You can listen to the radio. We have phones for communication between stations. It's hard not to fall asleep when there is not really anyone at the beach, like on a rainy day. I've taken NoDoz and drunk lots and lots of coffee. If you are just enclosed in your tower for eight hours it can drive you pretty crazy. You don't get a lunch break. You get something called a workout when for twenty or thirty minutes you swim or run. You're out of uniform, yet still must be responsible for your area."

Cindy, a firefighter, says her average day is punctuated by enormous adrenaline rushes. "A typical day starts at 8:00 A.M. with line up and the Captain announcing what is going on that day. Then, physical fitness, e.g., run or ride the stationary bike for an hour. 9:00 A.M. to 9:30 A.M.—get cleaned up in uniform. You clean the apparatus and station until 10:30 A.M. In between all this are calls. The cook prepares the meal. We eat at noon and play cards to see who will do the dishes. We'll go out later and actually lay some hose out, squirt some water, and do things that simulate a fire. We might also do fire prevention activities like building inspections. At 4:00 P.M. the cook prepares dinners. At 5:00 P.M. we eat and play cards again for the dishes. After dinner, most Captains leave the activities up to you. If you want to study for a promotional exam you can do that (I'm now working some hydraulics problems), or work out in the weight room, watch TV, or read a book. Of course, we're taking calls in between."

Lorie, a customer service technician for the telephone company, installs telephone systems. "Almost everything I do now on the job is physical. It is not very glamorous. My job is bringing business lines into buildings or installing jacks. Sometimes I mount a connecting block pulling all the lines in. I find the phone room in the business, make sure I have a dial tone, sometimes I pop out ceiling tiles and pull wires out or fish a wall drop (a string with a weight dropped down to where you then knock a hole through the wall). It's hard pulling thick wire floor to floor or across a big building. Sometimes I lay temporary wire at construction sites, too."

To do her job Pam operates a heavy piece of hydraulic equipment called a maxi sneaker. "The maxi sneaker has a piece on it that actually digs down into the ground. We thread our wire through this piece. As we lean forward the digger digs a hole and plows the wire into the ground. It is hard physically. I learned to do it on the job. I am a network technician, but the boss calls us the 'dirt crew' or 'plow crew.'"

Cheri recently got a job with a moving company as an accounts payable clerk, but, she works as a mover on the weekends and is happy to be physically active again. She described one day she spent moving some corporate offices. "I lifted boxes, turned desks over, put them on dollies, pushed them to the truck, moved boxes, carted things up. You work up a really good sweat, but I like it. It feels good. It's like working out. It's fun to watch the guys' reactions. They didn't realize I was working. It was like get out of my way lady, so I can move this stuff. It's funny. Guys tell my boss I pumped. I worked as hard or harder than the guys there. I was raised to believe that to get paid you should work 110 percent. As a woman I can go into a man's job and give 110 percent while guys stand around only giving fifty to seventy-five percent. It's like you build a mark in the sky. It's a job ethic."

Welding for Linda is akin to art. "So next thing I know I bought a tig welder and I'm restoring Frank Stella and Giametti. I also learned welding. We fix everything from semi trucks to ornamental gates. I worked the steel project on a big building on State Street. I set up I-beam columns. We're bound to be artists. Artistry is everything. I have to work with my hands. I'm not normal. I have a hard time punching a clock. I get to be a welder. I get to be a macho foundry person."

It took Kathy twenty-five years working for the telephone company to finally admit she likes her work. "I am working a nice job now, still driving an air-conditioned company truck. I have computer inventory equipment which is fun. In the field the computer does a lot of work for you. A year and a half ago I volunteered to take this all night shift because this job is cutting edge. Only seventy people in the company are doing this. We are doing preventive maintenance. I trained with three different men on three different shifts. Now, I'm working nights, which is a drag in summer, because I have to sleep all day. I like the freedom and it is fairly safe. I carry a little 'heater' which shoots pellets. It's not going to kill anyone. I could get in trouble with my company if they knew I had it. I work different areas of the city. The company has been good about putting us in better buildings at night. We work outdoors at big green boxes which are the cable feed for neighborhood homes and businesses, giving everybody dial tones. I park next to the green box and hook up the computer. I do some manual labor."

Madeline, a splicer who also works for the telephone company, finds her job has gotten easier as years go by: "My title is Network Technician which includes: splicing, installing, repairing and maintaining. Specifically, I take wire from the central office and make sure it gets distributed out to the terminals to businesses, government offices, and homes. I don't work with the public. There are basically three areas: 1) aerial on poles, 2) direct buried—working little green boxes on the ground (I don't do too much of that, that's usually for new people) and 3) underground—working with large cables. I work in twelve-foot manholes—little basement rooms four or five feet by five feet and six feet high. There's a neck leading from the ground. I drop down. I have a fan—a blower hose pumping air into the hole. My truck generator produces electricity. I put up a tent if it's raining to make sure the splice closure won't leak. The wire won't work if it's wet. Mostly you see spiders underground. Occasionally you find a snake. I don't mind being underground. It's kind of comfortable, safe in a wind storm, and warm in the winter. You are down there eight to ten hours. I take breaks. You have to or this work can ruin your back. Once or twice a year I do aerial work. If a great big east wind in winter time whips up the Columbian gorge, it will try to take your ladder away. But, you have to trust your equipment. Getting up there is the scary part."

Kathleen Tracy, Plumber, L.A. Unified High School District, forty-six years old

Kathleen has a deep voice, a big body and an efficient manner. She couldn't find a job as a teacher so adjusted to the nontraditional working world as a plumber. She was raised on a farm in Kansas with four brothers and a father, all of whom were plumbers.

"I went to Kansas State Teachers College in 1965 to become a teacher. I got a B.S. in Education but wasn't able to find a teaching position. I didn't know what else to do. I started a house cleaning service. One of my brothers dared me to apply for a plumbing apprenticeship. That's what got me in. When I went down to the local Union, in 1972, they said, 'There will be no women working at this local.' That statement made me all the more determined to be accepted into the union. I imagine my paperwork 'got the shuffle.' But, since the apprenticeship is funded by the state, they were required to accept my application for apprenticeship as a minority. Finally, in 1976, I got accepted into the plumbing apprenticeship program.

"I knew that being in the trades wasn't going to be easy. Being raised around males I was expected to work hand and hand with them. I was right; it hasn't been easy. Women aren't as physically strong as men. We have to use our brains to work around problems. When I was an apprentice I wasn't wanted and they made that clear.

"Once I went out on call to a job site. You take these little slips saying you are qualified and they are supposed to take you. They worked me that day but the next day the foreman laid me off. He said, 'We want a man and not you.' I tried to file a grievance with the Union and they wouldn't take it. I ended up going to Equal Employment Opportunity and got back wages and an apology. The employer had to hire me back. I only worked there six weeks and they laid me off again saying there was a work slow down.

"There are times I've been sexually harassed and verbally abused, but when a person puts themselves in the work position I have, they have to realize how people really are. I knew I could do my job as well or better than many men. I've had guys say, 'This is man's work; why are you taking a man's job?' I have all these years of attitudes. They write sexual comments on the bathroom walls like: 'Easy lay' or 'Gives head.'

"Now I'm forty-six years old and a home owner; I'm not so willing to put my job on the line fighting and bitching for things that seem insignificant to me now. At times it seems my boss doesn't treat me quite as fairly as the men but in some ways he treats me better. I'm not willing to get blacklisted or transferred. You can't have a chip on your shoulder; they play on that too. There is always the shit list and if you act out, you get on that list.

"When I first started I worked new construction on housing projects, Budweiser refurbishment, rebuilding the Olive View Hospital after the '71 earthquake, Lancaster B-1 bomber hangers. Now I'm working at the Los Angeles Unified School District in maintenance. They are a better employer. They have a little more class than the crude and rude animals at the construction site. Here I get more support because I'm around other female trades people. There are about fifteen women in different trades. In construction I was the only woman on the site unless a catering truck came. With other women if you're having a tiff with a fellow employee there is someone to kind of pat you on the shoulder and say 'Hang in there.'

"Women have more emotions than men. Men consider that a weakness and try to dig in on that point. But I've had a lot of support from men too. One of the guys at the B-1 bomber told me about the LAUSD maintenance job. He told me I was good enough and should apply.

"Most of the women who survive in the trades were taught by their father or brothers. Women haven't been taught how to lift and use proper body mechanics. Women generally aren't as tall, and their backs aren't as strong. It takes strength when you've got to use a powerful drill to not let it out of your hands trying to drill these holes. Since I'm 5 foot 8 inches and overweight, my weight has been a helpful advantage with leverage. Women get torn bladders from lifting. I've torn my knees up. My body is covered with scars from cuts and scrapes and burns. Your body pays working in the trades. Maybe I should have been an electrician, they don't have to move bathtubs. I might be putting in giant pipe and they put in little bitty wire.

"I have a good job, but I don't love it. I tell my boss 'It seems every time you got a stopped up urinal you send me in there.' I'm the only woman plumber and it's a very unpleasant task. I feel like the Urinal Queen, but I have to be able to do this. It's an honest job and I take a lot of pride in my work. Normally when I do something it's right, and they don't have to send someone back. When they send me out to do a job, I do it. A lot of people slide by and take a lot of short cuts. I use the proper tools to do the job and don't climb on top of tables instead of using a ladder.

"My dad was a self-employed general contractor and plumber and mother helped him. We lived on a farm in Kansas, but I left for college at eighteen. I was the only girl. My dad wasn't happy about my plumbing job when I was in new construction. He felt that it was a man's job. But I told him if he didn't want me to have a man's job, he shouldn't have taught me to use man's tools. My brother who challenged me has been really supportive. He was a contractor. When I had lean times with work he'd hire me.

"If I could find an easier job that paid more I'd be gone in a second. Construction builds confidence.

"I don't have a family or children, but I do have a significant other. I bring in the bread, but everybody has chores. Now I'm involved in building a guest house with a group of women. It feels really good to be working with a group of women and not having men tell you what to do. The stress isn't there. There is not as much competition. When you say something, people listen. There is more praise, I think. Praise goes a long way. I earn $6.00 less than working for the Union, but it's steady. I earn about $20 an hour with medical and retirement.

"At forty-six I'll soon have to get behind a desk. I could become a supervisor. Now, I'm in the ditches. If a pipe breaks and there is no tractor, I dig a ditch. Some schools add bungalows, and I have to run water and gas lines and put pipe in ditches underground. For work I wear construction boots, jeans and a T-shirt; it's what I wore all my life.

"Young women going into the trades need to have their eyes open to the actual harshness of the physical labor. Because they are women, men are not that supportive. Men aren't going to run over and give you a hand. Even now most of the guys don't want you there. Women have to get the attitude—I'm here to stay! You're constantly tested. Even if you're the youngest of the young, don't think you know anything. For example, I was working with a young guy who asked 'How old are you?' I said, 'I'm Forty-six.' He was thirty-three. He said, 'I can't believe you can keep up.' I said, 'I have one speed and if you want to bust your back for ten minutes going balls out to prove you're macho, go right ahead.'

"When I started plumbing in 1972 for the Union, I was the first woman in the apprenticeship program. Since that time twelve other women have joined the union. Now there are only two women left. The other women left because of lack of work or a given job was too difficult to handle. I like the freedom of working out of doors and don't think I would ever enjoy doing sedentary work.

Susan, Meter Reader, Southern C.A. Edison, Thirty-five Years Old

Susan is a very pretty woman who looks fresh and pulled together in her brown Bermuda shorts, orange bowling-style shirt and work boots. Her tidy uniform certainly doesn't take away from her femininity. She is married to a fireman, who is very supportive of her and her job. They have no children. Her husband just wants to see her happy. She's looking for a transfer, but in the meantime she has to contend with the commute from Palmdale to Santa Monica, California (about seventy-five miles one way). Her job is climbing over fences covered with leaves and cobwebs, always running the risk of getting banged up, bitten by a dog or even getting shot. Yet, she says this job suits her. She's always been a tomboy.

"I'm not really petrified to do this job, but there are yards I will not enter because of the dogs. We have made arrangements with the customers. Edison wants you to go in there. That is the difference between me and the men. The men will just go into the yard thinking the dog is not going to bother them. They are more macho about that. I am more protective of myself. I don't want to get bitten. I've been bitten once. My supervisor knows the women are a little more fearful. But I don't care because I don't want to get bit. Just come with me for a few months. You walk between buildings. You get the tree branches and bushes all over you. You get splinters and your hands get cut up opening fences. Sometimes you have to hop fences to read the meter. I am a pretty physical person. You have to be.

"My job consists of reading meters at apartments and houses all day long. I've done this two years. Prior to this I was a parking enforcement officer for the City of Los Angeles where at least half the workers are women. Before that I did clerical work.

"I got into meter reading because I wanted out of the city. I had a girlfriend who works for Edison. Most everybody who works for Edison was hired on as a meter reader. They had an opening in Santa Monica. So I thought I'd try it. Out of sixteen, there was only one other woman when I started.

"This job is a steppingstone. Meter reading is not where it's at. I get banged up and scratched and almost bitten by dogs. I'm trying to get a promotion in the company, but at this time they have a hiring freeze. I hang in there because it wouldn't be wise to quit. It pays pretty good for what I do—$15.00 per hour. I work forty hours.

"A lot of times you go into people's yards and you frighten them. It's an uneasy feeling walking into someone's yard even though they know that is how they have to get their meter read. It's an uneasy feeling for me thinking some day someone is going to shoot me because they don't know who I am. We carry an umbrella and mace for protection against dogs. You're supposed to open up the umbrella real quick. Also, I carry dog biscuits. It helps a lot to throw the biscuits into the yard before I go in.

"I like the outdoors. I've met some nice people and I look forward to going up to their houses and talking to them, and there are some dogs I can't wait to see. But, I am beat by the end of day. Then I have the long drive home. Physically and mentally I'm drained by the end of the day.

"Most of my customers don't even realize I'm a woman. They say, 'Oh, here comes a meter reader.' Sometimes I'm the gas man. Usually I have my hair up in a bun. I don't get hassled and it is not harder for me as a woman. Some customers might talk down to me. They are a little more sarcastic and don't give you the respect they give a man. They stare and, I think, what are you looking at?"

Our in—depth interviews of Kathleen and Susan give us new perspectives: Kathleen lets us see how she got used to this work. Her father and brother trained her early on working with tools. They worked her hard. Graphically, she describes cleaning urinals, but her pride at doing a stand-up job—even though a tough job—and coping in a tough environment, comes through. She does her work proudly. She's found regular employment with the Los Angeles City Schools.

Susan represents the many women who, even after getting into this grimy, outdoor work for the money, work so hard they are exhausted at the end of the day but wouldn't ever dream of working indoors. Though some complain, they continue. Susan just laughed at the idea of working indoors. That would be worse than all the hardships she endures daily.

Our notion of what is appropriate women's work is expanding. Women's work is no longer only traditional housework such as doing dishes, changing diapers, cleaning, vacuuming, or traditional careers such as teaching, nursing and typing. The profiles of these blue collar women show how they changed their feelings about what they could do. Both started toward traditional women's occupations—office work or teaching. But through a combination of circumstances, needs and opportunities they began jobs doing work that society defined as masculine. Kathleen's work was physical labor just as her father and brothers had done. Plumbing and meter reading are both physical, independent, involve some math and are dirty and hard. These are not careers that we see pictured for women in "Redbook" magazine or even "Working Women." The women we have interviewed for this book do physical labor. We can hear in their views expressed as they tell their stories that this new kind of work strongly fits their temperaments, backgrounds, interests and styles. Even when there are reservations, we see how this new kind of work can be rewarding and satisfying.

FIVE

REQUIREMENTS

"There was a physical agility test where you had to run a timed one and one-quarter miles, jump over a six-foot wall, drag a weight backward, hang onto a bar and do sit ups."

Betty, Police Officer

What It Takes Just to Get in the Door

It often takes tremendous feats of strength and will just to qualify for the blue collar jobs in the first place. Jumping fences, dropping into burning buildings, swimming a mile in the surf, driving a five-ton truck, using heavy, vibrating equipment, and walking unannounced into someone's backyard that may be guarded by an attack dog are all things done willingly by those who covet these particular jobs. After the initial challenge, it takes courage, physical strength and stamina; physical exertion sometimes to the point of exhaustion; being out in all kinds of weather; crawling around in holes underground; climbing up eighteen foot poles and digging in the dirt—these are the everyday requirements of these nontraditional jobs.

To become a firefighter, Cindy had to pass a grueling series of mental and physical tests. "There's an agility test with six events which somewhat simulate what you do on a fire. For instance, we have to drag 150 feet of hose off the back of the engine that is two and a half inches in diameter 155 feet out and 155 feet back, in less that thirty-nine seconds. It's all timed and if you can't do it in that amount of time then you fail it, and you fail the whole agility test. In another one, you climb up a 100-foot long aerial ladder. It's on a ladder truck and it's leaning against a five-story tower. You climb up that ladder with a breathing apparatus on and a belt, get inside the tower, jump down a hole in the roof, scoot down a ladder, jump off the fire escape, jump back in the window, go down an interior stairwell and go back to the starting point. The whole thing is timed. The initial agility test is just to find out if you can do those things—if you have adequate physical capabilities. There is a written exam as well as an oral. Once you pass, if you are in a top grouping you are asked to be in academy classes. Prior to that all you need is a high school education. Most people don't have a problem with it. They might be scared when they go up. Every once in a while someone freezes. I had always been athletic and into a lot of different types sports. It wasn't something foreign to me."

To qualify as a lifeguard Tanya had to swim a mile and pass an oral interview. This was followed by two weeks of training including CPR and first aid. Then she had to pass a written exam and an exhaustive running and swimming test similar to what is needed during an ocean rescue. The requirements for a lifeguard are suited only to ocean swimmers and surfers. Pool swimmers don't qualify.

Lorie, who is a telephone company service representative, literally forced herself up higher and higher ladders to conquer her fear of heights. Eventually she passed the fierce eighteen-foot pole climbing requirement to get her job. "Pole climbing school was a very negative experience. I was set up for failure. Several women had filed sexual harassment suits against the instructor for putting his hands on their hips to show them how to get up the pole. It was not positive. I have a weird phobia for poles. I'd drive home and say I could make it to six feet. Then I passed twelve feet. Eighteen feet seemed so high. I was just about ready to quit. I told my instructor I've got to get myself through it.

"Finally I went to a hypnotist for a one-hour session. It was very relaxing. I relaxed every part of my body with headphones. I heard waves and seagulls as she spoke all positives to me. I could swear I was ready to float out of the chair. She just reinforced all the positives and safety. I got my own tape for self relaxation. Later I laid on my bed quietly repeating the positives. The next Monday I went to the top of the pole having no doubt I was going to make it eighteen feet. I did!

"It was optional to pull a fifteen pound sack up a pole, but I was prepared to try it. The pole was new and you had to use more muscle. When you climb a pole you put one and one-half inch spikes or "gaffs" into the pole at certain angles for your only support. You only put the belt on at the top. It was strenuous because we had been going up and down the poles four hours a day and I have tendonitis in my knees. I 'cut out' and the sparks were flying. Instead of thinking of the positives the instructor says, 'You just fell eighteen feet,' I told him I wasn't doing it again. I had passed the test. He didn't understand."

For Betty, entering the police academy was a real eye opener. She had grown up in a large family who wrestled, but she had never really been in a fight before. "The most frightening thing for me was combat wrestling, because they actually try to put you out. I mean choke you out. At the time we were doing karate—really fighting people. I was always a very assertive, aggressive person but never to that extent. Every time I thought, 'Oh, today is the day for combat wrestling.' I'd get just panicked and think, Oh I don't want to do it. But eventually I did very well."

Betty also described the physical tests and the training classes she had to pass. "It wasn't discouraging. It was challenging because I had never jumped over a wall before. The first time I tried it I couldn't do it. I had always been able to do anything I wanted. I thought, I've got to fix this.

"I remember training in Long Beach. We had a five-foot high brick wall behind our house and a rose bush on the other side. I jumped that wall and jumped that wall until I had it down perfectly. I had to jump high and wide so I wouldn't get killed by this rose bush. The next time I took the test I just flew over the wall. Men use their upper body. Women have to use their feet to catapult more. I thought, okay, I can do this stuff."

Working outside also takes an ability to withstand social criticism. Many times female blue collar workers are sneered at for stealing away jobs from men. They are also sometimes perceived as masculine, lesbian types. The general feeling is that no feminine, real woman could possibly want one of those dirty jobs.

The first day Pam was on the job as a cable splicer her trainer took her past an unemployment line of men. He said, "look at those people out there. They are there because you took their job." Even her father and husband were discouraging. Her husband, who she finally divorced after twelve years, said from day one that he never wanted to see her dirty and on the job. Sometimes she left herself dirty and wore work clothes around the house to make him angry.

When Susan was hired on she was only the second woman meter reader out of sixteen at her job location. "It's a manly job. Most women don't want to be dealing with dogs, hanging off fences, climbing the trees, climbing over fences and walking all day long."

Required Attire

Besides the threshold requirements to get the jobs, women have to conform to dress requirements to keep the jobs. They must dress for comfort and safety yet some felt resentment at having to wear their boots or to cut their hair in keeping with specific regulations. They also complained that they can't find boots, gloves or even tools that fit.

"I felt like Jane Symour with a gun belt," says Betty, a police officer who feels her gun belt affects her femininity. "It's hard to walk with a feminine gait with a gun on your hips. You know, you got this gun, this weight on your hips, and men's shoes on, and pretty soon you're in a role. I never wanted this to happen. I had to cut my hair above the collar and I wear men's clothes and ties. I feel like a clown. I remember looking in the mirror and singing, 'I enjoy being a girl.'"

Besides, in her opinion, clothing requirements engender discrimination. Betty's retaliation for the strict manly dress requirements—down to the cotton underwear she had to wear under her uniform—was to hang Frederick's of Hollywood lingerie on hangers in the locker room when she knew the inspectors were coming by.

Mary, a welder, dresses for the weather. She never gets cold because the work makes her body heat up quickly. "I dress like the guys. I had a hard time in the beginning. Finally, I figured out the only thing I could wear was 501 Levi's. It makes me mad but they are the only thing that lasts. They're expensive and I try other things from time to time but they just wear out. I wear heavy shirts. All welders wear JC Penney's hickory striped shirts that are white with blue stripes. I don't iron. Even if it is 100 degrees outside, I would feel naked with just a T-shirt on."

Not required to wear anything special, Sylvia, a narcotics agent, dresses for comfort even when she's posing as a prostitute. "I wear jeans and a sweater—you don't need a tight thing."

Lorie, who is a customer service representative for the telephone company, dresses up to sell Mary Kay cosmetics during her off hours, to counterbalance the constraints of her masculine looking work clothes. "On the job I wear jeans and T-shirt. I have to wear long pants. If I'm working on a loft or ladder, I'm supposed to have work boots on for safety."

Her company provides overalls, yet only restricts Pam from wearing shorts. She finds her work gear useful. "I wear jeans and boots, a comfortable shirt and a hard hat. The phone company supplies us with lotion cleansers and on top of that I have baby wipes. Sometimes I'm filthy. If I wear overalls most of the time, I'm not filthy, but sometimes I don't put them on because it is really hot to wear jeans and overalls and a shirt. I am used to the hard hat—actually I like it, because it keeps my hair kind of clean, the sun out of my eyes and the rain off my head."

Tanya Richardson, Los Angeles County Lifeguard, Twenty-Seven Years Old

We met at the patio of a restaurant in Hermosa Beach, California. Sturdy looking, blond and pretty with great skin even without makeup, she looks very healthy—even the way she eats—eggs on muffins with spinach and mushrooms, hold the hollandaise sauce. Wearing shorts and a white shirt and sandals, her blond hair was pulled back in a ponytail.

Tanya grew up in Redondo Beach. Her mother put her in junior lifeguards to learn water safety so she could go to the beach by herself. She tried out at the suggestion of her junior lifeguard instructor. She started working as a lifeguard at eighteen years old.

"This job takes a special kind of person. You have to be flexible. For example, there are no women's restrooms, just one restroom and showers. You can't think of it as not having women's restrooms, just co-ed restrooms. When you go to take a shower you have to knock and make sure no guys are in there. Then you have to keep them out while you go in. But it's no big deal. You have to be a woman who is able to get along in a situation that is definitely male dominated. To me it isn't real difficult. Now, they are more conscious and we are getting our own facilities.

"This is a tough job because you have to be alert all the time and scanning. It is tiring. In the winter it can be real boring.

"About twenty percent of the lifeguards are women. I get some hassles from guys like, 'Hey baby, I'd love you to rescue me.' Those kind of comments you just have to blow off. One guy faked a rescue. It's tough because I had to go out there and pull him out, but you know it's a fake. I was really upset. He's taking my time away from other people.

"The male lifeguards are supportive now. When I first started, the older guys made remarks like, 'When I was younger, there used to be no women out here.' The general impression is females are weaker. The younger male lifeguards are supportive though. Women and mothers think my occupation is great. Socially, I have gone out with lifeguards. You have that connection. It's weird generally. Lifeguards are like boys in college and they get married after they are out there a long time. They like to run around for a while.

"I didn't meet my current boyfriend in this environment. He's getting a masters degree in bio-geography. I think all the guys I meet think it is pretty cool that I'm a lifeguard. My boyfriend thinks it's neat. He's pretty comfortable with our relationship. What I look for is someone who is comfortable with me.

"The general public looks at lifeguarding as an important job. Lifeguards have become more professional. Lifeguards use to be looked at as just people who sit up in the tower and kick back in the sun all day. Instead people are realizing how important it is to have somebody in the tower watching the water.

"I went to University of Southern California. I just got my teaching credential. For me this is a steppingstone. I'm looking for a teaching position. You can keep a seasonal lifeguard position for the rest of your life. It is something I will definitely continue to do. You have to work at least five days per year. I am a seasonal employee. I work full time starting about the July 4 weekend. After you get some experience, then you can aim to become permanent. The test for a permanent lifeguard is a little more intense. As a seasonal employee you are hired based on how you came out of the rookie school, how many days you work, seniority, weather conditions, amount of people on the beach.

"When I went through the test there were just two women. About 300 people tried out with ninety candidates making the cut. Two women out of the ninety made it.

"When I first started I thought it was very stressful being responsible for all the people on the beach. You constantly have to be aware of what's going on. You don't get a lunch break away from the tower You're always watching the water. No question it is a long day. You can listen to the radio. We have phones for communication between stations. It's hard not to fall asleep. I have started to doze off a couple of times. Especially when there is not really anyone at the beach.

"The money is great. I enjoy the team work with the other lifeguards. It is a good feeling when you actually save someone's life. It makes you glad you were there. I enjoy teaching now too. Personally I don't want to stay in Los Angeles. In some places lifeguards have to carry a gun while on duty, which I don't want to do. I like the combination of life guarding and educating our youth. In the winter time there is not as much action and I don't know if I could stand that. It gets exciting, too, with all the winter storms. I'm not scared of the big waves, though I have high confidence in my ability to get someone in trouble out of the water."

Factors found in Tanya's profile highlight the necessary requirements for these jobs. Something in their background or an accidental exposure led these women to try—the first requirement. In Tanya's case it was learning to swim at a very young age. When they have attained the general requirements as far as age, etc., they have to pass the physically grueling threshold tests just to get in a training program.

They have to qualify internally too—their personalities and attitudes must equip the women to fit in and adapt to their situation. Tanya, so naturally and succinctly, describes how important it is to be flexible. An unstated but fundamental requirement is finding a way to get along in a man filled world—adapting to the work situation at hand without insisting on immediate changes. Tanya's words illustrate that she meets that requirement. She doesn't resent not having separate bathrooms. Instead, she reframes the problem and has learned to turn her experience into a positive. She has learned to adapt.

Additionally there are rigorous external qualifications imposed by unions, employers, contractors, licensing agencies and government regulators. Requirements include tests and experience both of which often disadvantage women. What we learn is that persevering and focused women work hard to qualify. Nevertheless, employers need to look at present qualifications to make sure they aren't outmoded and don't automatically eliminate women who might be the most productive workers.

SIX

MOTIVATION

"I figured either I would have to get on welfare, earn poverty wages or get a better job. I didn't want welfare because it didn't pay enough, I didn't want to go out and look for another husband to take care of me, and I wanted another job."

Mary, Welder

In terms of aspirations and goals, we've never heard one of these women say: "All my life I wanted to be a plumber."

A combination of necessity, curiosity and luck led them into these jobs. Some of the thing that served as motivations for them were: an out of the blue phone call from a father, a chance comment from a friend working out at the gym, years of observing men working at strange looking jobs making better money than they were. Almost none of the blue collar women set out to be what they became. Outside forces such as the need to take care of themselves and their children pulled them along. Chance was their teacher— necessity their exposure.

Few high school counselors tell girls to get into jeans and apply for work underground. Few mothers or fathers spend years instilling in their daughters the view that it is desirable and advantageous to live a life of hard physical labor. However, these women were motivated to find a different and , for them, better way of life, and they learned of these jobs through unusual and unintended secret avenues. Once they knew where the jobs were they responded.

Some had not finished high school and were untrained, uneducated and unconnected. Work for such women would often mean earning minimum wage at dull and repetitive jobs sitting behind sewing machines or on factory floors. Then they found real job opportunities—allowing them to make real m-o-n-e-y— were in jobs involving work outside. By agreeing to do hard, physical work sometimes in difficult weather conditions, they could triple their earning power quickly.

Many took the challenge. Given a chance to try, they did. Often the work involved labor at which they had no experience and that presented difficulties most had never considered before. They asked themselves:

- Can I really drive a fire truck?
- Can I save a drowning person from the raging surf?
- Can I convince my male police partners that I can defend them?

Because they were motivated to try and succeed, these women were intrigued by the challenge. Yet they asked themselves, could they really do it?

They proved themselves by getting the jobs and learning to successfully do the work. What kept them there? The ones who stayed found that the work, in addition to giving them a better life financially, matched their background (sports, working with machines, rough housing), their interests (the outdoors, exercise), personalities (counter culture, independent, pioneering), and talents (mechanical abilities, the desire to help).

In addition, they liked being pathfinders. They were pioneers. It was exciting to be one of the only women to drive a big tractor trailer. It was a novelty to be the gas woman, or the telephone utility worker, showing people that women could be happy and successful in new roles.

A combination of necessity and commitment started a quiet revolution. More women now work in nontraditional jobs and their numbers are growing. High school counselors still don't encourage women to enter fields like construction and labor to find satisfying work. However, given the ever growing numbers of formerly traditional mothers now heading families, and the burgeoning unemployment and high school drop-out rates, more women need to find out about good job opportunities that provide great money, new skills and feelings of self worth and respect. They need to know, through a concerted social endorsement, that they have a choice.

Understanding what motivates these blue collar women is the key to unraveling the mystery of their nontraditional lives and a clue to help others break down the barriers that contstrain them.

Money and Power

Good pay is the primary motivator for most women entering these jobs. For single mothers, high-school drop-outs and welfare dependents, there are shockingly few traditional paths toward earning a good livelihood. Even many college-educated women, particularly those educated for currently overcrowded fields such as law and education, are unable to make a living in their chosen field.

These women represent a painful shift in the employment opportunities now available. Yet, despite the lack of opportunities, many women need to find gainful employment, because they are an emerging class of women who are the sole support of families. Such women do not merely supplement their husband's income. In a world where divorce statistics are rising, they may not be married, or, if they are, they may be the primary breadwinners.

The promise of money is often the dare— the lure— to try the unthinkable, simply because it's the best way to earn a living wage. This is so even if some negative consequences sometimes result.

Money also gives women who must work and who come from lower economic groups self esteem, status, the ability to buy the things they want and the power to leave bad marriages and raise children on their own. Lorie, who earns $675 a week plus $19 an hour for overtime, makes it perfectly clear that she took her blue collar job for the money. Mary makes $22 an hour as a welder plus fringe benefits like $2.58 toward a retirement annuity, paid medical and double time for overtime. What is even more important to her, she is absolutely addicted to what she does. "No one controls my life now because I have money. It is such a feeling of power to have money," she says. There's also a sense of power associated with the physical nature of the job. Pam, who earns $1430 every two weeks, finds a certain power in using machines that tear up dirt and rip through yards.

These women are the forerunners. They are taking advantage of the secret fact that many women in nontraditional jobs earn as much or more than men in the same professions.

Freedom

Because they couldn't stand some women who were catty in the operator's pool, the strict dress codes, and having to ask permission to go to the bathroom, women who once worked as operators for the telephone company willingly and enthusiastically responded to the freedom offered by the outside working world. Outside, no one was around to watch over them. Madeline explains that: "As an operator, if I even turned to talk to a friend, my supervisor was breathing down my neck. I had to put up a little green card to go to the bathroom, so everybody knew when I had to go. Sometimes I had to wait up to a half hour. It was dehumanizing." Mary says, "I like it because I'm by myself. They tell me to do something and I go and do it. I am left alone to do my job all day long. Miles of work is ahead of me and the time flies by. It's nice. It's creative, fun, putting a building together."

The Challenge

Betty was motivated to do something different. She really loves challenges; so when a friend who was the wife of a policeman suggested she try out for the force, she jumped at the idea. "I get bored. This job has never done that to me. There is always something else I can do." Sylvia, an undercover police officer, says she was always an athletic daredevil. Cindy took the firefighter challenge, because she wanted to help people. She had witnessed an accident and felt helpless standing on the sidelines without knowing what to do to help. Madeline left her phone operator job as soon as she saw a way out: "We were treated like machines. In fact, they are replacing operators with machines. My friend, Muffy, who is six feet tall, was having the time of her life. She worked really hard in all kinds of weather, but she got to decide when she went to work. She made good friends. It sounded like a great big party. It sounded great. There was a bit of a 'I can do that' challenge." Madeline also had a political motive. She liked being a woman doing physical labor.

Exchange of Information

Responding to information posted by companies, encouraged by their fathers, or influenced by other women role models, information concerning jobs inspired them to join the blue collar work force. Pam aspired to be an executive secretary and didn't know women could work in blue collar jobs until a friend showed her the sewers. She was surprised they didn't have rats running around underfoot. In fact, they were kind of "clean" dirty rooms. What was more surprising was she found out she was really able to do the work. When Brenda found out the guy in the tire shop, who sat on his duff most of the time, was paid twice what she made, she did everything in her power to get his job when he vacated it.

External Conditions

In the 1970s, the Department of Labor's Equal Employment Opportunity Commission (EEOC) forced companies to actually entice and recruit women into these jobs. Once the law suits were settled, doors began to open. In the 1980s, nontraditional employment opportunities again reopened for women, mainly because the economy was booming and there was enough work to go around. In the 1990's, rising divorce and unemployment statistics caused women to seek job opportunities in new fields.

Sense of Accomplishment

Women who worked with their hands to accomplish something appealed to Pam. She took classes through the company to get a frame attendant job and once employed, she also learned on the job: "I've done stuff I thought before I'd never accomplish, like school and regular college courses that I actually passed. If I had stayed in the office, I would still be there." A role model for her nieces, Madeline feels she's really helping people by linking up life sustaining telephone lines. "This is life and death for certain people—shut ins, invalids. Telecommunications is just as important as water; it enhances or makes their lives possible. I can go down the street and say, 'I put in terminals there.' If you work at a department store how great would you feel saying, 'Yea! I sold her perfume?' I have five nieces who see me. I'm strong, I take care of business, do stuff that's incredible to them. I'm making an impression on them. Here I am."

Getting A Workout

Sweating, pumping, training and using their bodies is a job benefit for many women. While over —exertion can be a problem for some women, most of them enjoy the release involved with physical labor. Staying in shape is a welcomed requirement for police, firefighters and lifeguards who get time to exercise included in their workday. For others, it is a byproduct. Jennifer gets a high from the physical exertion of combating a big fire. Cheri, who probably is stronger than many of the men in her profession, is happy that she gets to work out on the job. She'd never have the time otherwise.

For the Love of It

Mary is the epitome of many women who simply and unabashedly love their grueling jobs. "I love the work. I need to be out there. When I get up in the morning I'm almost hyper I'm so excited to go to work. The adrenaline is pumping. I just look forward to going out there and doing the job and doing my welding."

They don't consider working in the hot sun or in the cold and damp punishment; they find it liberating. Satisfaction flows from the money, independence, exercise and knowledge of the fact that they are pioneering the way for others. The lucky ones found satisfaction quickly. Others developed it over a period of time, in part through the admiration of others:

"You mean you really dig ditches or climb telephone poles?"

"You make what an hour with no education?"

"How come I'm stuck wearing hot sticky nylons making minimum wage?"

Pam's day goes quickly. "I just love the outdoors and playing in the mud." Mary enjoys the satisfaction of seeing what she's accomplished at the end of each day. She also finds the friendships she's made important. She has no husband or relationship outside of work, but gets her "tender loving" on the job. It is her sense that people who work outside join together to achieve a common goal. Sylvia, foreign born and uneducated, likes the flexibility, because she is a single mother. She can work at night while her child sleeps and still earn as much as her college-educated sister. Plus she's been able to learn a new skill in the pressroom. What Linda loves is the artistry of welding and, in her teaching role, breaking new ground for women who used to be afraid of fire and the foundry. For Sylvia, the narcotics agent, the thrill is putting the bad guys in jail.

Together these women love the power and freedom of having enough money and being in control of their lives, the friendships they make with their coworkers, the feeling of service when "The customer is thrilled," or the wonderful sense of accomplishment because they are able to successfully hang in there and do this tough work day in and day out.

Mary Michels, Welder, Member of the Ironworkers Union, Forty-eight years old

Mary definitely doesn't look like the stereotypical welder. She is petite and pretty. Yet she started welding thirteen years ago. At the time, she was going through a divorce, and barely supporting herself and her two sons on the little above minimum wage she made as an accounting clerk at a furniture company. Her father, a welder himself, suggested she give it a try.

"I like welding and having the work set out in front of me and saying, 'Oh my God, I have all this to do,' and then I seeing the work completed and saying, 'Oh, my God, I did all this.' Sometimes it seems so normal being the only woman on the job. I'm treated well, I think, because I'm easy going and I keep my mouth shut. Otherwise, I wouldn't make it. What's important, I definitely don't hassle.

"Still, I get upset. It is a real hassle with only five or six women out of 3,000 doing this work. I was talking to high school girls. I thought it was important because I love the job. It's not that the women do not want to go out there but it is too hard to get work. At this point I would not recommend women getting in the trades. First, we need really strong compliance people. But there is a brick wall in terms of hiring. Before I tell them how wonderful this is, we need compliance.

"My dad was a welder and when I was going through my divorce he called me up out of the blue and asked me if I would like to get into welding school. I told him I'd think about it. I knew it would be a pretty big change. I did think about it for two months as I was working as an accounting clerk making minimum wage, hardly able to make ends meet. I told him I would do it. He signed me up at the Pacoima Skill Center. At the time we figured I would learn to weld and then go into a shop as a welder. To my dad it wouldn't be acceptable to work in the field. Period. Women do not work out there. To this day I haven't figured it out. It's funny because at the time I had talked to a lot of other people about careers, but I never talked to my dad. I didn't want him to worry, and I really didn't think he could be helpful to me. But I get chills thinking about it because here he asks me, 'Do I want to be a welder?' It took five months, twenty weeks, 8 A.M. to 2 P.M. full time.

"It was bizarre because I was the only female in the class, but I was in my own little world doing my only little thing. It was strange but I got used to it. I had to become a welder and I had to succeed, or else I'd starve. Financially, being a female, there was no way I could earn money because women don't earn good money. We earn poverty wages. So I figured either I would have to get on welfare or earn poverty wages or get a better job. I didn't want welfare because it didn't pay enough, I didn't want another husband to take care of me and my children, and I wanted another job.

"Construction was booming in 1980 and they couldn't get enough construction workers and welders. Guys who graduated would come back to the Pacoima Skill Center and tell us how great it was. Guys would be working at Bush Gardens, a massive project in Van Nuys, California—really big, and they encouraged me to go out there. They told me it was not too hard and not too heavy and there were a lot of little guys out there who aren't that strong. They were very encouraging the whole time. There were a lot of negatives, though, too.

"Of course, I found out that some people flat out are not going to hire me because I'm female. I get real tired of it. It is different for the guys. You get jobs through your friends and I've gotten a lot of jobs that way too, but it is easier for guys. I don't have phone numbers. I can't be calling these guys at home; they have wives and wives don't understand why a female would be calling them. So, I have limited access. I've actually had my son call for me. Guys get together and have a good time and talk. I don't go out with the guys. The connections aren't there. There is nobody out there backing females. The Union is out of it.

"But in the early 80s there were so many jobs that if you persevered, you were bound to find one. I got my first job at Bush

Gardens. I worked every day for a year and a half except for bad weather. The guys were nice, very encouraging. I was never short of someone showing me something. I would be cutting something and because I was new someone would come by and show me how to do it. So I had a lot of teachers out there and I would never turn them down because I was always learning. I definitely had an advantage there.

"I consider myself the production welder. I put my hood down and I am welding the iron together all day long. I have a welding rod and a holder that holds the welding rod and a machine with leads or a gun with wire. The metal melts are coming out of the welding gun with electricity. It's fun.

"I was doing a parking structure with precast panels with metal clips, welding those metal clips to the metal on the building. There were a lot of iron workers out there. Some I hadn't seen in a couple of years. You always run into each other. It's really neat. It was an overtime job and I made a lot of money. It was eight days. I'm outside, but under a parking structure. There is usually something above me until I get to the roof. I love working outside. You could never get me inside again. I'd get claustrophobia. The weather doesn't bother me. I just dress for the weather. I never get cold because when I'm working my body heats up fast.

"Prior to the last two years, I worked all the time. Right now I'm kind of resting after all the overtime. Then, somehow I get angry and that motivates me to go look for jobs. I go down to the Union hall or to the job sites and ask to be hired. I usually have to get myself worked up, because it's hard going to a construction site and asking for a job. It can be very disappointing. If it's a company I've worked for before, they will hire me on the spot.

"Except for my dad's welding, there's nothing in my background that connects me to this work. I was raised to be a traditional female, to grow up, finish high school and get a husband. The idea I had was I would get married, wouldn't work and raise my family. I had factory jobs here and there, and I always worked and earned enough to pay the baby-sitter and a few doctor bills here and there. I was eighteen when I married and was married eighteen years. My working had nothing to do with the break up. I got the job because of the divorce, and I got that because he was going through his mid-life crisis. Our marriage couldn't survive his mid-life crisis. He was in the automotive business selling parts and upholstery. I worked for my husband as a gofer or flunky. The divorce was totally devastating at the time. It was like a death. I couldn't believe he would walk out on me. I planned to spend my life with him. Things weren't perfect but I never thought about divorce. It was always in the back of my mind that I couldn't survive on my own financially. I don't date now with the AIDS thing. The few relationships I had after my divorce were short. If I found somebody really nice, yes, I would get married again. I find guys on the job all the time, but I don't date guys on the job. I did at the beginning but it's not a good idea. It's common knowledge that I don't date. We're friends and they treat me like a person. I do get tender loving care on the job and it makes up for it.

"It is such a feeling of power to know I can do whatever I want, to know I have the money to go on my little shopping sprees. I can take myself out to dinner and it's so nice. I can help my grown kids—not a lot but I have the money. And when I retire I will have my ironworkers benefits—which will make my life very comfortable. No one controls my life."

Laura Jeffers, Off Shore Oil Rig Worker for Exxon, Forty-five years old

Learning what she didn't want in her life from watching the frustrations of her mother and family, Laura has an admirable story of her determination to provide for herself and her children. She works hard seven straight days on an isolated oil rig out in the ocean, running up and down seven flights of stairs carrying heavy tools. But she has carved out a career that has resulted in a Wharton education for her banker daughter and college for her sons. Not bad for a high school dropout from South Central Los Angeles who was born the fifth of seven children and raised exclusively by her single-parent mother.

"I work on an offshore oil platform in Santa Barbara for Exxon. Currently I'm an operator. I have the platform under surveillance. We take rates and pressures of liquid going through different vessels on the platform. Containers hold the oil on the platform. We pull 25,000 barrels of oil out of the ocean per day. We hold it for eighty minutes before it's put in containers. We remove gas. Oil tankers come by every couple of days. We are self sufficient. We work twenty-four hours round the clock. We do all the work mostly ourselves, including mechanical and electrical. We are trained in both. We sleep and eat on the rig. I work in shifts of seven twelve hour days, and am on call at night. We are the fire fighting team; we get up and do electrical. You come in maintenance at the entry level and they train you in mechanical and electrical and operations. The training is one to four weeks given in small intervals on different machinery. Now Exxon is asking new hires to have an electrical or mechanical background. I came to work in 1980. Back then they were not asking for technical background.

"It seems like it was just yesterday. I like it because it gave me a career rather than a job. I have three kids I was able to support. There are great benefits, including retirement and school scholarships for my kids. The company paid for my daughter to go to Wharton. I have a son who is a policeman; my daughter and another son both graduated from University of California in Davis. I raised them as a single woman. The father was not involved.

"I'm forty-five years old now. I don't mind giving up weekends and holidays. My kids and I have adjusted. We celebrate holidays before and after. I had worked on shore a couple of years before going out. It has taken discipline from the beginning. I had people sleep in the house when I wasn't there. It's something you just can't start. It has to be instilled in them before hand. My kids would die before they'd try anything on me. Even fathers working on the rig had problems with their kids stealing cars. My biggest problem was the phone bill. I've never been to the police station or had problems with drugs. We lived in South Central. My daughter told me they thought I would kill them if they did something. My mother was living a half mile from me. They were latch key kids somewhat, but I made up for it when I was there. They were the type of kids who would get up and go to church by themselves. It was a routine. Now I live in San Bernardino. I moved three years ago. My youngest son is in San Bernardino, too—managing a hotel. My daughter is in the East as a Vice President of Corporate Lending at Barclays Bank.

"I've had several women roommates on the rig. They never put me with the men. One woman started drinking because she couldn't stand the harassment. She wouldn't talk about it with anyone. We have eight flights of stairs with no elevator. She fell down.

"Now one other women works on the rig, but she works opposite me. If we have a lot of people I take a two-person room. It would be a catastrophe to put me with men due to personal hygiene. A couple of years ago we only had one VCR and they were getting raunchy. If I didn't like it I would just leave. I found out a lot of men didn't like it. Now we have our own videos. Exxon does things to keep us comfortable. It is a sacrifice to be out here in the first place. They cook excellent meals for us. All of us are healthy. We have a recreation room with weights. It's quite comfortable. The week goes rapidly. Younger people think after being on the rig five minutes 'Oh my god I've been here forever.' You can go downstairs and fish. Sunset and sunrise are astronomical. Peace and calm. Physically, though, it's challenging.

"I had been in trades prior to Exxon. I had done construction and residential housing. Here I make $18.53 per hour plus benefits. One of the unique things is we've never been laid off. Our benefits are going up and up— we don't have to pay Kaiser medicine anymore. This job is similar to a milk route. You check the machinery every day. If there is anything abnormal you shut stuff down. You have to go up and down stairs with tools that weigh as much as I do. But you have people to help you. No one is stupid enough to go it alone.

"It's a challenge working with all men. With women we have to be able to do the task. Men only have to show potential. We have to absolutely prove we can do it to be accepted. As soon as you get a new bunch you have to start all over and that gets old. Last year we hired 200 new people and they all go through the rig. Some people don't like the isolation—some don't like to get their hands dirty. I just think then they don't like to work. I don't worry about politics anymore. Before it was important, but after about four years I just said I have a right to work here. There are a variety of people, some even with masters. I'm just there to do my work and get my butt off. When it comes to the tools I know what I'm doing.

"I was raised with no dad in my family. My mother had seven kids. I was number five. My mom was a domestic. I saw her work. I saw her get up and go to work every day. I loved to sew. I transferred those skills to construction. I didn't get a high school diploma. I was sixteen by the time I married and had gone through that ya hoo. I went back to school at nights. I used it as a way to pull myself out of poverty. I just continued to work for something better.

I went through abusing myself with men and trying to find a father figure. I realized I had to be mother, father, sister, brother. I was married almost two years and another kid came along. We kept it up about four years. I never married again. I recognized I could be happy by myself. My family was envious and kept pointing out that it's a man's world and I really shouldn't be out there. My mom said go for it. That why I don't associate with my brothers and sister. Anyway, one-half of them died of drugs. Seeing it in my family, my kids didn't have to look very far. I spent the blizzard in New York talking and talking with my daughter and had a great time talking. She never came back, I wish she would.

"My children think I have always been adventurous. I would take them to work when I worked construction. They promised God and three other people they were going to get an education because they never wanted to work that hard. There were muggings in the neighborhood; they hadn't started shooting yet. My kids were identified as gifted kids, and that was the real beginning. I got flak from others in the neighborhood like, 'Oh the school system here isn't good enough for your kids.' But when they were bussed out I thought, 'I can continue my skills without worrying about them.' They were hand picked out of the neighborhood.

"My daughter was the first person to go to college out of the family. Some job counselor told my daughter all she had to do was get a MRS degree. I jumped on that woman with my two feet. I wasn't very tactful about it. I never knew how to do these things but I knew how to scan the papers to find the people who could help. I would get the kids into things and that's where they found some peace. They went to back to back summer camp. I never went. I kind of relived my life through them.

"Of the six women who started with me, only two are left, and we are the only two with children. If there is sexism—I deal with it. Harassment— I deal with. I don't let nothing go by. I have gone to upper management or outside sources. Management has changed, because Exxon has educated management to change. If my husband had pay and stuff it might have been a deterrent.

"I've been on panels at trade meetings for high school girls telling them, 'These are options in your life without all the hoopla and harassment.' And now they are talking to young men about how to treat women—that will help. When they would watch dirty movies on the rig, I would always tell the guys, 'That could be your mother, sister, daughter—it's not right. When I open a door I don't want to see this.'

"What motivated me was the abuse I've seen with my mother who had seven kids by five fathers. They had just came from the South, just learned how to read and write and were just grateful to get jobs. People don't even recognize it is being done to them. They just think this is the way it is supposed to be. I chose things I saw working for my mother and dismissed the others. I said to myself, 'I'm going to make sure this house is clean and so when the kids get home we can talk in peace about some of the things they did in school.' I learned from what I observed about my mother. The sad part about it is a young woman needs nurturing. But now I know there is a difference between nurturing and love. I thought with the kids' dad it was love and for him it was just lust. I try to tell my kids, and if they understand, that is the first step. I observed the long haul and made up my mind. By the time I knew how to make clothes, I could protect myself. I could sew nice looking clothes. You don't have to have the parent pay $100 for tennis shoes. We went to the outlets and that made the difference, because the kids could still look cool. I listened to them. I used to slip into school to watch them when they thought I was at work I told them you never know where I am. My mom got her nursing license when she was forty-five years old, so she was happy finally and got all her kids out of the house. One of the reasons I don't speak to my brothers and sisters is they used her. But if she watched my kids, she got compensated."

Yvonne Butler, Only Woman Sanitation Worker in Los Angeles, Thirty-four years old

After seventeen years of welfare Yvonne was very motivated to get off and make something of herself so she could educate her two sons. She now earns over $35,000 a year and owns a $200,000 house and a car. Her work is dirty and extemely hard on her body, but she says she's in it for the long haul. Perhaps her success story will inspire others to join this first and only woman in Sanitation in Los Angeles.

"I've worked in sanitation, trash, almost four years in April. I had a friend in refuge who told me when they were hiring. I went down and put in an application. You have to have experience on a vehicle of more than two axles, along with a written test, and then a performance test actually driving a 1,200 pound truck over fourteen feet high. I did good—scoring ninty-seven out of 300. I was the only woman. Prior I had driven buses for two and a half years. Basically I drove forty foot buses thirteen and a half feet high. I started driving the bus, because a neighbor suggested they were hiring bus drivers. The job was working for the school district and they train you to drive the bus, teach CPR for carrying loads of kids, prepare you for the test and when you finish the course, they hire you.

"Most times before that, I worked around Christmas in accounting. I always wanted to work. I had two kids out of wedlock. I didn't venture into going to college, but I always had a desire not to be on the county (welfare) for the rest of my life. When my son was five years old I had to figure out what I wanted to do with the rest of my life. Little did I know you should stay on the county and go to school, because when I got the bus driving job I was making about the same money and they (the county) cut me off. I was working about four hours per day earning about $5.00 per hour which is about $6,000—what I was making on the county. I worked there because I felt I needed to know what it was like out in the workforce. I had to take whatever I could get and learn what people had to go through to stay in the work force.

"I did it to be where I am now. Now I work and make about $35,000 to $40,000. I have a good home, and me and my husband just bought a new car. The kids are in more activities now, like Young Marines, and karate. I make almost three times what I did at bus driving and the county. The work is hard—don't get me wrong. I worked for everything I have. I worked for it. I laid down with my husband the other night and we was beat, but we said to each other, 'They can't say we didn't work for it.' I used to pick up trash cans ten to seventy pounds, sometimes working fourteen hour days—the whole nine yards—in rain, heat, even snow, in all kinds of weather. We work hard for our money. Our bodies pay for it with endless aches and pains. You get used to it and ignore it, go in and drop an aspirin. Over all, I wouldn't give it up, because of the money, benefits and coworkers. I've never had no problem with my coworkers. I get more of that from my supervisor. My coworkers have always been there for me: 'Do you need me to take a block (of houses for trash pick up) for you?' But higher ups couldn't accept women in the field. I just dealt with it. I was just there to do my job; just give me a route and a truck. I wanted to be able to prove myself. I knew I was the only woman and I had a point to make. Four years down the line I'm just one of the guys.

"My supervisor is a headache to everybody. He really hates to see a woman there. I tell him where to get off. I go over his head and he gets overturned and that is the end of it and I go to do the job. I would like to see other women get into this, especially now, because of the new trucks (which pick up with an automatic arm). Other women would be an adjustment because I get all the attention, but I still would like to see other women.

"When I started picking up trash cans my son was twelve and he was putting me in the bathtub, rubbing me down with alcohol and Ben Gay. It was an adjustment for the whole family. I already had taught my son to cook ,and he had to make breakfast for the youngest. He did a lot with Hamburger Helper. After six or seven months my body started getting adjusted. Now, with the new trucks, I can pick up 300 homes in four hours. But there is more trash on the ground now than three years ago. The truck is slower than the person. It takes more time now but less body work. I just started driving the new truck three weeks ago, because it was awarded on seniority. All that time before I picked up trash all by hand. Other people look at me with a lot of respect. I'd see people staring at me from ten houses down because they could see my pony tail sticking out of my hard hat. They are waiting to find out if they had actually seen dangling earrings. Just yesterday a lady said, 'Yea, all right,' when she saw I was a woman. I stop to tell women what kind of license they need. They have kept me going.

"I met my husband on the job and we married about two years ago. It was my first marriage. My husband has been in it twenty-four years. My boys are sixteen and eleven years old. My kids always were rooting me on. They'd seen me play the mother and father role to them for so long, they'd say, 'Mom you are tough enough to do it.' They encouraged me to go on gladiators and I would have done it if it was my first year, but after four years there is no way I would touch it with a ten foot pole.

"There is only one way to pick up trash. I used to work out before I got in trash and I think that is how I lasted. I knew what it was to push yourself. Still, it's rough. I use to pick up on two days with my upper body and two days with my legs and thighs. Trash weighing about sixty pounds. Your body adjusts. They don't really train you on how to lift, only in driving the truck—like never turn to the left, always turn to the right but no lifting up. A lot of guys have to have surgery on their knees, rotator cuffs. With seniority you might not have to bend or lift or pull. The chances, are basically, if you were in decent shape, after working a few years, you won't be. When you leave the City you definitely will not be. Doctors tell us our bodies are equal to pro football players. Stepping up and down out of the truck to the curb eventually your joints give out, or your back gives out. I hate the fact that it messes with your body, but I'm in it for the long haul. The only way I would walk now is if they go private. I'll work hard to go toward supervisor. But I don't like the way I feel some days, just trying to stand up. It's like pulling yourself. Also, I'd leave if they eliminated workmen's compensation. No way I'm going to hurt myself on somebody else's job and then get no pay.

"My father has shown more concern about my job than my mom. He knows physically it's weighing me down. He understands that more than my mom but she knows I'm strong and muscular. I go for it. I did what I set out to do when I had my first child. I knew I would not do like I seen so many other women around me do. I learned from that before I had my first child. I wouldn't be pinned on a income that comes to support my kids because it was not my support. I am very proud. Now, I live in a $200,000 home. I teach my kids that we have come a long way. We give a lot of thanks to God. I'm proud God gave me the wisdom and heart to press, because there was a lot of things that made me want to quit, like dealing with my supervisor. I wasn't going to let him walk all over me. It was about respect and I wasn't going to kiss nobody's ass. When I was telling him off I didn't care if I made it or didn't make it. He did respond for a while. I got respect. I still get on him. People say, 'Them two is something to see.' I tell him, 'You are silly.' But I learned over the years he has a personality problem. I tell him, 'If you have a problem, you have all day to sit around here and deal with it.'

"I spent seventeen years on the county (welfare). I had my first boy at eighteen. My mom and dad are from Texas. My dad played briefly for the Brooklyn Dodgers. Then he drove rigs across the country (now I'm about as close to that). He went to Ralph's as baker and mom was at the homestead. She had eight of us and she was a good mom. A lot of my sisters, we pattern after my mom. She was not a fussy person; she talks everything out. I've seldom seen her lose her temper. I've never heard her cuss. I'm proud and conscientious about the way I carry myself as a woman. The only difference between me and my mom is, I'm a lot sturdier and bolder, and not scared. I'm feminine, but tough. I have to wear their uniform five days a week with khakis and work boots and I hate it. So I wear dresses and heels, make-up and long hair dos the rest of the time.

"I hope more women get into this, and they might now, with the new trucks. I bet they will because a lot of women say they need the money. I have kids and I don't want to depend on this man."

An article in *Tradeswomen: A Quarterly Magazine for Women in Blue-Collar Work*, about Anne McLaurin also caught our eyes:

Anne was motivated by despair. She is now working for Contra Costa County Sanitary District, east of San Francisco Bay. "That's sewers, not garbage."

Practically the first thing Anne says is she is clean and sober, and has been for seven years. Then she starts to cry. But she's okay—in fact, she's great.

"I want to tell you that nothing I have today came from anybody else. Everything I have I got myself. I left an abusive, alcoholic husband in New Jersey in '84. I had two little babies and I was pregnant with the third, and I got out, with fifty bucks and my kids and the clothes on our backs. A year later, I realized I had a problem with alcohol and drugs and I got help."

She then showed a paycheck stub, highlighting $3,256 per month. "Five years ago I was on welfare, six years ago I was a junkie living in a drug-infested neighborhood in East County. So I'm here today to tell you it can happen."

While Mary and Anne at first were motivated by the money, they found the money had a larger meaning. It freed them from dependency and gave them the financial power to take care of themselves and their children. Mary is further motivated by an absolute love of her job. Having a forum for sharing her experience with others would make her completely happy. Yet she knows that society needs to take the lead. The government and the media need to take on the task of communicating to the legions of women out there in menial, below poverty-level occupations that there are huge rewards in working in these nontraditional jobs.

Some talk of the toughness of these jobs and some the harassment. Yet, women want them, take them, and keep them. It is stirring to see the persistence and desire that motivates courageous women to get out of unfortunate circumstances, poverty or dependence. Just as in Laura's story, determination keeps them going against tough odds, because they are motivated to carve out a better life. Isn't it heartening that so many women are motivated to take advantage of these opportunities? Theirs are tales of women who are appreciative and grateful to gain another chance for a better life, offered by government and business. They find pleasure and celebrate their discovery as well as their liberation.

SEVEN

DIRTY DEALS

"I have dirt in my wrinkles."

Pam, Ditch Digger

When a woman works as a laborer, there are, of course, many physical hardships, including physical and mental exhaustion. Dirt literally gets under their skin. Says ditch digger, Pam, "I have big dark marks on my face and fingers. I work with material that just likes to stay there. The grit in the wrinkles of my skin bothers me when I have to cook. I've had to learn to wear make up more often to protect my skin." Tanya also spoke of the hazards of her job at the beach. "The exposure to sun is our biggest concern. A couple of years ago we had a young girl, in her early thirties, die of skin cancer. I put on sunscreen all day, I wear a hat. Especially being a junior guard instructor, you have no shade all day. It is definitely draining. You come home worn out."

Cold and rain affects them. Lorie works outside in the subzero temperatures of Minnesota winters. Her truck has a bad heater; so many times she just lays in the hot water of her bath when she gets home from work to warm her body. " One cold, rainy, very nasty day I drove forty-five minutes home being so cold that my foot was shaking on the clutch, and I had to pull to the side. My whole body just shook. I had no control over it. It scared me."

Special uniforms and equipment complicate life. Betty almost lost her boyfriend. "I remember one day I got home from work, threw my uniform and stuff on the couch, then rushed to the market because my boyfriend was coming to dinner. He came into my apartment while I was at the store and saw the guns and uniform and just left. After I got home I waited a little while and called to see where he was—not knowing he'd already been there. He said he came in and saw my stuff and just freaked. He was afraid I would change. We actually stopped dating for about two weeks."

Physical demands take a great toll on women who are small and thin. Jennifer says, "The physical work takes more out of a woman; it takes more out of me because I weigh 112 pounds. When you have a fire, everything is hard. You have to haul a very heavy and cumbersome hose. It doesn't bend. You have to get it up the stairs. Ladders are hard. When you get into a burned building you have to clean and move heavy furniture."

Odd hours take their toll, too. Cindy loves her job in the firehouse, but complains about being awakened many times during the night. "This is a busy station. Bells ring maybe three times a night. The lights go on and wake everyone. I usually sleep in my running shorts and a t-shirt, ready to pull on the big, bulky yellow 'turn out' pants I have to wear to go into a burning building."

Pam Owens, Cable Splicer, United States West Telephone Company, Thirty-eight years old

Born in Illinois in 1955, she came with her family to Seattle in 1960. Both her mother and father were black ministers. She began working at the telephone company in 1973, during the summer of her junior year in high school on a recommendation from a high school counselor.

She started as a clerk, typing and ordering in the payroll office, and she liked it. After graduation she worked full time. In 1976 she moved to the typing pool, working evenings from 4 P.M. to midnight so she could be with her children during the day. At the same time the phone company was making a big push to hire women into nontraditional jobs. Two years later, her need for further income became greater, and the 1978 revolution in labor laws requiring a certain percent of women on the job made a further impact.

Owens started in a nontraditional frame wiring job. She took classes through the company to become a frame attendant, then learned on the job. She also watched women working with their hands, who seemed to be accomplishing something in a more "on your feet" environment, with people hollering over loud speakers. At the beginning, she made only a little more money than she had been making at her old job, but her friends told her the potential for increase was great. When she started some men told her women that would ruin the ladders because they wore lotion on their hands. She didn't answer, and didn't listen.

She worked frame for ten years until she went outside in 1989. It was scary because now she had to work underground and she didn't know what was under there. Some men who had been on the job for a long time told her a lot of stories, and she had nightmares about what could be down there—spiders and rats and snakes. But the guys got to be nice to her after they got to know her.

"More money was the thing swinging in front of my face. Plus I needed a change. I'm a nice person and I knew I should move on when I realized I wasn't so nice anymore. I was dealing with screamers who all thought their complaint was the first priority. People loved me up there because I always helped them out, but inside I felt irritated all the time."

The only job that offered change was outside. "One guy I knew, Skip, who worked on air crew, said I should go for his job. He took me to a manhole and showed me that when you're down there it's not that far. It's bearable. It was nicer than I imagined. I imagined it as being like a sewer, but there were little rooms made out of cement and sometimes out of dirt with holes in the wall so the cable could go through. I hadn't imagined they would ever look like that. They weren't sewers. He told me what he did and it was a nice job. So, I said okay to Skip and his job and took the test and passed. As a splicer your job was to maintain air pressure on underground cable.

"Then they offered me an air crew and splicing job in Tacoma. I asked a friend about it, and she told me they would never let me forget I'm black and a woman in Tacoma. Prejudice there and a "good old boys" network create a lot of problems for women.

"However, I was determined. I learned by observation, rather than doing. I'm small, but I fight and hit now. I holler and scream. For example, my first experience in taking bolts out of the utility lid—there are two bolts in each lid. I got one out but couldn't get the other. This guy came to help me. I said, 'don't you touch this.' I was so mad! But, they trained me on the maxi sneaker and they were fantastic. For me this is great. I like the outdoors—it's more physical. My body is deteriorating, though. I chose to do this too late. To me, its worth it, though; I love not having anyone over me. I determine where I go and what I fix.

"I never notice problems with what I do. I finally get the chance to play in the mud. There is more freedom outside. Inside a lot of women are petty. When I go in I see that's why I left. It's back stabbing and petty arguments. You have to dress a certain way. Outside people work together to achieve a common goal. I enjoy it. When I graduated from high school, my goal was to be an executive secretary. I didn't even know this job existed. Although I've been told horror stories of rats in holes and snakes, I've only seen a snake in one hole. I've seen one rat's nest.

"It's definitely not where I thought I'd be out here. I've had fun. It's been like an adventure. I've done stuff I thought before I'd never accomplish on the job and off, like school and regular college courses that I actually passed. That's been a great accomplishment. If I had stayed in the office—I planned to be a secretary— and not been positioned in the phone company, I would still be in an office type job. But I saw men and women doing these other jobs. Comparing what I do now to where I was, learning a lot of the technical things I didn't think I had a brain for took gumption.

"But, the physical labor is tough. By the time I get home I am ready to go to sleep and you can't do that if you have kids. You have to have time to get them ready for the next day, fed and settled into bed.

"I'm sure my job changed me, because I always wanted to learn more. I wasn't the sweet little quiet thing anymore. I became more assertive. I learned a lot at work through training. I'm sure from working eight hours a day I learned to take charge. Those were things I found out on the job. I even took assertiveness training.

"I don't really want to talk about the details, but my divorce was a result of broken down trust—other women. I was urgent about dating about a month after my divorce. I thought this dating thing would be good, but, nah. It's changed— the money thing— they want you to pay and I've dated guys I've known a long time and the marriage thing is right there. I'm not as ready to get that deep. I don't know if I want to go through getting to know someone but I'm lonely and I'll probably end up with someone. Now I'm just sitting back. I'm unclear about what I want.

"I'm the oldest of six, and I'm the only girl. They never said anything about what I do. I'm probably the most successful. One of them drives an ammo truck, one works in paper products, one's a jack-of-all trades, one's a dishwasher, and one's a UPS clerk. I'm like their second Mom. I suppose I have the best and most steady money in the family.

"Soon after I started at the phone company I gave birth to my daughter. She's now eighteen. The dad hasn't been involved. I was angry at him for making me pregnant. His mom took care of my baby and I paid her. I wanted more kids but not without a husband. As far as morals go I got a big bashing from people in the church. I was the preacher's daughter. My parents loved me and my kids and they would not turn us away.

"Now I don't work overtime or Saturday. I have gangs of family that help with the kids. My husband's mom watches my son. I plan to move to Seattle. It will be less costly. All my support and family and friends are there. I've lived in Tacoma four or five years. I have a girlfriend who is involved with day care and I trust her judgment. My husband wanted a five year space between kids. We had a son who is five now. I said it was now or never for another kid. He wasn't ready so I got my tubes tied. It was okay at the time. What hurt most was my husband would say, 'Pam didn't want any more kids.' I have taken all the blame for him not having more, but it was a mutual decision.

"I've had a couple of nights when my son wanted to do something and all I could do was sit on the couch and say, 'I just can't do it today.' I don't like that at all. I work ten hours a day, four days per week—a schedule I sort of chose. I am partners with another guy who wanted four tens and I had worked that before so I said I would try it. It works out okay. I get that Friday to do all my shopping and clean up and all the little things I wouldn't normally get to do.

"I drive my own car to the work garage to get the pickup truck and a trailer that carries the maxi sneaker. My partner and I do a little paper work then go to the sites and plow in their wire. It's new homes or taking all the wire out of the air and putting it underground. Most of our places are new development. I am a network technician, but the boss calls us the 'dirt crew' or 'plow crew.'

"I signed the sheet to do this because I wanted a change, and next thing I knew I was on the crew. It was the same money. I earn $1,430.00 every two weeks. No more money and harder work. I didn't exactly know what this was and that is why I signed the sheet. I wanted to know more about it and running hydraulic equipment sounded like fun. When I got the job I found out these people were installers and installing is a job I turned down for the last ten years. I don't like climbing poles and I don't particularly care for crawling under homes. New homes are okay, but when you get those grungy places that have been around since 1909 it is not real pleasant. So it's not a job I would have chosen. I like learning the new job. I like learning the trouble shooting.

"I've learned to pace myself, so I'm not killing myself on the job. The day goes real fast. The customer is thrilled you finally made it; so there is a reward there.

"Tearing up that dirt, ripping through people's yards; there is a certain power there. There are two other women on the crew trouble shooting but they give me the plow work. My partner, Mike Tulley, is thirty-five years old. We are alike—energetic people. It's good we're together. He told me at first he would not like to have to have a 100-pound woman pull him out of a ditch. I'm I very small boned person. This equipment can tilt. He would rather have a man there who could pull him up if he started to tilt. It's not that I don't have the strength but that they can't see it. It doesn't mean I can't carry out my portion of the job. There's nothing he can do that I can't do but he can do things maybe faster because of his strength. If we are digging a hole he is able to lift more and maybe get more out of his hole before I will get the dirt out of my hole. Running the equipment doesn't take any more strength. He gives me the paper work.

"I'm sort of a passive person, unless you make me mad. As a navigator I got him lost. He knows the area we work in better. He's from the country. After I got him lost he suggested I drive because I told him I wanted to learn to handle the trailer and back the trailer so he choose this time to let me drive. After he looked in the book and found out where we were going and everything was okay, he wanted the wheel back and I wouldn't give it to him. When he thinks I'm not doing something right he'll come in and take over. I think it is his personality; he thinks he can do things better. He is married. He talks to me about his wife.

"The majority of our work is running the plow. We have to dig a little hole on each end but sometimes if we are in someone's nice yard and they don't want a plow, there is a lot of digging. There is a lot of driving and plowing and digging. You are dealing with energetic people so lunch is usually in the car.

"I don't agitate to get another job because I have golden handcuffs. I can't imagine not being with the phone company; I can't imagine even knowing what another company would want to do. I like the idea of serving the customer. I am a perfect server and enjoy satisfying someone else's needs. This is okay, because I'm still learning. I am interested in fiber portion, so I'm trying to move in that direction. I am particular where I go. There was no turn down on this job. It's a new day."

Wendy Gaston, Alignments Repair, B&D Auto Repair, Thirty-years old

Wendy credits her success in auto repair to determination and willingness. Especially revealing is how she uses her time at work when she is not busy. She hangs around with the engine repair mechanics to learn more. She doesn't have to but she does. It invigorates her.

"I was looking for a job for a few months. My girlfriend said there is a school where you can go, train and find a job and they pay while you are training. It turned out to be the St. Louis Urban League/Toyota Automotive Training Center. I applied, and had to pass some tests and have an interview. The tests were basic math and English. The second test dealt with mechanical abilities. I didn't study for it. All you needed was an eighth grade education. Later I realized there were thousands of applicants. Apparently a lot of people had heard about it. The class only took ten applicants. I was grateful to be chosen when they narrowed it down to the final group . It was ninety to one hundred day program. I took brakes and exhaust. It was great, because they had state of the art equipment with all the tools. Toyota donated money, cars and trucks and we got to do hands on stuff on cars. They encouraged us to take the Automotive Service for Excellence (ASE) exam—a nationwide certification—recognized in the industry. ASE certified. Prior to the end of class I was employed as a direct result of school and the placement team at B&D Automotive. For a month I continued to go to school from 7 to 11:00 A.M. and work from 1 to 5:00 P.M. I started doing alignment. After graduation I worked full time doing alignments and brakes, but now I've gone back to part time. Just by being there and more or less hanging around in my free time I've learned a lot about mechanical engine repair. On lunch hour or after work I picked up on a lot of other things. That inspired me to go back to school. I took the Automotive Service for Excellence exam in November, 1993. The results came back in January and I passed. You need two years experience to get a patch (but you can use school and work time)—to get ASE technician, which allows you to open up your own shop anywhere in the nation. That's one of my goals, or to go for a dealership, but it's still too early to tell what I will do.

"I always wanted to know how to work on cars, because my dad always worked on his own car. When I had my own car I was always taking it to people who said it was this or that or charged me $100 to tell me my car couldn't be fixed. I know an honest, competent mechanic is in demand.

"I love what I do. It's challenging. I love working with my hands. I love applying my technical skills. There is never a dull moment. As far as alignments, I feel I can handle it. A dealership is limited to that line of cars but an auto shop works on a lot of cars. I want to take a class in fuel injection and engine repair. I asked my teacher who said community colleges have good automotive curriculums.

"I got into this at twenty-nine, a year ago. I started working at age of seventeen as a mail clerk at an insurance company, then a part time accounts receivable clerk for a commercial lighting manufacturer for two years. I moved up to full time credit analyst. Then I did all kinds of odd jobs; worked at a pizza place, part time for small privately owned party supply store. While going two years at a state college in electrical engineering, I did freelance work. I was into drugs, and I got progressively worse, had bad grades; so I just cut it loose and did cable and stereo repair and yard work. I support myself. Now I live independently in a sober living residence, where the occupants are all recovering addicts. We're nine women in this huge house. It's okay. I'm in a relationship away from the house. I have no kids, but I'd like them someday.

"I grew up in St. Louis. I was born in Texas but have been here since I was two. I knew all the tools my dad had. It was always, 'hand me this.' I was always working on my bike and interchanging parts with my sisters. I had my own set of power tools and a Black and Decker tool box. My dad had a work bench. He encouraged me. I was an inquisitive kid. I have two sisters— I'm in the middle. My dad was thoroughly mechanically inclined. He did his own plumbing, added on a room, put in the driveway, new wiring. He owns property and is very versatile. I was always tagging along behind. He works for the postal service. My mom died when I was fourteen years old.

"It's okay working with all men but you can't play around too much. They tend to get carried away. I have to prove myself. I might always feel that way. It's the old concept—this is a man's job—they know better. It's okay once you prove you can do the job. In any one area no one knows it all. When you do alignment it is designed so the car will maneuver better. I work in a body shop so car frames have suffered damage. It will never be like when it came from the manufacturer. At times you have to make adjustments with the alignment because the frame is not where it should be. You have to use your judgment to see how to compensate on the specifications. Sometimes this guy and I didn't get along at all, but now we can take in each others' opinion or advice. I can see constructive positive changes. I believe it's my willingness to learn—one guy calls me the sponge. My willingness and determination helps.

"I make more than I had hoped for. I will get health care. It's satisfying. The ladies in the house where I live ask me when something is wrong with their car. That motivates me even more. There is always someone asking for advice or help. When I don't know, I want to know—that's what motivates me. I could make a lot of money and help. I've excited by knowledge.

"The other day at the bus stop I saw a lady driving a huge truck. I did a thumbs up, because you just don't see women out there, and I like that. I'm not really this activist or into this equal rights but, if a person is really determined enough, regardless of race, creed and color, you can do anything—if you put your mind to it. Everything is changing and I see how my electronics will help fix cars. Mechanical and electrical will be interchangeable—like in smog checks. The grease monkey is a thing of the past because of all of this high tech. Nowadays it is a lot easier to replace rather than rebuild. Right now I work four days, four hours, and one day eight hours. I want to work full time. It took some time getting used to the unevenness; one day I worked on five cars, and another day I only worked on one. More work made the day go by faster. Now I've learned to fill my time by helping somebody or watching. I'm still learning."

Besides the challenges, adventures and increased earnings, there are not only physical drawbacks but emotional ones, as well, such as fear, sexual harassment, discrimination, patronization, disrespect and resentment. These psychological pressures and hardships go hand in hand with all the hard work. In addition, there are small, practical nuisances, such as grease under the fingernails, tools that don't fit smaller hands, lack of separate bathroom facilities and sleeping quarters, or trainers unwilling to show how to lift and pour. then there are the social issues of being accused of taking away men's jobs, stealing other women's husbands, and not acting like "proper women;" the objections of colleagues, companies, wives, families and the public, and their own doubts, insecurities and exhaustion. All of these may sometimes be part of the job for women in blue collar employment.

PART III

BEHIND THE SCENES

"We're like a lightening rod for all their anger."
Madeline, Splicer, United States West Telephone Company

Women in blue collar jobs are sometimes subjected to sexual harassment, discrimination, patronization and disrespect. In certain jobs their colleagues and managers fear and resent them. When this happens, gnawing prejudices work insidiously against them to lessen self esteem and courage. Doubting looks, whispers and other hardships, as well as open rejection, can be serious problems. In such atmospheres, few are out there to support and urge them on. Even if the women are later admired for their accomplishments, they have to first break down the threshold barriers on their own.

In jobs where disrespect is the norm, nobody is looking out for women. Instead, once they manage to get hired, they are often accused of taking jobs away from the men, says Mary, a welder, who really loves her work but says "The negatives are now and always have been." She feels the strain of not being "one of the boys" when it comes time to get her next job. In fact, she's actually had her son call the men at home to get work information, knowing that if she called herself it would upset their wives. "It's much more difficult. A lot of companies flat out won't hire me because I'm a female. It's a real struggle."

Many men who work in jobs outside have made it very clear that they want to work with strong male partners. Pam, who loves her construction job digging in the dirt, still has problems with her partners' prejudices about her small-boned frame. "He told me at first he would not like to have to depend on a 100-pound woman to pull him out of a ditch."

Moreover, once women have these jobs and are successfully working at them, they have to deal with their own feelings about what they do and how the public feels about them. For some, it's hard to admit their job involves crawling around in sewers or in the dirt when talking, for instance, to ex schoolmates at a high school reunion. Syvia went to an all girls' school in Mexico and when she goes there on vacation, it hurts her to answer her friends' questions about her job in the pressroom. "They are all professional—doctors, accountants. When they ask what I do, I say, 'Oh, I work in a pressroom.' I always feel I am not complete because I haven't got a college education. It's a good paying job, but it doesn't have the status I'd like."

EIGHT

SEXUAL HARASSMENT
AND DISCRIMINATION

"So, I get in the car with my new partner, Moberly. The first thing he tells me is: 'Look, I'm going to tell you right up front. I've never worked with a woman, I don't want to work with you!"
                    Betty, Police Officer, Los Angeles Police Department

Although some women in non-traditional jobs have good work experiences and are well treated, one wonders what makes a woman want to stay on the job when she's not wanted and not respected, where she's harassed and the butt of crude language and jokes? Perhaps such women's definitions of sexual harassment are different from ours. Perhaps their threshold for anger is higher. Or, maybe they just want their jobs so badly that they are willing to put up with anything.

Sexual harassment can be defined as a continuum of behavior ranging from the coy wink of an eye to crude and overt advances. Any but the most sheltered women, and nowadays many men, in the workforce usually experience some form of sexual harassment and discrimination during their careers.

For women in nontraditional jobs, these experiences can be more frequent and glaring. Of course, it is a difficult and explosive subject. Historically it has not been openly discussed, but recently more and more individuals and groups are exposing the problem, through discussion, legal means and legislation.

Like many other aspects of our increasingly industrialized life, such as wages, work hours and working conditions, the boundaries of sexual relations at work are monitored by government. Equal employment opportunity and affirmative action groups define the hiring and protection of women and demand that employers should make no difference between men and women in the workforce. Legislation in the early 1970s was directed towards equal access, which was actually an emphasis on equality. Any whisper of inherent differences was viewed as discriminatory. In reality, this attitude blinded us to the tensions of differences.

However, as more women entered the workforce, they were guarded by protective legislation. High turnover and absenteeism, plus the loss of productivity and lawsuits, were clues to the discomfort of females in a hostile male-dominated environment. More recently, we have learned the many different ways in which women are not equal but different, from uniform size to competitive natures. We have an emerging sense of the value of diversity. Despite this, women and monorities have fared much worse than traditional white males in work situations. They are untrained and undervalued because their approach to work looks different —particularly in jobs that depend on physical skills and large body types.

However, sexual harassment is just the tip of the iceberg. It is an unfortunate metaphor for the lack of understanding between men and women. It is symbolic of the chasm existing between the sexes today.

Many women in the nontraditional workforce have encountered varied forms of harassment. For example:

- Specific sexual overtures, though not reported very often, such as a man pinching or grabbing a woman's buttocks as she tried to do her job. For example, while she is climbing or descending a ladder.
- Hostile working environments that spawn innuendoes or crude language and pornography, such as "What you

need is a good you know what from a real man." This also includes referring to women doing blue collar work as lesbians or dykes.

- Patronizing behavior by male colleagues such as indoctrinating a woman on the police force by insisting she be the one to frisk the crotch areas of a group of gangbangers.
- Public questioning of a woman's competence or appropriateness for the job, as exemplified by men saying, "A real woman wouldn't try to do men's work," or other women snickering when they see women in grubby clothes with dirt under their fingernails.
- Resentment illustrated by an irate wife standing over a utility hole because her husband is down there with a woman colleague. Another woman, because her husband slept in the fire station dormitory near a woman colleague, eventually caused him so much grief that he ended up with high blood pressure!

Some women's stories reveal how they were discriminated against while on the job or even before they have the job. In other cases women had to sue just to be hired at all or to pass muster on a physical agility test because it was traditionally graded on the curve. Then once on the job, several women encountered no on-the-job training, inadequate or inappropriate training not adapted to the female physique, strength and background; poor facilities, ill-fitting uniforms and equipment, men who refused to work with them or even talk to them, and those who were so patronizing that they wouldn't let women learn by trial and error. Because of these problems, in some cases, women are still relegated to desk jobs doing paper work because their chiefs, colleagues and the public at large are unable to accept them in these psychologically threatening nontraditional roles that test comfortable stereotypes.

Legally, women are now protected, but they use this protection reluctantly. Even other women, and many men, believe women bring on these problems themselves and question why they can't handle their own situations. Many men resent the encroachment of women into their jobs in the first place, so a legal suit can produce irreversibly adverse effects between men and women in the same department. If women want to hold nontraditional jobs, then they must consider how to distinguish the important issues that go beyond irritation and really threaten their power, authority, self esteem, career and personhood. Negative reactions from some men are fortified by an emerging public backlash that views harassment claims as a ruse to shore up the underskilled. There are now legitimate complaints of misuse of legal protection. Some women can be argumentative, oversensitive and eager to make mountains out of mole hills. Sex discrimination suits can be a convenient avenue for revenge, offering overly broad protection and stifling normal male/female interactions. However, despite these cautions, there is a real need, to provide protection for women; so they can get and keep these wel-paying jobs.

Because there are gray areas as to what constitutes sexual harassment and normal interaction, many women are left with questions such as: Where do they draw the line? How do they best stand up for themselves? Have they exhausted every alternative? What will be the repercussions of fingering someone or some system? Isn't it better to suffer the consequences in silence? How can they continue to live with their male colleagues who may resent them? Just what is the price for legal action?

Though the answers to some or all of these questions may be disturbing, each individual, without sacrificing self-worth or self-respect, must let her own conscience be her guide as to the action to take.

Betty Kelepecz, Female Los Angeles Police Department Patrol Officer, Thirty-eight years old

Betty is a tall, attractive woman. She wore makeup, black stockings and high heels for our interview. She has a lean, lithe body showing the results of regular excercise. Betty is married and has no children, because finding the time is a challenge. When she came on the job in 1980, only two percent of the police department were female officers, few in patrol. Now women make up thirteen percent of the force.

Betty never really planned to be a police officer. She met Janet, the wife of a Los Angeles Police Department officer, while working out at a Jack LaLane's gym. Betty told her she was not happy. Janet suggested police work, because Betty met the height requirements and the force was looking for women. Once she met with the recruiting people Betty never looked back. What really motivated her were the challenges.

"I love challenges. I can't live without daily challenges, goals and things to go after. I get bored. This job has never done that to me. There is always that something else I can do. There was good pay. It offered me more career moves.

"I was first assigned to work with an old guy. He went to the Sergeant and said: 'I'm not working with a woman.' The Sergeant refused to listen. So, I get in the car with my new partner, Moberly. The first thing he tells me is, 'Look I'm going to tell you right up front. I've never worked with a woman, I don't want to work with you. It's not going to be easy.' I said, 'I understand it's the boys club, I'm accepting of that, but can you give me a chance? Teach me something tonight.' The first thing he does is pull over a bunch of gangbangers. He tells me, 'Okay, I'm guarding, you're searching.' When you do a cursory search you have to check the crotch because they keep their guns there. All the gangbangers are laughing, because a young woman has to search them. It was embarrassing, because it was the first time I really searched a suspect and these are gangbangers. By the end of the night my partner said, 'you handled that pretty good. I'll never work with another woman, but I'll work with you again.'

"Back in 1973, Police Chief Davis made a 'unisex' academy for all police officers. Women could work in the field but we still didn't have women above the rank of Sergeant. Prior to this time Davis said he wasn't going to hire women, and he hadn't for a long time. Police women had been restricted from working field assignments and consequently from going higher.

"There was the famous Fanchon Blake suit for discrimination, because women couldn't go above sergeant. The suit was settled in 1980. I had been waiting on the list for police duty until the suit was settled.

"In February 1980 there were 140 officers in the academy and about twenty women. We graduated one hundred officers with about ten women in the field on patrol. A woman was a rarity in patrol in a black and white. I went to Wilshire, and there were no women. There had been a female sergeant who had been a detective.

"I expected the worse. I had resolved I would not be accepted. I would be harassed everyday. I would be hated and nobody would want to work with me. My first day out that's what happened. I came in late, because for one and a half months I had been on a special assignment . Because of this, I didn't have camaraderie even with the other new males.

"I was treated very well, though. Then I went where the Captain asked for women. I feel I've paved the way. I went along with a lot of joking that wouldn't be appropriate now, but it was all in the interest of getting along.

"You had to cut your hair above the collar to standardize, to make you one of theirs. I wore men's clothes, men's ties , men's shoes, and I felt like a clown. Women had to wear cotton underwear—no Frederick's of Hollywood.

"I can remember the first time I combat wrestled I was carpooling with a guy about my height; they put me with him. He didn't beat me and I didn't beat him, but it embarrassed him because he should have been able to beat me. In the car on the way home he said 'Why did you do that to me, Betty?' I said 'Do what?' He asked, 'Why didn't you let me beat you?' I said 'You think I'm going to let you beat me in something like that? No way.' 'Well, you could have at least let me' —'No, I'm not going to do that. I'm here for the same reasons you are.'

"I made detective in four years, which is fairly quick. I was a very young detective and I was a female. There were a lot of men that didn't want me there. They were still police officers working for a female detective. There were a lot of angry people.

"There were these two old time dinosaurs that had a lot of time on the job. I'd walk by and they'd make filthy comments. If they would say anything, it was negative to me, and it always had to do with gender or sex.

"I didn't want to work the traditional women's assignment of sex crimes. They wouldn't put me into robbery investigation, they just wanted me to do the administrative robbery. I didn't want to just do phone calls. I asked to be put into the general robbery investigation.

"They did two things that really upset me. First they put me with a Detective 3, a staunch Mormon. I was a very strong woman and wasn't going to let them step on me. This Detective 3 didn't like me. He told me I couldn't wear skirts. I said, 'I can wear whatever I damn well please as long as I catch my suspects.' He was very sexist. In one conversation he asked, 'How can you do this, go home and make dinner for your husband?' I said 'I don't. He either makes it himself or goes out. We share.'

"Traditionally, on Friday everyone went to bonus shoot. This dinosaur tried to get me to bonus shoot and I don't like to bonus shoot. Shooting was only required once a month. I don't mind guns. I can handle them. But I'm not a gun nut and don't love to have it in my hand and go shooting all the time.

"One Friday he said, 'Don't forget to go bonus shoot.' I said, 'okay.' When I came back he said, 'What was your score?' I said, "What do you mean?" He said, "I told you to go bonus shoot." I said, 'I know what you told me, but I had investigations to do and I didn't bonus shoot.' He said, 'Didn't you hear what I said?' I said, 'I heard exactly what you said, but I'm telling you I didn't bonus shoot and I'm not going to bonus shoot and you can't tell me to bonus shoot.' He said, 'If you don't I'm going to put you on an administrative assignment right now.' I said: 'Oh, you are. You do that right this minute and I am going to go to my Lieutenant because you can't force me to do that.' So I went straight to the Lieutenant and told him I wanted to file a complaint. My lieutenant said, 'Oh, don't do anything, I'll take care of it.'

"They put me with the old time guy who was a jerk who didn't like to work with women, and didn't like to work with me, because I was a snot-nosed kid. Next they put me with his partner. They were really trying to get rid of me and make my life miserable. He was a jerk. For the first couple weeks he ignored me. Finally I grabbed him and took him into a room and said, 'Right now my life is miserable. I know you're a dinosaur, but you can make me or you can break me. Or you can take the opportunity to teach me what you know. You can have me as your protege and tell everybody you taught me everything you know. You can do one of those two things. If you try and break me, I'll probably be broken.' We had a long talk. Finally he said 'Okay, kid, I'll give you a chance.' We became good friends and he taught me a lot."

"I have mixed feelings about the special qualities or sensibilities a woman might have that would make a contribution in her work. My thoughts have changed over the years. I can remember, I hadn't been out in the field long, we got a call for a person suspected of being on PCP. He had been breaking out windows, screaming and yelling. You could see he was under the influence. His hands were all cut up.

I knew it was a very volatile situation. This guy could go off at any moment and tear my head off. I said, 'You know what; let me try on this one.' I approached him and started talking. You have to remember this was eleven years ago. He heard the woman's voice before he heard anything else. I started saying, 'you know everything will be okay. I know you must hurt.' He kept screaming he was on fire. I walked up behind him talking very gently and softly and finally said, 'now will you let me put handcuffs on you and help you.' My partner said if I hadn't handled it we would be in a big huge fight and someone would have been hurt.

"Women are changing. We are becoming more androgynous. I have been allowed to be more sensitive and not get caught in the competitive male thing. Now men are allowed to be more sensitive. Women are an asset to the organization because diversity is an asset. Also this sensitivity has allowed me to be more of a free thinker. I'm not bound in the tradition of the way police work is done, because I'm nontraditional in the first place, being a woman. I have a reputation for being nontraditional in my thoughts.

Jennifer August, First Female Salt Lake City Firefighter, Thirty-five years old

When former playmate of the year, Jennifer August, became a serious Salt Lake firefighter, she had to live as the only woman in a fire station that had no separate women's sleeping or bathroom facilities. Eventually she got the men to share the cooking and cleaning chores; however, she continually had to contend with their irate and jealous spouses. She didn't complain about wearing the men's fire fighting uniform and boots, lifting weights, and dragging heavy water-filled hoses. But, after conforming for years to the mandated short hair regulation—cut over the ears and to the collar—she put her foot down. Finally Jennifer complained to the Chief, saying, "If you don't have tits you ought to be able to have hair."

"At the time I applied to the Salt Lake Fire Department I was thirty-four years old with no direction. I had been racing horses for nine years, not a very secure position, following jobs lawn mowing and house painting.

"I've worked out for ten years. I met a guy from the Salt Lake Fire Department at the gym. I was without a career at the time, and he suggested I try out for the fire Department. Luckily they were taking applications and I applied. I didn't make the cut off on the physical agility part which was graded on a curve. Women just can't be graded on a curve.

"I took it to a lawyer who took it on contingency because she liked it so much. The Equal Employment Opportunity Commission even contacted us. Finally Salt Lake settled out of court and gave me the job. There were three women.

"The physical test changes every year. That year it was a job related combat test with five tasks. I had completed all the tasks but failed the test. Some of my male colleagues couldn't get past that fact. That was all they could see. So I just gave up talking to those people.

"I was in training for two weeks prior to the resolution of the case so I was not paid which was very difficult. For the next two years the great pay raises were also delayed an extra twenty-one days. It was just comical. It's a kick butt academy. I mean it's a killer academy and I was doing it for free. It's like, 'I want this job; I've got to do this.' Every morning you have book learning. Twenty-six different categories you have to learn. In the afternoon you go to the drill ground completely suited up. The whole afternoon is doing the very strenuous physical work of the job; especially the first few weeks when your body's adjusting. You're raising ladders and pulling charged hose lines (a hose with water in it). It was a character builder.

"Living in the firehouse is really no problem at all. The first firehouse didn't have doors but you had your own room. That worked out fine. The second firehouse was a dormitory. I'm an early 'to bedder' and one of the guys came up later. We laid there a while without saying anything and finally he said, 'Boy, Jennifer, you must really feel weird.'

"The dorm had a locker room with no privacy. I've always been around non traditional stuff. The race track helped me a lot. I saw jockeys in their underwear. It's just a state of mind. I haven't seen them much. Mostly its by accident. Somebody walked into the shower on me one time when I was in my underwear. He was a good guy, and I had no problem with it. You just tell the guys you're going to take a shower, and they stay out. We finally put up a curtain. Before the curtain, I'd just put up my hand and we'd giggle and laugh. It was no big deal. Ninety-nine percent of the guys are nice; one percent are very bad.

"There were two times that I had to go before the big Chief. One guy patted me on the buttocks. I just kind of laughed it off. I'm from that era, okay, fine, get it over with. I thought in order to take a case farther you had to complain and I hadn't. One of the officers decided it wasn't kosher; we ended up going in front of the Chief over it. The Chief said, 'well, Jennifer, what remedy do you want?' I said I didn't want any remedy. I was just sorry it went that far. Now that I'm a Lieutenant, I would have to report something like that.

"I was very upset by it, because I've worked very hard to promote my public relations in the job. That destroyed it for a while. I got phone calls asking why I did that.

"Another time there was just very bad language. I'm used to bad language; I use a lot of bad language myself, but this was just very offensive. It was meant in a bad way. I went home that morning with my knees shaking. Specifically I had worked a shift at the other firehouse when my relief came in. One of the 'one percent' guys said, 'Oh, did you relieve Heather? I just wondered if one cunt relieved another?'

"It just hit me, because he was talking to another guy. Everybody let this guy ride over them. For a whole month I was very upset and felt I needed to talk to them. Well, I never got around to it. It ended up in front of the Chief again and one guy I liked got in trouble, too. It makes you look bad and that's not fair. They start out not being fair. Luckily most of the people know these guys. About one month later the guy I like denied saying anything rude. I took him by his collar and shook him saying, 'I've lived with this every day since then; you did say it.' He had said, 'Well, you might as well fuck a cunt because you can't fucking well talk to a cunt.' He said he didn't mean to hurt me. I just said we'll think about it. I'm definitely from the old school, brought up to please people. It's a way of life.

"When I first came on the job we had to have the same military hair cut as the men. It can't extend over the ears or the top of your collar. It's very short. I had to wear short hair the first two years, and I'm a 32A. I had people saying, 'Yes, sir, can I help you?" I became very dejected. My self confidence was just going down the drain. So I thought, okay. I'll go and try and get this fixed. I went before the Chief. I told him. 'If you don't have tits you ought to be able to have hair." Now guys and gals can have hair.

"It's a lot of fun in the firehouse. I had to cook, not because I was a woman but because I had no seniority. I hate to cook. I never had a date. They didn't ask. Nobody. I was unattached. We've had a lot of verbal play. There were some I would have dated.

"The physical work takes more out of a woman; it takes more out of me because I weigh 112 pounds. I work out because I love to work out. It's not that often when you do physical work. Most of our stuff is emergency medical calls. When you have a fire everything is hard. You have to haul very heavy and cumbersome hose. It doesn't bend. You have to get it up the stairs. Ladders are hard. When you get into a burned building you have to clean and move heavy furniture. But most of the time it's not that difficult. You get back to the fire house after you're worked hard like that and everybody is kidding and joking. Everybody is very happy. You're high. It's like you're on drugs.

"My parents both passed away before I became a firefighter. Mom would have loved it. Dad would have freaked out; he was very gentle, kind, old-school: get married, have kids, cook dinner every night. I had a horse, and that freaked him out. I could get injured. But my mom was a very untraditional women. She was a barmaid and she loved all that stuff. I'd hear her cry at the races, 'That's my daughter out there.' When I finished training for firefighter one of the neighbor's came up to me and said, 'Your mother would be so proud.' I was struggling not to just ball. My brother plays charades; 'Guess what my sister does?' He loves it. There are seventeen women in the Department out of 830 men. I was the first.

"I was raised like a boy. I was a tomboy and wouldn't wear dresses. Since I hated my name, mom called me George. I hated Jennifer. It was just so feminine. I loved working on cars with my brother. I didn't want to be a girl. I have one brother four years older and we are very close. We just took a four-day trip to Utah on our dirt bikes. He's too strange to be married. My Dad worked for AT&T. My parents were divorced. Dad lived in Saint Louis. We'd go visit him in the summer, and he'd make us be in at 9 o'clock. My mom didn't even know if we were out at 2 o'clock in the morning. Mom was just not there.

"One time she came to the door. Her clothes were torn, she was bloody, and I looked at her. She had this glint in her eye and I asked what happened. 'A guy tried to rape me, but I beat him with my shoe.' She had three-inch heels on.

"At work we just started a women's group. There are times when all of us need a little encouragement. Men and women are different. It will be good support. We need restrooms in the firehouses. Administration wanted to have this group. Women think differently. Men are little boys. I've met many men I thought were adults, but I don't think they make it. They really don't quite ever grow up. I get tired of acting like a kid, but they don't. Men avoid a lot of things. I don't know how they get away with it. They don't care about the physical testing we're going through. Maybe they are ashamed.

"I've watched other lieutenants deal with my Chief. They fight him; It's like a competitive thing. It's like a good game. Men read new recruits differently. A guy will think a new recruit looks like she doesn't like him, but I think she just looks confused.

"You get tired of fighting it. You are friends, but you are not as good friends. They are never going to accept you like a guy. Regretfully, I am never going to be as strong as a guy. I can do as good a job at emergency medical, but in a fire emergency I am never going to be as good. Maybe I'll be better as an officer. I think I have good reasoning. But I grew up in the era of trying to please people and its painful that I can't, completely."

"I rode horses since I was three years old. Years ago a woman I worked with encouraged me to work at the race track. I was small and one of the guys I worked for got me riding. I was actually happier with that than the Fire Department. It was pretty exciting, but it was: go no where and get injured a lot. It was nontraditional. It's not a woman's place.

"I watched many jockeys get rides who I knew were crocked, doing drugs, and were drunks, but they were men. I was actually getting bitter and frustrated. I didn't want to do that any more. I suffered a few injuries. The horses I was riding were trash; old, broken down. It was because I was female. I would take chances the guys didn't have to take. I was getting on horses nobody would get on. I was struggling to make a living and the men could pick and choose. For the most part they were not going to let women ride. Even a guy I was dating for a long time who had a string of eighteen race horses only let me ride two—the two that were no good. I ended up going to

Billings, Montana; they would ride you there. I rode every race, every day. You don't make a lot of money and the horses were even worse up there. The insurance wasn't any good, retirement isn't that good, and injuries are often and bad.

"Back in 1971 I was a Playboy bunny, and that was interesting because I'm very small. I'm a 32 A on a good water-filled day. So, I was just flabbergasted I was invited to do that. I had a lot of fun. I've told interesting stories about that over the years.

"I got pregnant in my last year of high school. I had the baby, got married— that lasted the typical year. My husband raised my son, which was fine with me. I'm not a mom. I had my tubes tied when I was twenty-four years old. I saw my son maybe once every four years. Now he's twenty-four, not a good age, not going anywhere at all, and I don't appreciate that. I feel some guilt, in that I didn't take more control before. I was young, though. I didn't know. I thought he had it okay. I was like a surrogate mother. I bore the seed, had the child, and that was it.

"I'm engaged for the first time since I was seventeen to a gentleman who has 400 antique collectible motorcycles. We're purchasing a building to make a museum and residence. He is a very witty, entertaining man. He's never been married."

What worked for Betty was confronting the harassing perpetrator directly and engaging him in a project to train her. She was able to handle the harassment herself by the force of her personality without invoking a higher authority. Fortunately, she was successful. She was able to jiggle the system in a way that provided a model for others, a positive face-saving method and an educational experience for her reluctant male colleague.

Jennifer had a threshold legal complaint against the discriminatory agility test. If she did not file that complaint she would not have gotten the job. Still, she is not completely happy in the department. As a woman she is not taken seriously, and even her promotion is questioned.

Brave women take legal action and move mountains in solving the problems of sexual harassment and discrimination on these unusual jobs. Speaking up raises consciousness, even though women are personally at risk in doing so.

As a result of this new awareness, standards regarding pornography, vocabulary, unwelcome advances and joking are becoming company policy. Differences in style and comfort are being shared, reducing the likelihood they will sharpen into harassment charges. More frequently, the women's point of view is being solicited and listened to. The legitimacy of these issues is coming to the fore, as it is more and more acceptable to talk about and confront.

Organizations are taking more responsibility for the offending individuals, within the system, and for the system itself. Organizations are also providing preventative training in how to confront sexual harassment and how to gain expertise and comfort in speaking up about problems and different points of view. In providing protection and support, both for the offended and the offender, through education, human resource specialists and consultants, and legal guidelines, organizations are proactively trying to ward off the problems before they occur.

Sexual harassment occurs in a context. It is tolerated, ignored, unnoticed, or even endorsed. Individuals and systems must confront these trends. Individuals need to speak up, and organizations need to go beyond listening to ferreting out pockets of sexual harassers. Organizations can create a climate of decency with an emphasis on understanding different points of view. Preventing harassment and discrimination goes along with honoring diversity through communication, respect, trust and support. We all can learn from experience. That is why it is so important to listen to women who have had this experience and can guide us through the process.

NINE

OTHER WAYS TO SOLVE A HARASSMENT PROBLEM

"I try not to whine."

Lorie Swenson, Customer Service Technician,
United States West Telephone Company

There are lots of ways to solve a problem. As these women know, it's fascinating to learn how different people approach their own problems, whether they are large or small. From the profiles, we get a big picture of how each woman's resolution fits into the patterns of her life and shapes the complex outcomes. What makes one woman file a legal discrimination suit, another complain, still another confront, while others swallow their pride, go around the problem, or joke about it?

Enormous pros and cons accompany the decisions to speak up or not. We are taught to speak up in school; we speak up to defend our individual freedoms and rights. Speaking up is the American way. But, what are the ramifications?

Complaining

Complaints bring dignity to some situations and give women a right to be viewed as professionals. They set the boundaries and relieve the stresses. What is more, complaining is cathartic. It just feels good to complain. Often their complaints are successful, especially when they focus attention on the problems so that they can be better understood and addressed. Jennifer's complaints produced the changes she wanted, and Cindy's were instrumental in getting short hair restrictions lifted for both men and women. The women on the police forces successfully got hiring and maternity policies changed.

Yet, complaints often invite negative reactions such as attributions of hysteria, bitchiness and weakness. Many times they divert precious energy and resources away from work. For example, in Silvia's case, she was ostracized by her female co-workers in the pressroom for being too prissy when she complained about harassment. Her male counterparts named her "the bitch."

Confrontation

Confrontation differs from complaint in that it is a face to face difference of opinion or belief, in which two people or groups, one of which dissents from the other, tells the opposition in clear, certain terms his or her problem.

Sweeping It Under the Rug

Looking the other way, reinterpreting, making allowances and not making waves do have their price. Kathy continues to work nights even though she is entitled to a cushier situation. "Now, my dilemma is: should I bump a man who is less senior so that I can work the day shift? I could do that, and I really would like to work days, but I love what I am doing and I don't want to create any waves. Maybe I will work out a compromise, and work all vacations for the guys working day shifts. That should be enough for a while." She sounds accommodating and fearful that she will lose her job if she attempts to step on any of the men's toes. Mary, the welder, gets along with everybody. She just keeps her mouth shut and works on in her easy-going way. Lorie also is accommodating. "I just walk away if men's language is too crude. I don't want them to have to change." She overlooked the pat on her tush from her pole climbing instructor who caught her coming down the eighteen-foot pole. Was it just accidental—part of the training and his protection of her, as he stated, or an inappropriate "feel" as she suspected? Here was her dilemma—to make a federal case out of it or brush it aside. Since she needed his tutelage to learn a very difficult skill, she decided to keep quiet. However, it always gnawed at her and distracted her whenever she went up those eighteen feet.

Cindy Fraylich, First Female Los Angeles County Firefighter, Thirty-seven years old

We met at the fire station where the yellow coats and fire hats all hung in rows in the truck area. The station has a big communal kitchen/recreation room area, and a dormitory that consists of individual little cubby holes without doors, a unisex bathroom, a shower area and a large weight room.

Cindy is five feet nine inches tall and a solid 155 pounds. She is attractive, intelligent and strong looking, with hair slightly graying at the temples and restrained in a ponytail bun with a big ribbon. She was dressed in a masculine-looking firefighter's uniform with the name badge reading "Fraylich." Lipstick was her only makeup.

Cindy feels that sexual harassment in the fire station is minimal, and that she hasn't been harassed unduly. However, she complained about the pervasiveness of pornography, in particular, rented porno videos played in the living room at night.

"The other problem was the hair. We had a policy that women had to have their hair cut above their ears and not below the top of the collar. I did take that to the Chief. It was important because everything else you do is like a man. Your uniform is like a man. I felt you didn't have to be a man to have this job. I had always had long hair and I wanted long hair. The Chief told me to take it to the Union. The Union wouldn't go for it. Finally, we had to negotiate with the top brass. They were pretty good at getting what they wanted. I could not appeal to the Chief directly, face to face. I had to go through these others. I didn't know who my 'enemy' was. It's like there's this blindfold in front of you and you don't know if you are fighting the people in the negotiating room or the Fire Chief. I finally found out it was the Fire Chief. It took a lot of my talking to convince everyone it was appropriate to have different standards for men and women. It was not a lowering of standards; it's important to have gender differences. It became very apparent that people in the

Department didn't want this standard changed; they didn't like the idea of a difference; that women don't have to do the same things to get on the Department. They don't want anything that threatens them. If you have a difference, they think you meet a lower standard, and they try to use this to keep women out. If you are not going to look like a man you are not going to have this job. But I did a lot of research. They had fought this in the early 1960s, with men who wanted long hair, and had tried to say short hair was a safety reason but it wasn't. Basically the resistance was based on the personal preference of the Fire Chief. His wife has short hair. He thought long hair looked straggly. He's very neat. A clean uniform and looking good, looking sharp is important to him. I had researched what other departments had done. I ended up getting pretty much what I wanted. I wanted to be able to wear my hair down, but we have to restrain it. It was important to me because a lot of women wouldn't want this job if they thought you had to become a man. It was important to retain some femininity.

"I took this job because I wanted to help. I felt I had to deal with these issues along the way. Some guys would just never like you and some guys would like you if you proved you could do the job. One guy's wife was petrified when she found out he would be sleeping in the fire station with women. He was the kind of guy who would fill up the Cadillac and the Mercedes with gas if he was going on a fishing trip so that his wife could drive first one car and then the other and wouldn't have to put gas in the car while he was gone for the weekend.

"Anyway, I began to learn the differences in paramedic duties as a result of the Emergency Medical Treatment (EMT) training. I was twenty-six years old at the time and I just started asking about the fire department. Los Angeles-City is strictly paramedics; they are not firefighters and their promotional system is very limited. I ended up applying to a bunch of fire departments. I took a test and passed an agility test. That was in 1982; I got hired in 1983.

"I was the first female firefighter in L.A. County, which handles fifty incorporated cities. (There were women in San Diego). I didn't know that going in. I hadn't ever heard of a female firefighter. I don't know how much I even really thought about it, but the more involved I got the more I realized this was something exceptional, because women just aren't around.

"There's an agility test, which somewhat simulates what you do in a fire. You connect six different hoses to opening on the valves of hydrants and then you disconnect all six to get coordination of spinning on these hoses and the coupling. You have to do it to hand tight. You have to pick up sections of hose and load it over your head. This involves upper body movement. I had lifted weights specifically for this. I had always been athletic, so it wasn't something foreign to me.

"The initial agility test is just to find out if you can do those things—if you have adequate physical capabilities. There is a written exam, as well as an oral. Once you pass, if you are in a top grouping, you are asked to be in academy classes. Prior to that, all you need is a high school education. Most people don't have a problem with the test. They might be scared when they go up. Every once in a while someone freezes. I had always been athletic and into a lot of different type sports. Plus, I have a degree in Kinesiology from UCLA. I have a lot of familiarity with the weight room, physics, and mechanics. I never really thought this was a strange thing for a woman to do because I tend to go for jobs that are more unusual or male oriented. They tend to be the higher paying ones. I figure if I'm going to work, I am going to earn more money per hour. Usually, to me, most of the male oriented jobs are the fun jobs, not as mundane and confined to an office. They are more physical—more outdoors. We're paid really well. It's not like you have an action-packed day. Typically you do certain things on a daily basis.

"It's different to be around all males, living with them in the fire stations. You can't believe how crude males are when they are all together. It's not like mixed company. I was shocked to find all the pornographic material all around. Not just like "Playboy," but really gross stuff. It's everywhere in the bathroom and in the rec room. And they would rent porno videos. It's tough to take. I didn't want to file a complaint and get an individual guy in trouble, but I was offended. It's degrading to women and then it's hard to work as professionals. I was trying to write a memo to the Chief so as not to get any one individual in trouble but just to say it's an unprofessional environment. I thought a policy was coming out three years ago but it just came out. After the riots a lot of people were in the stations and it was embarrassing.

"It wasn't fun to pioneer these issues. It was a pain in the butt. I took this job because I wanted to help. I felt I had to deal with these issues along the way.

"It's not bad living with men. Sometimes it's a problem, as I don't have much privacy, like in the bath room. Also males tend to be more competitive. There are times when the guys go outside and just duke it out. Not often, but they do. Also, if the public is emotional, men are more confrontational, while I don't take it personally.

"Working with all guys is like family. Flirtations are minimal. I used to work with my boyfriend. We met on the job in the same firehouse, but not too many people knew. Sometimes guys do things as a joke to test you, and viewed with a different twist it would be harassment. I haven't felt harassed unduly. It's all within the parameters of what other people get.

"The job doesn't really impact my femininity. Whether my weight is up or down impacts me more. My hair, the man's haircut, affected me most because before, when I went off duty, I still had to have the short hair, and I didn't like that at all. Aging also is a concern. I think I'm in better shape now at thirty-seven than I was ten years ago. My optimum potential might not be as great, but I realize more of my capability. So, overall, I'm in better condition.

"I was married about ten years ago for three years. I am talking about marriage now with my boyfriend but children are a major issue. He's forty-six and has an eighteen year old daughter and has been fixed. So we might not get married. I'm not sure how to deal with it."

Silvia Carrillo, Pressroom Apprentice, Los Angeles Times, Thirty-seven years old

Raised in a middle-class home in Mexico, she regularly witnessed her father's abusive behavior toward her mother and his constant belittling of the women in her family. Consequently, she has sworn off marriage, but not the idea of motherhood. Still a virgin at twenty-nine, she invited an English rock musician into her bedroom so she could become pregnant. Now, a single mother, she works the graveyard shift so she can be home with her son during the day.

She's confrontational on the job, not afraid to speak up if she feels she is mistreated. This only aggravates both her male and female coworkers. They have labeled her a hussy and a troublemaker.

"The most difficult part of working in the pressroom is dealing with men's sexuality. They see us not as coworkers but as future lays. Their language is terrible. Just breaking the barrier where we are equal isn't an easy job. The hardest thing for me is working with blue collar men. Being a naive person, I came into the pressroom from a job where they expected you to be ladylike, courteous, 'Yes, I'll be happy to help you; I'll get back to you' — very civil like.

"I've filed four sexual harassment cases. I had been working in the pressroom about seven months when I bent down to pick up a rag. A coworker kicked me. I ran away and he cornered me. I said, 'You better leave me alone.' It was graveyard, 1989, on a weekend. It took management two days to respond, and then the guy started to follow me again. I lost it. I cried and shouted. One of my supervisors came by saying I was making too much out of it. I was scolded. They didn't like the way I was handling it. I told employee relations about the problem. Employee Relations said, 'Oh sweetheart, we'll take care of it.' I had gone to medical, so Employee Relations called it assault and battery. This man actually bruised me.

"Men were having a difficult time adjusting to females in the pressroom. At first there were five women and now there's twenty out of 175. I was 'the bitch.'

"The men don't even like each other but they have allegiances as men. They don't help women. I had a difficult time hooking up the ink hose, which really is simple. The guys just won't show you. They use their body strength, but I tell them, 'No, can you relate to me as a small person?' I get the feeling it's a burden for men to relate to me. They still think women belong at home. I've been told by some of the women I'm a priss.

"Toward the end of last year I worked on an outstanding crew. To show appreciation they gave us a trip to Oregon to see one of the mills and go fishing. The office told the guys about this trip and didn't tell me. I said I wanted to go. I was part of the crew. A lot of the girls asked, 'What is she going to do?' I got hustled at the poker party the night we were in Oregon, and they all blamed it on me, saying I shouldn't have gone in the first place.

"I work from 8:30 P.M. to 4 A.M. I like this shift, being a single parent. I requested to work graveyard. Also, I don't have to think. This way, when I get home I try to get some sleep. I get up, get my son ready and off to school, and then go back to bed. When he gets home from school at 3 P.M. I get up and supervise his homework and get ready to go back to work. I interrupt my sleep. At this time I'm living with my mom and she watches my son while I go to work. That is one of the reasons I live with my mom. Dad lives in Mexico.

"We are originally from Guadalajara, Mexico—nine siblings—a large Catholic family. I'm second oldest. One passed away at twenty-five. Seven girls and one boy left—all live here in California. I was twenty-two when I came here— a year after my mom and brother and sisters. Mom had a sister living here. My parents are separated. My dad physically abused my mom, and was very abusive verbally. I was rwenty when they separated.

"In Mexico I was a flight attendant, but I was always attracted to the United States. Even though we had a good life in Mexico we were very influenced by the American way, learning English from an early age.

"I'll tell you when we came here my mom moved to Highland Park and we all went into a culture shock. We were used to Mexican middle class private schools. We had a car; socialized at private clubs. Here in Highland Park, it was poverty town. My mom used all her savings in one year. She started sewing clothes and waitressing. I can remember when I arrived she said I had to work — do anything. I said, 'You mean I can't go to school?' She said, 'No, there is no money.' I got a job as a cashier at minimum wage and that was devastating. As a flight attendant in Mexico after five years they give you a car, even though it was a Volkswagen, and my life style was posh. I wanted to go to college. Once I started working here I just never got around to it. I still have a goal of going back to college. I'm sorry I haven't yet. My one brother; my mother supported him, so he could go. Her attitude toward it was, 'Well, he's the boy and he has to go to college.' I was devastated with the lifestyle in the United States the first two years.

"For a group of intelligent people, it took us a while to realize we had a lot of potential. A lot of our relatives are successful—when we go back to Mexico for weddings we see they have jobs and careers. My dad always put down women. I was always told I was limited because I am a woman. Otherwise I might have tried harder to get my college degree.

"Even though I was in my early twenties I had to do what my mom told me and that was help her financially. And things got better.

My mom is a very strong person, character-wise, and she had a lot of influence over us. I started as a cashier at Tiny Naylor's. I got a receptionist job. I worked for a Japanese importer for two years, starting at the bottom and ending up in promotions—a sales rep. I learned a lot about the business. I liked the traveling.

"Then at twenty-nine I decided I wanted to have a child. I was still a virgin. I never thought about getting married, but I do like motherhood. My mom being physically abused put me off marriage. My best friend and I were in search of a father for my child. She introduced me to a friend from England. We got along. A romance occurred and I did get pregnant. He knew my purpose. We dated about three months. He was a musician from Liverpool and had to go back to England. I thought, 'Oh well, it was wonderful.' After he left I found out I missed my period and I was happy. I told him I was pregnant. He is very open minded. He said it was wonderful and told his mom and we corresponded. When my son, Andrew, was five we traveled to England and we met his family. We saw him and his girlfriend. Andrew and his dad correspond. That is the only time we saw him, but it's a nice relationship.

"I'd seen a lot of broken marriages in my family and that didn't really attract me. I love my culture and I don't want to put it down, but in Mexican culture, men are verbally and physically abusive. Men can have lovers, but demand a lot of girls. You have to be a virgin. You can't have sex before marriage.

"My Japanese boss, who wouldn't let pregnant women travel, laid me off when Andrew was a year and a half. Then, I got a job as an RTD driver because my father had been in the bus business. I did it for seven months, just to show my dad it was okay for a girl, but, I quit because it was part time and had no benefits. I got a temporary job at the Los Angeles Times in Employee Relations as a record keeper. After one year I had access to a computer. I started looking around to see how to make more money. I realized I didn't want sales. It's too competitive and stressful. They had an apprentice program, as long as I didn't mind doing certain things: working three shifts, wearing a uniform and doing heavy duty work—pushing, lifting heavy things, getting inky, getting dirty. Clerical work is hard and it's not worth the money. I didn't want a 9 to 5 job, and have to do a lot of thinking. This is automatic. They started me at $13.00 an hour. Now I'm making $22.00, soon it will be $23.00. You start as an apprentice and every six months you get a raise. But, you have to be careful regarding safety. In the past two years, three coworkers got hands caught in the press. Two of them are still on disability.

"This is a great job for a single mother, foreign born, who can work nights and take care of her child during the day. I can do this without a college education and earn a good salary. So, there are many advantages."

In September 1993, Silvia earned her journeymanship with great reviews.

Even though Cindy didn't feel harassed sexually she pursued the hair issue through her tough and accommodating demeanor. She knew about the short hair requirement going into the job, and really tried to live with it. But the severely short hair was so threatening to her self esteem that ultimately she had to complain and challenge the restriction. She gathered enormous amounts of information about how other departments dealt with the same issue and even found statistics on hair burning. She wanted to know the source of this restriction and why and what support was available to her. Adding to her cause, many men felt restricted by the short hair policy as well. What probably helped the most in her case, however, was that she was so well-liked and that she did not take on the department right off the bat. She had proven herself for years with the department before her challenge. Also, her choice not to complain about midnight porno videos reflected her desire to get along with her fellows. She demonstrated fluidity of style in bold, purposeful confrontation on issues critical to her, and tolerance about the videos to keep harmony.

On the other hand, Silvia filed harassment suits one after the other to the frustration of her male and female colleagues. However, by defending herself, by defining her own limits, she was able to stake out a livable environment for herself.

There is a price to these actions. Women don't usually take these jobs for political reasons—to make policy. They take these jobs for the challenge of helping people, like Cindy, or to get a high paying nightshift job, like Silvia. To keep their own sense of self they often have to use some of their work energy to complain.

But the price of complaining can be high. Many women who make waves find that criticism can follow them endlessly. Silvia was scorned by both male and female colleagues. Fighters are labeled and accused, ignored and taunted. Women who choose to speak up to defend themselves must be prepared to incur others' wrath and resentment and deal with lingering hostility. They are often targets for all the bad feelings caused by women's encroachment into this segment of the work force.

PART IV

ALL IT TAKES IS
A LITTLE ATTITUDE

"Since I was a kid, I've always been the kind, if you dare me to do something I do it. I always had that in me. Maybe that's why I don't get freaked out about it."

Sylvia, Undercover Narcotics Agent

A positive attitude is a survival must for most working women. Some gather their positive strength from within, while others go outside for support. Most are able to accentuate the positive without being Pollyanna-esque. They can call to mind the best about their circumstances. Their health and hearts benefit by a positive, balanced picture of their situations. We've compiled a list of attitude adjustment mechanisms that work both on and off the job:

- *Don't bring the job home.* Though Sylvia, the undercover narcotics agent, is still the happy-go-lucky person she always was, she has to continually fight not to become callus and hard. She says, "When I go home, I sometimes feel like he's the man and I'm the woman." Tanya doesn't   mix up her social and work lives.   Her boyfriend is not a lifeguard. Even so, she enjoys the admiration her job brings her from the guys she meets outside of work.

- *Have an outlet.* To gain a positive attitude, Lorie sells Mary Kay cosmetics. "I come home in jeans and work boots, and an hour later I leave decked out to the hilt. Believe it or not, I go to Mary Kay and get all this confidence. When I don't go I miss that fix; all the positives. I think it's all the hype and all the support. There is no backstabbing. I've met a lot of nice, warm, genuine women who help each other out and cheer each other on."

- *Work out.* Physical activity has been essential to many blue collar women all their lives. They know that working out serves as mental as well as physical release. Madeline can only stand her work as a splicer by swimming competitively every morning, and Tanya gets twenty minute workout breaks every so often as part of her daily routine to relieve the stresses of constantly guarding the beach. Cheri, however, admits that she doesn't have the time to work out outside of work; so she looks forward to the exercise she gets as a mover for Bekins.

- *Get support.* Support comes in many ways. Mary, the welder, gained support and instruction from others on the job. Cindy spoke of the men in the fire station being her family—the ultimate form of support. Some of the women to whom we talked at the phone company have the healing function of the "Outside Looking In" workshops where they learn others have been there too and are there for them. Madeline resorted to going to a counselor when she couldn't cope with her work anxieties. Hypnotists, psychologists, loving husbands, gay partners and men on the job inspire and keep them going. However, more times than not, the women must rely on themselves, digging deep inside for the support they need.

- *Reject unhelpful support.* Pam, the cable splicer, told patronizing men to bug off. "I was trained by the only black man on the crew. I had to get away from him to learn my job more. He babied me. He always did the heavy stuff. I was his grunt—just doing light errands. I learned by observation rather than doing."

- *Define limits.* Silvia, the press room operator, did not choose the traditional bonds of marriage, because of her frightening parental model. Pam had to leave her marriage, partly because her job changed her into a much more assertive person. Also, her husband couldn't stand her looking dirty—a necessary evil of her ditch digging job. Lorie worked very hard to complete the pole climbing test, but drew the line at dragging a fifteen-pound sack up that pole when it wasn't absolutely required. On the same note, Betty didn't like to bonus shoot, and wasn't going to be bullied into it. It wasn't a requirement and she didn't need to prove herself by doing it.

- *Have fun.* Because Betty was required to wear cotton underclothes as part of her uniform, she hung out her Frederick's of Hollywood lingerie in the fire station to release the restrictive tension.

- *Make a statement.* Laura says, " I don't let nothing go by. If there was harassment I dealt with it by going to upper management or outside sources."

- *Just ignore it.* Madeline let the dirty remarks go right by her during her training. "I tried not to be a confrontational feminist. I figured, if you want to learn the job, you have to kind of hang out with the guys. They tried out a lot on me. We made jokes all the time. We were twisting wires and they'd say twist your crank when we twisted wires. They'd just start laughing. Crank is another word for penis. It just went over me.

I didn't care. I just laughed. I could either laugh or make a big deal out of it."

◆ *Hang in there.* Kathy has been on the job for twenty-five years. Though it gets harder physically as she gets older, she really likes what she does now. Madeline, who has been doing her work for fifteen years, feels it gets easier the longer you do it. She gets great satisfaction in outlasting some of the best of them, defying those who believe women can't hack it. She's been at her job for fifteen years.

Accentuate the positive. Most of the women who make it and hang in there remind themselves of what is good about their work. They come from somewhere else. They see the benefits of what they are doing despite the difficulties. Many women who end up content make the most out of their training. They have realistic appreciation of the opportunities. Victoria exemplifies a good natured acceptance of difficulties and has wisely chosen a work situation—working for the state in her painting trade—that maximizes work stability and minimizes hostile environments. She was able to persevere in her tough apprenticeship, because she focused on the light at the end of the tunnel. She ended her interview with what is foremost in her mind about her job—not the aching bones or the paint fumes or the name calling, but how much she can do in her life now as a result of her trade.

TEN

HOW TO GET AROUND
WHAT'S AROUND

"I'm sure my job changed me because I always wanted to learn more. I wasn't the sweet little quiet thing anymore. I became more assertive. I learned a lot at work through training. I'm sure from working eight hours a day I learned to take charge. Those were things I found out on the job. I even took assertiveness training."

Pam Owens, Cable Splicer,
United States West Telephone Company

A tremendous energy is generated by women who have high self esteem. Those who can calmly talk about their work and present what they do to the world optimistically are the most successful in deflecting the problems that come up. They can get along without noticing slights, encouraging provocations or fighting the ego battles that often happen on job sites. These women have learned to muster up thoughts of money, freedom and power when dealing with their everyday job hassles.

Younger women seemed to be matter of fact about their jobs. So, Cheri works as a mover, Linda is a welder, Tanya guards the beach and Sylvia is an undercover narcotics agent. So what! Their attitude is, give 110 percent. For them, this attitude is sustaining and liberating and gives them the energy to work successfully, while others waste it trying to defend their positions.

It's understandable how they got to be this way. Their generation has been more tolerant about the changing roles of men and women. With their contemporaries they saw women fly into space, go into combat, serve on the Supreme Court and make millions playing sports. They have also seen men stay at home and change diapers, while their wives work to bring home the money. There's nothing to stop them from digging ditches and working the presses. Protective laws and gate keepers now exist, and they know they can go after different goals.

Linda, the rig welder, believes that certain welding jobs are more suited to women. "Most men are too clumsy for thin delicate work and when you do it for a yacht it has to look good, pretty and delicate. Most men can't do that." Her self esteem comes from doing work she loves and at which she knows she is good.

Tanya says you have to learn to be flexible. She doesn't think there's any problem in not having bathrooms designated for females only. Instead, she calls the available facilities coed bathrooms. She's neutralized the situation. Sylvia, the narcotics agent, has also turned discriminating behavior into a positive. "You have to be strong minded. You can't be thin skinned. You're dealing with policemen everyday who have the idea that this is a man's job. You still get a lot of that. I've felt I've had more opportunity because they need a woman—a Hispanic who speaks Spanish—so I feel I have an upper hand on that. You're still working in a man's world. I didn't come on this job to change policy or people or men's attitudes. I came on because this was something I wanted to do."

Cheri's self esteem comes from being a survivor. Her mother was mentally disabled; so she went to live in a foster home at five. There she had a foster mother who stabbed her on the back of her hand with a fork. She has no tradition to buck, so she successfully takes care of herself and her daughter without rigid social constraints. She never thinks twice about the social implications of her job. She's just very comfortable working as a furniture mover.

Mary's self esteem comes from financial power. The money she made sweating over hot flames liberated her from the confines of an unhappy marriage. It offered her independence and comfort in her role of single mother. She is elated that her work as a welder has given her a choice.

Glimpses of the sources of many women's self esteem appear in their nontraditional backgrounds. They've found work that fits their natural aptitudes and interests. Their mind sets enable them to do this work. They get a rush from breaking barriers, being role models, having a laugh over shocking someone and successfully taking the job challenge.

Linda West, Welder/Artist, Twenty-nine years old

At five feet seven inches and 138 pounds of muscle, she is pretty and very self assured. She is also very pleased with herself and her work, especially her role as a teacher. She doesn't hesitate to challenge the macho myth that working with the fire in the foundry is dangerous and difficult and only suitable for men. Her casual 'no issue' approach to her nontraditional job, and her strong and upbeat attitude, go along with her nontraditional lifestyle. Now pregnant, though not married, she plans to raise her child in the foundry.

Both her mother and sister are homosexuals. Most people think she is, too— she is muscular and wears her hair short on top and closely shaved around the sides and back of her head—but she is not.

"I don't find any down side to my work. I am a born woman's libber. It's natural that way. I don't have a problem getting boyfriends, because I've found most guys like strong women. My job and work enhance my life. I'm not restricted by anything. A rapist would look at me and go, 'Eh, too difficult.'

"My Dad is an attorney. I have two older brothers. The oldest brother Bob is thirty-seven, Jim is thirty-six. My sister is thirty-three. Bob is a tree cutter. He was the maniac. We'd build forts and work on motorcycles and I'd hand him all the tools. He showed me how to use a torch, and so I was cutting away with a torch when I was really young. At maybe five or six I gained a knowledge of tools by helping Jim work on his motorcycles. He'd have me find tools by calling out it's name and then describing it. I'd go over to the pile of tools on the floor and locate what looked like the tool he needed. In school I had a lot of shop and art classes. I would stay after school to work on projects too big to finish in class. The teacher would encourage me to learn how to service and understand the machinery, like replacing blades on the saw. There was one other girl in my high school shop classes. Most of my friends were boys. I was real athletic. I was always the person showing them how to do it. Usually the teachers would take me in and show me how to take apart tools. I would take the classes a little further than others. All my mom's family worked with their hands. They were crafts people.

"I got out of high school and decided to go into art early. One of my design projects was to do a carving. I went to the beach and dragged back a big piece of driftwood. I wailed into it and did some abstract thing. My teacher said I have to get into sculpture. The school had a foundry; all the tools. They were just building up the department. I took to it like a fish out of water. I apprenticed for another sculptor who had a large commission to do a state capital in Nebraska. I got involved in casting a large abstract bird—900 pounds of bronze. Pretty good for someone eighteen years old. There is a lot to casting, acid treatment; heat up the bronze and brush it on, and create color and modeling that is natural to the metal. You can do lots of stuff. It's kind of like painting.

"I got a scholarship to a school in San Francisco. I applied through City College and won it, and proceeded to get my bachelor's degree there. I took a big load of my own tools up there and had a pretty good idea of how to handle them. I was still a gas welder—used oxygen acetylene—a hot burning, flammable gas— and oxygen to make the 6000-degree blue flame. It's a flame process rather than electrical, but requires manual dexterity. I messed around with stone carving and welding. They didn't have a foundry. They did have a good welding department; so I played around. It shocked the instructors when I just went in and fired up the torch. I got a job running the foundry in Santa Barbara right out of school. Here I was twenty-three years old teaching a college class. It was kind of strange. Just about everyone in the class was older than I was. I started up an aluminum class which they hadn't done before.

"I joined my students taking a tig class. Next thing I know, I bought a tig welder and I'm restoring Frank Stella and Giometti. In reality, the first tig welders were all women, during World War II. I met one in a bar who used to weld in the war. There were no men to do it because tig welding is so delicate. I also learned arc (stick) welding. My entrance to welding was through sculpture. I kept taking welding so I would be able to get a certification—a practical and written test for doing structural welding. It takes a lot of time and skill. The most difficult test is vertical and overhead on one inch steel plate or pipe. You don't have gravity on your side. You have to be able to work in awkward positions. I really don't know why I wanted to do this. I'm a fanatic. When I was an instructor I was being paid for ten hours and working thirty. I already have lots of equipment and machinery in my shop, so it's feasible I could go out on my own and do these kind of jobs.

"When I saw my teaching coming to a close, I applied for a job as a tig welder. I went over with my hood and gloves ready to weld. I'm a relatively confident welder. I was the first one in for the test. He had a little test for me—a little thin pipe T-weld. I grabbed the torch and I found the smallest filler rod. I was really confident but I was shaking. Maybe I had too much coffee. The job was minuscule. So, he sees that I can weld, and I got the job. When I saw all the other attempts I saw why I got the job. They were pathetic. Most men can't do delicate work.

"I worked there one year. Their biggest department is structural. It's a welding company. We fixed everything from semi trucks to ornamental gates. We did a steel project on a big building on State Street. I set up I-beam columns. I've gained a good reputation and gotten a good rapport by doing work there. People find me by word of mouth. I get boat jobs from the harbor and contacts with the art community for restoring art work that usually takes a fine delicate hand—almost like sewing. I have a good eye. The boat people especially want someone who has an artistic eye, and I gained a reputation for making marine hardware (boat jewelry) look nice. When I'm not welding, I'm doing my own art. I pay attention to detail. Most people don't have the patience.

"It's give and take on art and welding. When I sell a lot I usually put the money right back into equipment. Most of the works I sell are large figurative aluminum or bronzes, combined with painting. They're large, colorful, expressive and they sell well.

"When I sell $10,000 worth of art I feel I can kick back and relax. Now I'm in the yellow pages. This brings in little, low paying jobs that sustain me and help pay the rent. I don't expect to make a lot of money but don't want to get so involved with welding that I sacrifice the sculpture I want to do. Making $12.00 an hour and barely making my monthly rent was so stressful I'd go home and have nothing left. Then I'd have little jobs once I got home. I was really doing three jobs at once, which was ridiculous. I quit for my one person show. Now I'm pregnant, and I continue working. I can make $25 to $30 an hour, on my own. I can work one-third as hard and make the same money and have time to pursue sculpture. I have a shop for little jobs and a foundry in the same space. I can dissemble my foundry and roll it away. All the big equipment is on wheels—low overhead. I've lived in my shop. I have a house because it is rough to raise a baby in a shop, but as an artist it's great to just go downstairs to work when you're in the mood.

"I have to work with my hands, and I love teaching. I teach welding at city college. I'm not normal. I have a hard time punching a clock. I'll do it if I have to. Artistry is everything. I get to be a welder. I get to be a macho foundry person. When I was taking the foundry class the men would tell me to stand back and look at the big fire. When I taught I tried to say: 'Hey, you could learn how to fire this up, and you could do this.' I had a lot of women in the art department. They are following their dreams. You run into women in the art department not afraid of fire —women in nontraditional roles. When guys did it, it is such a big deal. But I said, 'Let's get in there and have fun.' I'm a really strong woman. I surf. But when it comes to aluminum almost anybody can handle it. I totally changed the way the foundry was run. One of my female students got a scholarship but was told she couldn't take a foundry class until her second year. There is a big foundry mystique which is very macho. This woman overhears talk that they don't know how to do aluminum casting. She says she knows how and they look at her like, 'What?' The next thing you know she is conducting the whole pour. She knows everything. She is really relaxed. They then say maybe they'll let her take it next semester. That make me feel good. That was the fun part of teaching—breaking role barriers.

"People react to my physique. I'm pretty strong. I've been working eighteen years and I'm very active. I have big muscles. I try to convince them you don't have to be big old strong women. I try to break that down.

"My family knows I'm a crazy. My sister is a pilot and my brother a nurse. She was in the army as a helicopter pilot. My mother is a strong woman type. My dad is a typical proud dad. It's not a typical family. It's utter chaos. We never went to church. We did a lot of camping. My dad put on a suit but as soon as he got home off goes the suit and he was fixing and repairing. My brother had snakes. Unlike most mom's my mom said we should not fear them but touch them—it is not a bad thing. Mom and Dad split up when I was about eight years old. Dad had a major drinking problem. Mom is real liberal. She was on the school board. She'd raise hell about changing the dress code, hair code. She's real outspoken and forward. When she introduces herself she's forward. 'Hi, I'm Janet West.' She's not inhibited—a strong female role model—real cool. She was brought up with five brothers. She was the only girl, always trying to get her brothers to show her how to work with wood. Her dad would say, 'No you can't learn wood. You're a girl." She didn't allow that kind of restriction and encouraged me. 'Oh, if you don't want to go to high school, okay, go on to city college.' She sort of trusted me to find my own track. There was no down side for me. I did well in school. I didn't bomb out. I found it boring. It went so slow. They have to make sure every moron in the class gets it. I was a bit too precocious for that.

"I took advantage for awhile of the drug scene—making money selling drugs. That turned my Mom into a psycho bitch from hell. I got kicked out of the house, but even with all that I stayed healthy and went surfing and hiking. It was semi okay. I kept on track. Now I have a BFA degree. When I got into school other kids were in the 'Gee, I'm free stage,' and started using drugs, but I was serious because I already burned out on that. It became necessary to be serious.

"I was married once. I'm just going on with the kid business without being married. I'm living with an older welder. He's an instructor and helps me out. Now, I'm too pregnant to do some jobs. I wonder how this is going to effect my career and time and am I going to whig out on this? Will it be a struggle? The kid will go to the shop with me and be raised in an interesting environment. It will be scary because I have a lot of tools. I have hazards in the shop. I got it set up so I can work and have a kid, though. The man I'm living with has a flexible schedule and can help out. He has grown up kids. He's low key and has taught me a lot. He once worked for Rocketdyne as a tig welder. He is a perfectionist—one of the few guys who has a sense of detail.

"I don't know what a normal life family life is. When I was married, my husband had his shop in his truck and I had my shop in my truck. When we split up my situation didn't change that much. I am self reliant. There weren't too many joint possessions.

"My mom and sister are gay. I get called a dyke all the time, but, I guess it could be called a compliment because a lot of my friends are. They are all strong intelligent people.

Lynn Shaw, Electrician, Thirty-nine years old

A very pretty thirty-nine-year old, Lynn is tall with dark eyes and hair. We met at the Hyatt Hotel, where she enthusiastically chose the Japanese breakfast buffet. Her independence and adventurousness shows even in the food she eats—eels and other odd looking dishes. She made our time together fun.

Married with one stepson, she comes from a hard working, midwestern, Scandinavian family. Her lifestyle continually alarmed her parents, but they never tried to interfere.

"One of my favorite games when I go to a party is to have people try to guess my occupation. No one ever does.

"I think the biggest significance of women working in nontraditional work is breaking down gender roles. People need to get jobs on the basis of interest and abilities. In our society, there are strict race and gender lines. Only a few people are doing this work. Gender roles are very limiting. People don't have choices. Increased numbers will help break down the perception that this is man's work. But it is more than numbers. It will take a huge, deep, societal change. If more people knew other people of other races and other job preferences, it would help break down restricting stereotypes.

"It's not for everyone. Women need to learn to cope with all the things on the job aside from the job itself: being isolated, being a woman, men threatened by your presence, men going out of their way to help you (because then how else are you going to learn), men not helping, men sabotaging you.

"I formed the Job Protection Committee in 1981, when layoffs started. We kept track of the layoffs, tried to keep people informed and tried to persuade people not to work overtime. Finally, the mill was totally closed about five years ago. Some of mills along the river were torn down and replaced with dog tracks, water theme parks, etc.

"I moved to Southern California, desperately seeking a job. I worked in a limestone mine. That was my worst job. I was looking in the yellow pages under labor unions, and found electricians taking applications. I took the test which was mainly math and mechanical aptitude—very basic. Only twenty-seven percent pass but it's not advanced. I was a good candidate. I am big—5 foot 9. It really doesn't matter but contractors like big. Apprentices work full time and go to school at night. I was the only woman for six years. That was really hard. I completely lost my sense of humor because I felt so isolated. I felt like I was 'the other' to the guys. They would do things in class that I strenuously objected to. Like the teacher wanted to show the fight and I didn't care one bit about the fight. So I would say something. I was constantly at war. They hired a stripper for a retiring teacher. I left. It made you feel really alone. I felt like I should be able to be there, but I felt out of place. I felt I was missing a lot. They would go out together and study together. Even if they'd invite me, I didn't want to go. It would have been so much better if there was even one other woman. You don't get viewed as yourself but as 'the woman.' That is a really huge burden—representing half of the human race. On the job everyone knows you—when you go to the bathroom, when you eat lunch, when you screw up. You are so visible.

"My first nontraditional job was in 1976. I started in a warehouse in Menlo Park. I heard through the grapevine they were hiring at a dried fruit packing plant, and I got a job until the season was over and I was laid off. Through the same Union I then got a job in a liquor warehouse. In about 1975 they had changed the names 'men's jobs and women's jobs' to 'light and heavy' labor. They would send women out on heavy labor jobs, but when they got there they were immediately put on light labor. Heavy labor was at the end of the assembly lines where you lift the boxes off. I insisted on heavy labor, because I wanted more money. Eventually a lot of women took over the heavy labor shift at night, because night fit their child care needs, especially the single parents. Women could come home, take care of their kids, send them to school and then sleep.

"A sedentary work environment didn't suit me. I didn't like to sit all day indoors. I felt if I had a Union I'd have some recourse if I was treated unfairly. In the early 1970s organized labor was mainly in manufacturing; clerical unions came latter. Most women were on the assembly line, and they were susceptible to a particular injury, caused by a twisting motion of the wrist due to taking bottles off the fast moving assembly line.

"Then I went to Pennsylvania—United States Steel Homestead. There were 7000 employees and about 500 were women. Women did everything. They started at lower seniority jobs. I bid on all the open jobs. You can imagine there were quite a few; it was really booming. I got awarded a motor inspector job which was an apprenticeship program for electricians. You worked five weeks, and the sixth week you go to class. I worked about one year, then got laid off when the steel industry went down. I really liked the work. I thought it was great because I was learning a skill. Women hadn't done it before.

"We had a women's group in the shop, which was part of the civil rights committee. I finally got laid off, but I worked from 1978 until 1981. I loved it. I would still be there. I got a house right there in the community. When ingots came out of the ovens glowing orange they were put on railroad cars. They glowed at night. I could see them from my house. Ingots went to another mill and into rollers to get the right thickness for whatever they are making: boats, cars and then to the shipping. The entire mill was about four and a half miles long. I met someone new each day. It was like a little town. You moved from day to swing to night shift. Ninety percent of the people worked "turns." You can imagine how that controls your life. That was the most difficult thing. The solace was, everybody was doing this.

"The apprenticeship usually takes four years, but it took me five because you also have to have so many working hours. Every six months you get a raise. I loved the work. I liked actually building something. Even though it is a gross exaggeration, you say 'I built that building.' It's a very visible, practical, useful, beautiful, concrete thing. When you clean your bathroom once a week, you still have to clean it next week. In building, as you work you see progress, in both the building and your skill. I love learning new things, new tools, new material, new people with different approaches. I think it's the perfect balance."

Confidence and self esteem run through these stories. Linda is not diverted by self doubts. She's bold. We hear her pride, as an amused twinkle characterizes descriptions of her own adventures. 'Wailing on driftwood sculpture, defying macho foundry fire myths,' she demonstrates an acceptance of all the phases of her life. She's never allowed herself to get diverted. Reading Lynn's story, we see her growing self esteem, built up by years on the job, producing tangible things. Continually learning new skills, her confidence spills over to others as she actively works to break down gender barriers.

Since self esteem is so crucial to success, educators are now beginning to concentrate on teaching it. Nontraditional women's support groups and meetings have recently begun to include a component on self assertiveness and self esteem. Trade women have found that a positive approach is conducive to success. This means a realistic assessment, a balanced vision that keeps the negative in perspective but accentuates the positive. Such an upbeat attitude gives off an energy that contributes to performance and a sense of pride and accomplishment.

ELEVEN

JUMPING OVER THE HIGH BAR

"One night, instead of waking my 6-foot, 2-inch tall 200-pound husband when I heard a strange noise in the house, I took my gun and got up to investigate. When I came back to bed my husband said 'What happened, why are you up, why do you have your gun in your hand.' 'Oh, I just heard a noise.' He wanted to know why I didn't wake him and I go, 'what for?' I didn't mean to say anything mean to him. He's like, 'Oh, okay. I probably would have just gotten in the way.' His old football buddies ask him how he can let me do that."

Sylvia, Undercover Narcotics Agent

We found some women have a special quality, something beyond ordinary persistence, that keeps them on their determined path in spite of the risks and dangers bombarding them. It's as though they are born with it—this courage—this willingness to dangle at the top of an eighteen-foot pole with only a leather belt strap for support, to drive a police car through the riot-torn area of Los Angeles and be a prime target, to jump into someone's yard without fear of attack by either a person or dog, to live in a firehouse when irate and jealous wives undermine their image with their peers, to fix men's urinals, and to forcibly tell a man who is harassing them to back off.

Courage propels and protects many women who have it. It leads to success and brave actions defending boundaries while warding off malicious intruders. Instinctual courage, called up in a flash, can be a trainer for further courage. Women can remember they were courageous and therefore have the potential to be courageous again. Narcotics agent Sylvia survives each night on dangerous streets pretending to be soliciting sex because she has bravely done it many nights before. And, the next generation of young undercover policewomen can reference Sylvia's bravery.

Courage builds on itself like a pyramid of confidence. Thus, courage, acted out, builds up a repertoire of learned courageous responses. Women need chances to be courageous and—just as importantly—to glorify their courageous acts. The amazing things Silvia, Kathy and others do, just as a matter of course every day of their lives, is inspiring. Where's the public relations for women's courage? We underpromote ourselves. We need to hear stories, such as we find in this book, of courageous women like Sylvia and Kathy, and of other women who show extraordinary courage. These stories celebrate that virtue.

Courage can be thrilling, serving as it's own reward. Being the only female in the apprenticeship program, rescuing a drowning child or capturing a drug pusher gives off an electricity that continually feeds on itself.

Despite this inspiring virtue there can be a down side. Courage can invite loneliness. It was brave and right that pressroom worker, Silvia, demanded she accompany her selected outstanding team on the trip. Yet her courage was labeled "stupidity" and caused trouble with her women colleagues.

However, courage does not occur in a vacuum. It doesn't come magically, but from a set of understandable conditions. Courage depends on training that prepares women when the need arises. It depends on self esteem so that women can mobilize the strength and talent they already posses. Attitudes of firmness and steady resolve are components of courage. Electrician Penny Whistler remained firm in her commitment to finish her apprenticeship program, despite its negative impact on her relationship with her boyfriend.

The dictionary defines courage as 'the ability to conquer fear or despair.' Courageous women find ways to believe in themselves without being derailed by the multitude of potential fears lurking around job sites: fear of job loss, femininity, status, socially respectable standing, family roles, confident point of view and power. Bravery sets boundaries that serve as a weapon deterrence system.

Sylvia Ruize, Undercover Narcotics Agent, Twenty-eight years old

It's hard to believe this petite and feminine twenty-eight-year old Hispanic woman works as an undercover narcotics agent. Constantly exposed to the dark, seedy side of town one would expect a tough, hardened pro, but she is fresh and bubbly in the face of all the dangers she encounters daily. Her husband is very self-assured and though he understands and accepts what she does, admits that he's often scared and worried about her. Yet, the job is perfect for her. She's a daredevil, with a lot of femininity mixed in.

"There was one time when I should have said no (laughs) and I didn't. It occurred when another undercover woman, Tracy, and I walked into this very hot location in East Los Angeles to buy drugs. It's full of guns, and gang members selling PCP. They open a bottle and dip a cigarette—called a 'dip,' which they smoke or sell. It goes into your skin and does a lot of crazy stuff. I get a headache and a rush just by smelling it or touching it, and it's, 'Oh boy, now I'm going to get a headache for the rest of the day.' I have to write a 157 form saying we were exposed and if we have weird children we won't sue. I'm not worried about that.

"Anyway, Tracy and I go to the location, a residential street, just four corners filled with gang members, mostly young guys ranging from twelve to twenty-five—all guys. They've got little children on bicycles riding around checking for the police. They have the whole little system worked out. They start whistling if they see the police. That particular day we were short a backup officer. We're talking to about five different gang members, okay. They are going to get us a thirty dip—thirty dollars' worth. Because we're girls, they're trying to talk to us. We go along with it. 'Yeh, we party over here sometimes, do you know so and so.' We say we know certain people. We just use these gang member names. 'Hey do you know Chavo?

What's he been doing?' We've actually arrested these people and we say we know them. Sometimes you make it up. We're standing around waiting for the guy who went into the alley to get us the stash. 'Oh sure, you're police,' and we tell them, 'Hey are you guys stupid? What are you talking about? We've been here before.' I have my hat on and my ear piece is making like a buzzing noise. I got this guy right in my face. That's the part that freaks me out the most—when they see my wire. I just say, 'Oh, I'm listening to some music.' Then the guy comes out with a bottle of thirty pour, which he drops while handing it to Tracy. By this time I'm giving the backup guys a signal that it's a 'go' because more rowdy gang members are coming out. I'm leaning into Tracy's body wire going, 'It's a go, it's a go.' Nobody is coming. Our backup couldn't hear because news helicopters were flying overhead. Now, we're trying to walk to the corner to maybe get out of the area and a low rider drives up with six gang members. Two we've arrested before and testified against in court are saying, 'They're the f—en cops. She's narco, she's narco, don't sell them anything.' So we're up against the wall yelling for help but nobody sees us. These guys all rush us. Maybe there are eight gang members in front of us. We're saying, 'What are you talking about, what are you talking about?' I was scared. I was thinking we couldn't even pull out our guns because they were so close to us.

"Two guys are brothers—one 6 feet 2 and thin, the other about 300 pounds. He's a big kid. The big guy grabs my jacket saying, 'Let me see if you got your radio on.' I pushed him back. The 300 pound guy turns around and socks Tracy on the side of the head. I kick him in the groin to push him back. Finally the black and white units come in. Tracy and I start chasing the kid that hit her, because we wanted to definitely have him detained. We arrested about six gangsters. Tracy was really upset. She started yelling at everybody saying, 'Where were you, why didn't you see what was going on? We were there for twenty minutes without any help!' The worst is when you feel like nobody is helping, because you rely on your back up.

"I love it, though. I enjoy coming to work. I enjoy going to court and testifying against these people and putting them in jail. Unfortunately, first time offenders can plea out, do half that time, and be out in three months. But it's satisfying when they get three to ten years without parole. Hobos downtown just working for somebody—just to get a buck—are good because they are breaking into cars and robbing decent people. But, our main objective is gang members with guns making a living out of selling drugs. Sometimes you think, 'Why don't they buy their mother a better house?' They have all this money. Why don't they better themselves? They just don't have the sense.

"What excited me was working in a patrol car and in a uniform. I got in the academy within about seven months of when I tested. I did six months academy time. You have to take law classes. You get there at 3 or 4 A.M. so you're prepared and in your uniform. You have to be perfect. I remember we'd be outside in the morning saluting the flag. Then, you'd do physical training. They have you running up hills everywhere—three to six miles. I had a great time in the physical training because I love working out, but some women just came in and died. It was quasi-military. They made you know you were a recruit.

"The thing I hated out of the whole program: they take you to this huge old warehouse where they throw gas bombs inside. You put on a gas mask the first time to get the feel of breathing through one. Then you have to go through it without your mask. That is the worst feeling. You think you're going to die because you want to hold your breath.

"I was the first female on a bicycle. You wear a uniform and helmet. The bike has a little emblem on it, Los Angeles Police Department. Our main objective was to clean up the park area because there are peddlers everywhere. I go with a partner. We have our utility belt with our baton, gas, extra magazine for our baretta, handcuffs. If we see the transaction we walk up and arrest them.

"Then I got a job in vice working the PED unit—Prostitution Enforcement Detail. Our main objective was to go to locations and arrest prostitutes with warrants. I worked from 5 P.M. to 1 or 2 A.M. "I've arrested pregnant women. I've bought from a huge woman, eight months pregnant, who was 'mouth dealing.' She spits the rock cocaine out of her mouth to sell you. A lot of times they swallow the dope and when the police come, hey, you don't have any evidence. I warned the chase units coming to arrest her to watch out because she's pregnant and could swallow. I was so concerned about that. She did swallow about twenty rocks in her mouth and died that night. Her baby lived. It was an overdose. I was like, 'Oh no! she's going to swallow.' I kept telling her, 'Spit it out, spit it out, it's not worth it!' I knew what was going to happen because it happened so often. She was so pregnant and all I thought about was, 'Oh, God I don't want to buy from this lady.' I did it because she was there and it was a target. There were two ways I could think of it: 1) she is out here selling drugs and her baby is about to be born, and 2) she doesn't deserve to be out here in the street living like this. At least if she were inside she would be cared for; they'd take care of her baby. For the amount she was pregnant I didn't think she would swallow it.

"Normally in that area they package the rock cocaine in little chips of rock in film containers and they pour it out. They are out in the open, if you are not in a black and white or blue uniform. I don't ever try to be hard-core because that doesn't fit my demeanor. I don't need to be like that. I talk to the people. It's not me to be yelling at people and calling names.

"You just do it so much its routine. When it's something different, you can anticipate—say you get a hot call with a man with a gun—then I feel it more and I'm little more apprehensive. But, when it's just for narcotics, you get a little lax because you do it so often.

"At the motel we have this room set up with officers inside in uniform. My job was to get a John to say, 'Give me a blow job for $10.00.' I said, 'I have a room right here inside.' Then, I bring him in and they take him down.

"You have undercover officers standing on the corner. Maybe one is acting like a bum laying on the floor and one across the street. Supervisors are in cars listening for your body wire. I have no weapon. I never had any problems. You do feel apprehensive because you are out in this awful area. My security is knowing people are all around. If someone were to come up and stab me or pull me in a car, they would have to react to what is happening. I'm always careful not to get too close to a car or reach in. That's why I say I've got a room right here. We don't have to go anywhere.

"When I'm out I change the way I speak and look. Just like now when I go out and buy drugs I speak Spanish. I talk slang the way they talk and talk stupid. It's fun to do actually. Like you are being an actress playing a role. Like when you're buying the drugs it takes more because you have to go into the whole role. When you're playing a prostitute you don't have to say much you just say, 'Whhaata?' I wear jeans and a sweater and sweat shirt. You don't need a tight thing.

"I worked nine months in PED and then got into Narcotics. I buy drugs out on the street everyday, but, I'm not buying now because I just got pregnant. Right now I'm working in the wire car—a transmitter where you can hear voices. I'm listening about three blocks away. Since I'm pregnant I'm considered light duty, They don't want you anywhere where you can be a liability. They have terrible policies for pregnant women. We have no leave; we have to use vacation time.

"My partner Martha and I are two female Hispanics. We can fit in anywhere. We can go to the black locations, Hispanic and white locations, and guys pretty much talk to us. In certain locations where there are a lot of gangsters that is the most dangerous. They say if we feel uncomfortable we don't have to do it.

"The south central part of Los Angeles is the worst to buy drugs because they are the smartest. They don't just sell to anybody. If they don't know you, if they haven't sold to you before, they don't even want to talk to you. They look at you and figure you're a narco because how would you know their location. We have funky cars. I have a lot of success driving into locations by myself. They just think I'm stupid or something. I'm not afraid. Once, when I went to South Central, two black gang members are standing in the street, off Avalon—residential—selling rock cocaine. When I'm by myself I don't ever get out of the car. They are in the middle of the street. 'Hey,' I ask, 'Where's Little Joe at?' I just made up a name. 'Oh, he's not here right now.' They ask why I'm there to see him. 'Because I deal with him sometimes. I talk to him and he gives me some stuff.' 'Oh, how much do you want?' 'I want twenty ($20 worth of rock cocaine).' That's the lingo—rock, twenty, dove, caviar. One of them has a knife in his pants. I'm watching that. He's being fine. He's not being stupid or anything. I say over the wire, so my backup knows this guy has a knife, 'What do you do with that knife? That's pretty big.' He says, 'This is my weapon.' He asks, 'Where do you know Little Joe from?' I say, 'If you're going to be taking up my time I don't need to be hanging out. If you're not going to sell it to me I'll be on my way.' He pulls out the knife and says, 'You're a narco, aren't you?' 'No, I'm not and just get out of my face,' and he pulls out the knife and comes toward me. He says, 'Let me see your money.' 'It's right here.' I had the money in my hand ready to give to him. The other guy is leaning on the car. So I'm going to run this guy over if I have to get out of here (laughs). I'm already giving a go. I hit my blinker. I give a sign because this guy already offered to sell to me and now is just asking for my money—that's robbery. I don't think they filed on him. So, they came in and took him down. He was only a foot away leaning on my door with the knife out.

"When I came on the job I thought it was going to be just great. But there are certain things you find out. I've only had five years. I still know more than when I came on. Women can talk better to people. They're more sympathetic in certain situations. It's a great job for some women. My father always told me if there is something you want to do nobody should stop you. And that's how I feel. But, still you get angry. I don't know. I think the thing that irks me the most is men in the Department who look at you like you're still a woman. Like there are still certain things you can't do or shouldn't do. There are rumors that I got this job just because I'm a woman.

"This job has made me a little tougher only because of everything you see everyday and the people you meet. I told myself I didn't ever want to let myself get callous and mean and just not care about people. You know it has to harden you a little bit. But, I'm still the person I was before—happy go lucky. I want the best things for me in life and I don't want to be a hard person anyway.

"I've always felt whatever I think I can do I'm going to try. Training definitely helps but working undercover you are put in all kinds of different situations. The main thing is me and Martha talk about stuff. We have been working together for a while and know what we're going to do. You can screw yourself up not knowing what your partner is going to do. After each buy we talk about what happened. If somebody got screwed up we yell at each other. We get upset because, 'This is my life what are you doing?' Our supervisor says you guys go over there and talk it out. My partner and I are best friends. We even do stuff with our husbands off work.

"My husband works in athletic sales. I met him when I was already on the job. He helps because he doesn't stress me out. Even when I have to work on a Saturday or day I'm suppose to have off or overtime. I guess he's just one of a kind, and that makes my life easier. When I go home I'm a different person I'm a wife and expectant mother. My mom said she will baby-sit. But, I think that's fair to the baby because I'm still going to be a career person. There are certain stories I don't tell my Mom. She says she just prays for me all day. I was born here though my parents are from Mexico. I have two years of college.

"Since I was a kid I've always been the kind if you dare me to do something I do it. I always had that in me—maybe why I don't get freaked out about it. When I was younger I was tough—not like a tomboy—but, a combination. I was a cheerleader and played soccer. I was always athletic and feminine. I was always the daredevil type, off investigating something—always real curious."

Kathy Shaughnessy, Outside Preventive Maintenance, AT&T, Forty-three years old

Kathy is slim, smart and possesses strong good looks, a great sense of humor and tenderness. Twenty-five years ago she started working for AT&T in Minneapolis, Minnesota where on some days she experiences a wind-chill of minus fifty degrees. She was instrumental in developing and expanding the "Outside Looking In" workshop for blue collar women employees of United States West Telephone Company. She showed such a sophisticated side when traveling, coordinating and speaking in front of groups of her peers that we wondered about the other more glamorous career paths she might have taken.

"I have had some strange things happen. I work night shifts alone out in the fields, near the poles. Recently while I was checking the situation from my computer van, I heard what sounded like a cap gun. Two minutes later a cop car drove up to my vehicle and asked if I had heard any gun shots and in which direction. That kind of bothered me. He had a police dog with him. He took off and I was there five or six hours more. I was really aware of it but it remained quiet. I like this job very much. I haven't really wanted to tell anybody because it could jeopardize my situation.

"Another woman put up a tent over the green box interface one windy night. She was working in her van and went back to her tent, and lo and behold, there was a guy in the tent. She asked who he was, then thinks, 'What the Hell do I care who he is?' and calls 911. It turned out to be some drunk. But, it's pretty scary for her to walk into her tent and see this kind of apparition. I told her not to tell anyone about this.

BLUE COLLAR WOMEN
AT WORK

ABOVE: Linda West *(standing left)*, a welder and artist, works in the extreme heat of a once male dominated "kitchen."

BELOW: Police Captain Betty Kelepecz *(right)*, now a detective with the L.A.P.D., proudly displays her badge; Yolanda Valdez *(left)*, a professional painter, poses with her sign and paint shop truck.

Kathleen Tracy, plumber for the L.A. Unified School District, at the helm of her utility vehicle.

An American flag serves as a backdrop for Los Angeles Police Officer and undercover narcotics agent Sylvia Ruize.

Truck driver and Teamster Brenda Lancaster navigates her big rig through a loading dock area.

ABOVE: Vivian Price *(right)*, an apprentice electrician and Ph.D. student, at work in the field; Tanya Richardson, lifeguard, stands a bit inland of the coastal waters she usually patrols.

BELOW: Lynn Shaw, a married electrician, carefully makes an adjustment to an electrical box.

ABOVE: Margaret Ferguson performed top secret work during her World War II stint in the United States Navy.

BELOW: Frances Cuerras, then a railroad and defense plant worker, assisted America's war effort for as little as .87¢ per hour.

"I just love my job and I don't want to jeopardize it. It's on the cutting edge. It's clean. It's not the money. It's more the freedom. There's a lot of down time which is great. I can do other things and still get my work done. I am very productive. After twenty-five years—finally I love my job.

"My mother said 'Go with a utility;' she was concerned with benefits and things like that. Where did women go twenty-five years ago? They started as an operator. That's what I was hired as—an operator. I was downtown in the main building doing typically female jobs for thirteen to fourteen years. I was a long distance operator; then worked in a repair bureau answering calls from customers who weren't happy because their phones weren't working.

"Becoming a frame attendant was a steppingstone because it was a semiskilled job. I wore a little tool belt. It was a good, fun job with no supervision. You were on your own. I liked the people and liked the boss a lot. I heard about the 'frame' openings when I was sitting at a desk. It was more money and looked good. I did that two to three more years from about 1977 or 1978. Traditionally, the frame job had been totally a male bastion. But when I went in there were women forty and fifty years old. I was thirty. We climbed ladders inside, wore tool belts and had a solder belt. We learned from the other women. Men started calling us 'frame dames.' Women were very good at the job, because there was a lot of detail. They could easily handle the ladders and tools. No hassles or very little. It was a nice tranquil job.

"Then I found they were looking for outside workers. It was more pay, more work, and more school. If I knew then what I know now, I am not sure I would have done it. It was rough. I think it took a lot of good years out of my life. It was very physically demanding, and you worked in all types of weather. It was good though, because I'm doing what I'm doing now as a result. I ended up staying in the manhole environment for about ten years until I got the computer testing job. It was good dough. Many days I just threw my clothes away when I got home because they were so dirty. I didn't even wash them. I worked for a supervisor then who was pretty easy going. There was a lot of screwing around but it still was tough and we got the work done. In the beginning you had to be 110 percent right if you were a female and if you asked a question. I never had it really bad but there was always innuendo, always having to be so sure of yourself.

"I remember a co-worker, a gal, and I were sent out to a building to splice two cables. But the cables weren't there. We looked in the damn building; the cables weren't there. It was a tall new office building being built in downtown Minneapolis. We looked for half a day. When we told the foreman (not our boss) we couldn't find the cables he said, 'Well what do you mean? You two couldn't find the parking lot to the building.'

"If you try to do your share and don't come off really femmy you're all right. I didn't say if I had my period which irks a lot of men. When I finally found out the men on my crew needed help, I felt a lot better. It didn't take too long too realize that they weren't so totally confident all of the time either.

"I would get hassled from women on the street because I had a man's job and I was taking money from working men. I got irritated at one women who was nasty to me so I told her I had a husband in prison and three kids I had to take care of. I had a hard hat and was putting safety cones out. I was very noticeable walking around downtown on my lunch hour. I was aware of being noticed—usually negatively—when walking in ritzy stores with jeans, a vest and dirty finger nails. A lot of people look at you, but I knew I was probably making five times what they made working in the same store as clerks. I had only one other, horrible woman on my crew with me; she was no help. She wasn't liked by men or women. There were a lot of good men out there in my peer group and for that I felt fortunate.

"I got into this work maybe because I'm a tomboy. I liked sports. I always enjoyed men and what they talked about. I'm not prudish and could laugh at their jokes. I liked the independence. It was something different. I started at the phone company when I was sixteen years old. I worked part time through high school and for a few years of college. I went to court reporting school, graduated, and was certified but when I finished it was a tight market and I just didn't pursue it. I might have if the field was a little less competitive but it was too much hassle at the time. It's also a very stressful job, and I have little or no stress with my job now.

"A lot of days I think about how nice it would be to get dressed up in a suit. A lot of days I don't see anybody and I kind of like it that way. I think about going back to school now and it would be possible, because the company would pay for it and my current job has a lot of adaptability. I could retire in five years. I'm forty-three years old now. I own the townhouse I live in and rent out some condo property. I also own a home at the lake. I'm very comfortable, do what I want to do, and don't want for anything.

"I didn't marry, but came real close. When I wanted to he didn't and when he wanted to I didn't. But, I'm happy now. It's okay not having children. I have my two nephews. I love them like they're my own but the best part is they're not. I have a lot of good men and women friends. I never got a lot of pressure from my mother about marriage.

"What I do is not glamorous. It carries with it a blue collar labl. But, I wouldn't trade places with a lot of women I know. I've learned a lot about meeting challenges and I've gained lots of confidence."

Pam is proud to have negotiated difficult waters: having a child out of wedlock, divorce and meeting the job challenges despite her small size. She has a strong sense of self and her ability to do this work. Sylvia's daring resolve flows from her confidence. Kathy quietly maneuvers to get what she wants without making waves. Linda recognizes that she is different, but has no problem accepting who she is.

These excellent jobs which women have gained are not without problems. Before they start these out of sight and behind the scenes women are sometimes scared off by unwelcoming attitudes, resistant gatekeepers, horror stories and tales of abuse. Contractors on federal projects say they can't find qualified women. Police and fire departments recruit women yet grade qualifying physical exams on a combined male female curve that is geared in favor of the men. Unfortunately, for those who do prevail and get the jobs, harassment saps energy and distracts from possible satisfaction. Too many absorb the hardships at personal expense.

These women's individual stories illustrate the multitude of problems and a variety of their coping strategies. Here we've seen examples of how women deal with external problems by involving federal and state laws, EEO, the courts, Department of Labor, apprenticeship regulators, organizational grievance procedures and one-on-one confrontation. We've also seen strategies devised by women's organizations that demand compliance to the labor laws.

Also inspiring are the examples of internal resolution, positive attitudes of courage, self esteem, fortitude and relief that sustain them. They frame situations to give a balanced picture of the positives and negatives. Although the women have problems they deal with them well.

In general, women would benefit from counseling or support groups to help understand the difficulties faced by women and to provide greater compliance. Also, both men and women need assistance in individual problem solving, confrontational techniques, and coping strategies to expand understanding and acceptance. Creating a more humane work environment, embracing both men and women, goes beyond mere compliance and invokes real human cooperation and empathy.

PART V

LIFESTYLES

"I'm out the door by 5:15 A.M. leaving Carrie, my six year old sleeping alone.   She wakes up and eats and then walks over to the baby sitter who is three apartments away.   She is allowed to go in and out of the apartment but not to let anybody in.   She has to follow the rules, do her chores, make her bed and clean up the breakfast mess."

Cheri, Furniture Mover, Bekins

Most of the women we interviewed in depth come from nontraditional backgrounds. The pasts of many include multiple parental divorces, foster care, alcoholism, early pregnancies and abuse. As children and young adults they took on the roles of tomboys, ball players, mechanic helpers, jockeys, playboy bunnies and paramedics.

Only one woman out of the random lot with whom we chose to do in-depth interviews is in a traditional family structure with her first husband—the father of their two children. The fact is, most of the women we interviewed are single and one-half are single with children.

While the women work their children are tended by day care centers, ex-in-laws, old boyfriends, extended families, neighbors and homosexual lovers. Some seek out counseling, file harassment suits, leave lovers and divorce—all to alleviate the stress of working in jobs where there may be inadequate training, lack of support and harassment. Some garner outside support from other less demanding jobs such as selling Mary Kaye cosmetics; others seek additional opinions through the Tradeswomen Network, unions, gay organizations and social clubs.

Because they have chosen nontraditional employment, they often must struggle to reinvent families and communities, gather support and renewal for their life and work. Because of the nature of their lives, these struggles sometimes reach intense levels which foster loneliness and alienation in a way those more traditionally employed will never know.

It is from that sad and difficult struggle that real freedom flows. Released from the confines of more traditional lives, independence often emerges and they become freer, attain a kind of liberation to explore, to experiment and to test. Many develop an exhilarating if sometimes precarious independence that results in amazing creativity. Their independence and lack of need to travel traditional roads is what makes these women so inspiring and their attainments so significant.

TWELVE

WHERE THEY COME FROM

"When I was about ten, my mother tried to commit suicide and told me I was the whole reason she had a miserable life. That is one thing that has stuck in my heart forever."

Brenda, Teamster Truck Driver

Being raised as a foster child, having a mentally ill mother, hearing a stepmother offer your grandparents $100.00 to take you for a year and being discredited as a woman by an abusive, macho father did not lay the comfortable foundations of traditional family homes for some of the women we interviewed. However, these tough beginnings helped these women reject the polite, social, conventional, happy home and hearth picture and carve out different lives.

Brenda, a product of a broken home, has a mother and father who each have been married four times. Brenda will never forget her mother's biting words when she told her at age ten that Brenda was the cause of her miserable life. By the time she was fifteen she finally ran away from home to escape her sexually abusive stepfather. Brenda's grandparents gave her the only stability she ever knew but early on her mother stopped allowing her to see them. As a result, Brenda is a very assertive and strong lady. She speaks out when anyone attacks or takes advantage of her.

Because Cheri's mother was mentally ill, she was forced to live in an abusive foster home from ages six to twelve. In fact, one foster mother stabbed her on the back of the hand with a fork at the dinner table. Later, she lived with her dad and stepmother. Since her dad traveled all the time she never really knew what a real family was like. When Cheri was sixteen years old she ran off and got married.

At first glimpse, Linda's early homelife had the appearance of tradition and stability. Her father is an attorney and she has two brothers and a sister. However, her father's drinking problem made her early life very chaotic. Though her parents' marriage broke up when she was eight, her mother was a strong role model. Her mother and sister, an army helicopter pilot, are homosexuals.

One major reason Silvia has deliberately rejected marriage is because she couldn't stand the way her father treated her mother. Moreover, her father gave his daughters little attention and denied them the educational opportunities he gave her brothers. Her resentment toward her father and the way she was brought up made her choose the single life, but, coming from a large Catholic family she missed children. So, at twenty-nine, while still a virgin, she sought out an English rock star to help her get pregnant. Now, her working choices revolve around raising her son.

Jennifer's mother started out as a barmaid. Growing up Jennifer refused to acknowledge being a girl, wouldn't wear dresses and answer to her own feminine name. She wanted to be called "George" instead. Not liking the activities in which girls normally participate, Jennifer happily worked on cars with her brother.

Because of their temperaments and interests, these women sought out employment and chose lifestyles which were less conventional and suited them more than women's traditional roles.

Brenda, Motion Picture Studio Truck Driver, Member of the Teamsters, Thirty-nine years old

Brenda is about 5 feet 4 inches tall with long blond hair braided down her back. Married for the third time she earns a lot more than her husband.

"I'm a product of a broken home. My mom and dad were born on the same day but are total opposites. My dad is a college professor—a Ph.D. in chemistry and physical science. I was almost aborted. My mom was fifteen and my dad was seventeen years old when they had me. They separated when I was one year old. My mom, now, is an alcoholic. Life with her was Hell. I can't remember her saying she loved me or giving me a hug even once. I didn't see much of my dad. They've both been married four times. My mom is now divorced and will never marry again. My dad is happily on his fourth. It's been a crazy, tough life. I am the kind of person who can do anything. I've been on my own since I was fifteen.

"I had two half brothers and one half sister on my mom's side: five, ten and twelve years after I was born. I raised them all until I was fifteen years old. My mother had allowed me to visit my grandparents on my dad's side during the weekends. When I got to be ten she made me call up my grandparents and say I couldn't come there anymore. That was totally devastating to me, because I really loved my grandparents. They used to go to work on Saturdays and I would be in the house by myself, down in the basement, teaching myself to play the piano. I am a musician so that was my love—piano—and seeing my grandparents and once in a while my aunt and my dad. It was an escape from my mom. When she made me make that phone call it just ripped me apart. Nobody came to my rescue on this. Just this year I sat down and typed out this long get down letter to my dad saying, 'Where were you all these years?' He called and said he felt really bad. He's great. I always loved him. Still I was scared of him because I knew I couldn't live up to his expectations.

"My grandfather was wonderful. Whenever I think about him I cry. He died when I was a runaway. I was told when he was in the hospital dying he was begging people to find me. It just killed me. When I was child he bounced me on his knee singing these Hill Billy songs. They were from Kentucky. He used to make the greatest vegetable soup. Homemade. He took me to the farmers' market early in the morning and then made this wonderful soup. And we would go to church. I didn't see my grandparents after that call.

"You want to hear something funny? One time I found out about one of my mother's marriages. Here I am in a laundromat talking to a total stranger and we hit on something and whoa! I found out her brother was married to my mother. 'Whoa, you got to be kidding me.'

"At fifteen I left home when my stepfather tried to rape me. You know I am a smart kid and I could have done really good at school if I had been raised by my father. I probably would have been in outer space doing the astronaut thing, because my dream in life was to be the first woman astronaut, but the life I had with my mother was constant hell—constant mental torture. I grew up always trying to please her in some way so that she would show me some love and affection. I grew up love starved. I always took the blame for things. My mother's mother was nice and did love me with a deep love. Poor thing. We lived with her between marriages. She would catch Hell if she bought me clothes.

"When I left home, I went to downtown Detroit. I thought since I was a runaway they would help me. I got involved with somebody and got pregnant and was on welfare. I now have two girls. From what I've been through you wouldn't believe what I've raised. Unreal. Selina is at Santa Monica College, eighteen years old, and Harmony is nine.

"My first driving job was driving a "Good Humor" ice cream truck. It was only seasonal due to the weather. I was looking for extra money. I could never stand to be in an office. I am an excellent typist, but I like the freedom of smelling the air. I had a dream to put together the best all female band that ever existed. It was either New York or California. I almost signed with Capitol records. I play keyboards.

"I started off as a Security Guard at The Burbank Studios. I was putting out applications all over the place because I really wanted to start working right away; I didn't want my funds to run out. I got a call from two places the same day. One was an insurance company and one was The Burbank Studios. I went to the studios and had an interview with a woman. She said, 'Well, we have an opening in security,' and made it sound like I wouldn't like it. I said, 'I'll take it, I'll take it.' I was on the graveyard shift and I don't remember seeing any women. It was okay I was used to being in all male bands. It was exciting for people who came to visit me from out of state.

"I was with security about a year and a half when I saw this guy who was kind of kicked back sitting on a chair by a gas pump and whenever a car would pull up he'd pump their gas and check their oil and then he'd sit back down and do nothing. I asked somebody how much he made and it was double what I was making and here I was stuck working weekends and holidays. A week later he wasn't around. I go to the boss and asked if there was an opening. He said he'd give me a chance. He didn't give me any problems but the drivers did. One time this guy made a real lewd remark to me, and I grabbed him by the thumb and pushed him down into a bench and said, 'Look, don't ever talk to me that way. I am a woman and demand respect and that is all there is to it.' And, he never did talk to me that way again. I was the only female auto service person on the books for eight years. It got a little more involved when I started picking up executives' cars, bringing them down, hand washing them and delivering them back. I was pregnant with my second daughter while I was washing these cars. Boy, if you wanted to see a funny sight, see a big, fat, pregnant women climbing into the back seat of a Corvette trying to wash the rear interior window. I don't know how I did it. Another part of the job they never really got me involved in was breaking down and changing tires on trucks and cars. I had a feeling if they ever wanted to mess with me they would use that and they did. I knew they couldn't fire me; I was a good employee. I was never late or never called in sick. They asked me if I could run the tire shop. I said I wasn't sure. I asked the Union and they said I didn't know until I try. They asked me to come in on Friday. I did everything they asked me to do. I jacked up a big generator truck, used the big power jack, got the lugs off and split rims which are dangerous. I felt so good about myself. I did it all. But they said I couldn't cut it and kept me laid off long enough to lose my seniority.

"During the time I was laid off I asked the Union about becoming a driver because it was the same Union—Teamsters Local 399. There was a stipulation I had to have a truck driver's license. The Union paid for truck driver school but after that they put me on the shelf for three years. You have to take a road test with a semi tractor trailer.

"During those three years I drove a cab. Someone I knew was saying he was making all this money driving a taxi. Wow, sounds pretty good. He was talking about bringing home $150.00 a day or more. I went down to Wilmington to Long Beach Checker Cab. It was just a little old cab company like you'd see in the movies—like Taxi on TV—in a dirty, run down type place in a part of town you're really not crazy about being in. They took me right away. There were two older women who had been doing it a long time. I was about thirty-three years old. My best friend took care of my kids. There wasn't much training at all with radio procedures. I did it for three years. It was a fun job. Sometimes it's really rewarding and other times it's really a stinky, thankless, nasty job. If you haven't really spent any time dealing with the general public you haven't even a clue how funky the general public can be. But, I enjoyed the Japanese tourists. They were happy, gracious, thankful people. They were never afraid to spend a buck. One time I had four Japanese; it was their last day and they wanted to go on a tour—with hourly rates. They not only paid me waiting time while they ate at a Mexican restaurant and toured Universal. They even took me. It must have looked funny—four Japanese and a white girl in a Mexican restaurant.

"There were times I felt very uncomfortable. You never know who's going to come out of a house; it doesn't matter where it is. Once I picked up a guy in a gang and had to take him down to his turf loaded with gang members at dusk. I couldn't wait to get out of there. I've gotten into fights between two people, one wanting to be driven and the other not. I've driven customers to their banks or the Police Department to collect the fare. I've kicked people out.

"When I went to work at Universal they put me on a five-ton truck, but at Fox they never put me on more than one ton. I love this job. You can't believe the places we go; we'll see the most gorgeous desert or mountains or funky street gangs. I sling furniture into these trucks, walls, greenery or construction supplies in a crew cab or take people in a maxi-van. I like who I am. I'm strong. In order to go to school in my neighborhood I had to be strong."

Cheri, Furniture Mover, Bekins, Thirty years old

Cheri is a big woman who likes to dress in bright colors. She seemed blustery and loud but what emerged, however, as we talked about how she survived in a totally dysfunctional family, was vulnerability and a wonderful sweetness. In fact, as the hours went by, she demonstrated surprising common sense and actually became a pretty woman.

"I'm a jack of all trades. I work for American Eagle on the weekends doing moving. American Eagle is a small local division of Bekins Box and Ship.

"I've only worked for Bekins for about one year as an accounts payable clerk. About six months ago I asked Eric (my boss) if he had any work on the weekends. He asked what kind of work. He was amazed when I said moving. I wanted the money. They paid a lot more than I was making. I'm a single mother. I don't second guess those types of jobs. It's just a job. Oh, I suppose I could've gone to Bullocks, but here I can determine when I work. I can pick if I work both days on the weekend. At first, the guys were saving me for packing. So I'd go to the packing job and end up doing everything from packing, to hauling, to moving furniture on dollies. The guys were surprised I did all that.

"I'm originally from Oregon. Because of the environment I come from I played softball with the boys. For me it's abnormal that women go, 'Eek, I broke a finger nail!' I worked on a farm in Oregon bucking hay for a local farmer friend. It was no big deal. I just hopped on the truck with the guys and went to buck hay—putting on gloves, baling hay in small eighty to one hundred pound bales, wrapping it in bailing wire, and picking it up with your hands or hay hooks. It's called bucking because you have to pick it up and throw it on a truck.

"I took the moving job partly to give me a physical activity to do. I try to keep my weight down. I try to work out but my hours are long because I commute from Anaheim. I was really active until last year when I took this accounts payable job. I put on more weight. I love to play softball, boogie board, bowl, golf. All these are sore subjects with me. Before I started to work for the company I always thought, 'Wouldn't it be great to work in an office where people golfed together?' but they sure as heck don't ask me. I haven't picked up my golf clubs in a year and a half.

"My education doesn't allow me to walk into any company and say I want a $20,000 a year job. I have a GED—General Education Diploma. I left high school after my Junior year. My parents didn't really care. My family is a long sordid subject. My mother is 'touched'—mentally ill. I don't know her very well. I was about five or six when I went to live in foster homes. My dad was a police officer and became a trucker. I remember bits and pieces. I remember one time my dad coming home and he had been hit by a 2 by 4. It was the first time I ever saw him cry. He was a very gentle person. His idea of punishment was thunking us on the head. He was a large man. His hands were double the size of ours. He commanded, not demanded respect. What I remember of him, he was a nice man.

"During the years I was in foster care I saw my dad twice. I don't really know why he didn't come visit. I saw my mother once. After foster care, when I was about twelve, I resented it. I resented the fact that I didn't have a normal mother or father. I feel sorry for my father. My mother gave me life but deserted me and it took me a long, long time to get over that. I think my mother was weak. I have no contact with my mom now. I think she's still alive. I lived with my father and my stepmother for a short while but after I was in child foster care, I didn't have any contact with my dad until a year ago.

"I have a half brother and half sister, a full younger brother and sister and a younger stepsister. They went to a different foster home. It was all right—not that great. I was with one older couple for a year. They were church people. There was a generation gap. Then I went to a woman and her daughter and the daughter's adopted son. I called her Grandma and Joyce, Mom and Ben was her little boy. Joyce was mean. She stabbed me on the back of the hand with a fork. But I survived it. The grandmother was nice but she always sided with her daughter. She never stood up for me. After it was all over and we were all out my dad said, 'Oh, we tried to get you and we wanted you with us,' but, it was a little late. I lived with my grandparents for a couple of years when I was about fourteen.

"The problems were really beyond my father. My dad was always on the road. We were never a family. It was her house, her husband, her furniture, her food. She kept saying, 'You are eating off my table,'—everything was hers. That was one of the reasons I never went back. I tried—after I had moved away and gotten my divorce and been successful. I tried to put my foot back in the door and make amends. It finally dawned on me he wanted to be with her, and if nothing else, that deserved my respect. When I did come back after living with my grandparents for two years, I did everything she asked me to. If she asked me to jump, I jumped. I was the best kid I could possibly be. But, when my grandma brought my cousins back from their vacation, my stepmother, right there in front of everybody, she asked if my dad gave my grandmother $100 would she put me through high school. I didn't argue with her.

"Instead, I got married at sixteen years old. Grant was my girl friend's brother. I didn't want to go out with him. He kept asking. I said fine as long as his sister came along. When I didn't want to go out with him anymore his mother called, 'Please do something he's so miserable.' It snowballed. I grew to love him. Anyway, my grandparents were going to send me back to my parents.

"My sister-in-law was getting married and they were going to surprise me with a little part of the ceremony when Grant and I were going to step up to the alter. I called my dad and got his wife on the phone. I go, 'Oh, come to my wedding. I'm going to be married.' She said, 'Well he's going fishing that weekend and it's the last time this year.' I'm very bitter.

"I was married three and a half years. If you put a positive and negative together the negative is going to bring the positive down. I went out of my way because I wanted him to succeed. He'd say, 'I want to do this' and I'd go and enroll him in a class and he'd go for a while and get down and I'd pump him up. He'd leave the carburetor on the kitchen counter and I'd put it together. Other men were noticing me and he wasn't.

"We lived a block from the high school and I wanted to finish school and I didn't see any reason why I couldn't. But he couldn't hold a job so I quit school. I worked at Winnebago. I worked at Burger King. He had like a loyal thing he did with his family every year and I couldn't get that weekend off. He said, 'Either you quit your job and go or there will be hell to pay,' so I had to quit my job. He divorced me for a lot of reasons. I let him have everything. We had three cars. I didn't know I didn't have to let him have everything.

"After my divorce I worked for an old woman as a live in housekeeper and nanny. Then, I got a job at a chicken flinging place as dishwasher and baker. I love to bake. One thing about this environment I don't have time to bake or sew. I love art. If I won the lottery today I'd quit my job and be an art major.

"I also did taxi dancing on Olympic Boulevard, downtown Los Angeles. It's like a time card and they punch it in. No alcoholic beverages are served. You go, sit with them, have a sandwich and talk. Guys hassle you but you have to have a firm personality. I was like the enforcer for the place. I'd leave my customers and go over to other customers if I saw something wasn't right. The club didn't allow certain things. We called ourselves 'Club Paradise Dyke Dodgers.'

"I moved to Los Angeles ten years ago. Actually, I didn't move. I came down to get some money on some big business venture and it was just a guy hustling me. I stayed two weeks partying and then I decided I never wanted to leave. So I called my friends and told then to get rid of everything—my furniture, clothes, bird. I ended up doing construction for a neighbor in Arrowhead. I helped the guys. A lot of the guys didn't know how to do electricity. I'm not afraid. If I can figure it out, I'll do it.

"I was twenty-two when I had my daughter with one of the guys on construction. I loved him a lot. I knew him about a year. He was from New Zealand. We had a wonderful relationship, but it wasn't traditional. We'd hike and go find a big rock and read. He ended up making all the breakfasts. I made him two meals in the year. He would have gotten married, but I knew his heart wasn't in it. He wasn't comfortable in this environment and it wasn't fair. I lived with a girlfriend I met through Amway while I was pregnant.

"I love my daughter—she's the best. She's six. At first, I worked the night shift for a security service because it didn't require a lot of schooling. Oh, I worked different places like malls—3:00 P.M. to midnight. I lived with a friend who would baby sit at night. I didn't have to pay for child care. If I worked any days I had another girlfriend watch her. I slept in the morning on the sofa and Carrie would watch TV and play and color. If I really needed a good sleep I'd take her over to another girl friend who had kids.

"I had another girl who I put up for adoption. I was not conflicted because I got to pick the family and knew the baby was better off. I knew the baby wasn't safe with me because of the father. If it weren't for him I wouldn't have put her up for adoption. But, it wasn't traumatic because I did it the way I wanted to. I was in control. It hurts at times and I wish things had been different but the reason for doing it remains the same.

"I'm getting married in February. He's my best friend. It sounds silly. Sex is always good, but we don't have to be bunnies. I vowed I wouldn't marry again unless I was sure. We get along. I want another kid. He wants to have a baby too. Like me, he's a mover. He finished college with a financial analyst major which is one of the reasons his father doesn't like me. I'm not good enough.

"A girl in the office said, 'What are you doing this weekend?' 'Moving,' I answered. 'Why?' she said. 'For money,' I replied. I don't care about their reactions. I think it's funny. They don't expect me to pull my weight. The guys passed me by in the beginning. I've gotten more respect and manners out of the guys than any other girls. I feel they wouldn't respect me if I didn't do my part. I was raised to work really hard. I was raised believing that hard work would get you where you want to go. I would do it (moving) full time, but I don't want to do the physical stuff all the time. I want to work my way into a position."

Simone Fisher, Ship Captain, Matson, Thirty-eight years old

Simone grew up on the water and followed in her father's footsteps. This occupation was not nontraditional to her. It was in her life from the beginning.

"I grew up in Florida in the country. I'm in the middle of two sisters who are both married with kids. I knew about ships because my father was a Chief Engineer in the United States Merchant Marines. I went to the Academy at Kings Point, New York. My dad is a graduate of that school, so I spent many football games and homecomings on that campus. I was fortunate as a child to have wonderful parents. We always had a family boat which we lived on during the summer. My dad would come on vacations and we'd cast off and cruise. I've been in the Inland Waterways all over Long Island Sound. We always had a dingy or small dingy sail boat. When I was older we had a Boston Whaler beside the big boat; so I was always active on the water and enjoyed that aspect of my childhood. We kept the boat in the Florida Keys.

"I went to Florida State. In my first year in a news writing class, I was required to read all major publications and I saw Kings Point was opening their doors to women. It was the first Federal academy to allow women. I entered in July 1974. We were the test guinea pigs. People flew us to West Point to see if we were physically capable They had us run through a confidence course swinging from ropes, climbing walls and balance running through tires.

"Kings Point was a four-year program with two six-month periods at sea on board ships. We had to complete a sea project on board a commercial ship. When I shipped out I came to San Francisco with States Line and American Presidents Lines, the largest container carrier, and Matson services on the West Coast and Hawaii. I graduated in 1978 and the requirement was to get a license as a Deck

Officer Third Mate or Second Assistant Engineer—both lowest level officers. You had to decide if you wanted to work deck or engine. The deck navigates from point A to point B and is responsible for the crew and cargo. Engine requires real heavy math and science and is responsible for anything that has to do with the ship.

"I sailed on cruise lines for nine years, constantly upgrading my license. You must have 365 actual sailing days to get the Second Mate Chief Mate's license. We started with fifteen girls at Kings Point and finished with eight. Some sailed, some had shore jobs, some married—like the guys.

"I don't want children. I'm beyond that. I'm too selfish. I went with a guy for eight years when I was shipping out. I was madly in love and felt like he was my soul mate. Now he's married with two kids. It was my heartache it didn't work out. Maybe it was competition or jealousy. But I'd love to have a relationship now and I'm ready. I just haven't found Mr. Right.

"I'm a high achiever and when I set out to do something I do it. I'm qualified to be captain on any ship on any ocean anywhere in the world. But, when push came to shove, I found out I wasn't going to be captain. Nobody ever said it. I figured it out myself. All the young guys were promoted and I wasn't in on that phase. I finally left in 1987. It was time to move onto bigger and better things. Why should I waste my time? I had enough. It was a very stressful position. The captain is there to call if you need him but when it comes to brass tacks, the Chief Mate is running the show. A lot of responsibility is involved. I sailed the East Coast, Gulf and West Coast. Finally, I was offered a job as a captain on the Matson Lines.

"I love this job. It is worth all the crap I went through. Most of the older guys are retiring. There are only a few of the sticklers left. I'll be full fledged this February. I'm well accepted by my partners. I do my share, pull my own weight, never get out of anything. I'm respected and accepted. As far as the industry, the steady customers know me. Sometimes new customers say, 'Oh, My God, it's a woman—Ms. Pilot.' They are sucking their teeth in. I tell them not to worry.

"I know I can do my job. When all is said and done, at the end, I ask if I did a good job. They have to say yes. I ask them to tell friends.

"My dad is proud—my friends are proud. Everybody says, 'God, Simone, this is great/wonderful.' I just consider myself one of the captains. I disregard the fact that I'm a girl. I work one week on and one off starting and ending Wednesday at noon. I have a house in Aspen and it's a given I go home. In the winter I ski and in the summer I hang out."

Brenda and Cheri are tough, strong women both physically and emotionally. And it's no wonder. They have had to be because little in their backgrounds provided support and guidance. Their family life and education didn't conform to convention. No one took the time to direct them. They were left to their own devices without conventional parental figures and role models to define their own life patterns. On their own they had to draw deep into internal resources to develop satisfying lives.

Both only saw glimpses of love, mostly through their absent fathers. Yet, they are apparently able to give love to their own children even while they struggle through unsuccessful marriages and relationships themselves.

Workwise they have done very well. They have successfully carved their own niches and survived. Perhaps being unfettered by loving memories was for the best, because they never had to experience the benevolent straight jackets binding many of us. They have freely charted their own course by taking new, innovative paths. Most importantly, the end of their journey has led them to good paying work they like and in which they take pride.

The lives of Brenda and Cheri offer hope for those whose lives are difficult and unrewarding in that they have struggled and survived so admirably without the benefit of protective convention.

It is not only women with troubled back grounds, but also women who come from privileged backgrounds who chose unconventional worklives. Sometimes solid family lives and tolerant parents who respect their children's abilities cause young women to chart a course usually planned by a male child. For women like Simone, who is a captain's daughter, her work follows a family lifestyle tradition. Her work as a ship captain flows out of her experience and interest, thus providing her with a leg up on success.

THIRTEEN

THEIR FAMILIES AND
THEIR LIVES

"Ironically I got involved in Mary Kaye cosmetics. I come home in jeans and work boots and an hour later leave decked to the hilt. Believe it or not, I go to Mary Kaye and get all this confidence. When I don't go I miss that fix—all the positives."

Lorie Swensen, Telephone Company

Decades of women's magazines offer vivid color pictures that subtly instruct us about family relationships, and women's chores such as decorating and caring for the home. More recently magazines like *Savvy* and *Working Women* show us successful professionals in navy blue suits attending the latest financial planning seminars on how to invest the fruits of their labor. Dual career marriages, finding the best day care and how to dress for success are recurrent themes.

No magazine illustrates the intimate lives of women doing men's jobs. We gain a murky picture of their homelives and through our imaginations, often create mysterious stereotypical assumptions. If women work in men's jobs do they play like men, parent like men, relate like men, make love like men? What happens after they park their vans, check into the garages, take off the jeans, keys, gunbelts and boots?

In this book we wanted to reveal what really goes on inside the homes of those who labor physically. We were curious to know how they raise their sons and what their daughters learn about work and their role in life. What do they wear off the job and to sleep? What do they do in their leisure time? What does their family unit look like?

Among the women to whom we talked, about 31 percent are married, 42 percent are mothers, 1 percent are "out" gays, 31 percent have serious boyfriends, 32 percent have been divorced, and 1 percent have given up children for adoption or to their ex-husbands.

Only a few women out of many live in traditional families. Two women have given up their children for adoption, several have deliberately decided to be single mothers, one is expecting with no intention of marrying her partner.

The questions emerge:

Were they somehow free psychologically to take these jobs in the first place because they were less bound by traditional family life, their upbringing and their own family?

Or did their jobs liberate them from the confines of traditional family life? Did their income and attitude cause or allow them to divorce themselves literally from that world?

We weren't surprised that so few have traditional families. Everything about what they do in these jobs assaults gender roles in the rawest way: wearing men's clothes, earning men's wages, doing men's physical work of labor, combat, protection and defense. On top of the masculine behavioral requirements is the endless questioning of women's femininity and propriety of doing this work. That barrage can undermine the security that a marriage needs to flourish. Some research showed that in many cases, additionally and indirectly the man who would have such a wife feels threatened. The husband does not relate to his nontraditional wife on an individual level, but must do so in a larger social context that literally says, "How can you let your wife do this?"

The flip side of insecurity, growing assertiveness, accomplishment and independence also shakes settled relationships. Women must make fundamental marital changes. Time and exhaustion also take their toll.

Inevitably these problems spill over to the family. Pam's husband tells her directly he never wants to see her (a ditch digger) with dirt on her face. Of course, it makes sense, since he was raised, as many of us were, with conventions and stereotyped images who certainly didn't serve the family meals dressed in dirty overalls.

Traditional male/female roles change when a woman takes on a "male" job. Lorie suffers enduring tensions in her marriage as their basic marital contract has shifted over the years. Strength and a sense of independence gained on the job along with earning power and exhaustion has changed her relationship with her husband and children. Now, she makes more demands and accepts less of his stereotypical dependence and deferral. Her husband was extremely jealous and resentful when he had to stay home with the children while she went out of town for three weeks of training. She is not, after twenty years, the girl he married. Dramatically that is true for both of them.

Undercover agent, Sylvia, happily married, still says, "I have to go home after working ten and twelve hour days, you don't get home till 9:00 P.M., and either clean house or make dinner. A man would just get off this job and say 'Oh my God, I'm exhausted' and you would have to care for him. You have to go home and be a wife along with this. You can't just lie on the couch and say 'Feed me, I worked all day.' I think you have to be strong That's why it took me so long to have a baby, because I'm not going to quit my job." Strong financial independence gained from her nontraditional welding job, allowed Mary to live without the unhappy marriage bonds she once thought were necessary for survival.

Nontraditional jobs impact the children. Although like most working mothers, these try to spend quality time with their children. There are some liabilities which come with their physical labor. Guilt doesn't override ditch digger Pam's deep physical exhaustion and make her get up off the couch to play with her eight year old child. Guilt colors the morning when she rushes and corrals without time for soothing wake ups or comforting transitions.

The pluses and minuses of their work necessitate changes in family patterns. While their job didn't cause these choices a lot of women become the major wage earner for their extended families. They earn more than their parents or siblings, they help aging parents with mortgages or support their dependent grown children.

In addition, mothering choices reflect both unconventionally and independent thought. One of our interviewees made the conscious choice at twenty-nine years old to become a single parent. Jennifer and Cheri gave up children for adoption. Jennifer was young and not interested in mothering; so she gave custody of her baby son to her ex-husband. Though Cheri kept her first child, Carrie, whom she had out of wedlock, she willingly gave up the next child. "I had another girl who I knew wasn't safe with me because of the menacing father. I put her up for adoption. I got to pick the family and knew the baby was better off."

Both Cindy and Betty struggle with the question of whether to have children and how that would fit into their work and life. Betty has always been concerned that children would interfere with her career. How could she commit the time and energy to both?

Moving from welfare to an apprenticeship program, taking assertiveness training at work, leaving the family for a three-week training unconsciously redefines the particulars of family life, without the luxury of self reflection. Too busy and hassled, piecing their lives together, getting to work, eating and going to school, they don't have the time or assistance to view the new lifestyles they have created in terms of triumphs or failures. Most of the time they just do what they believe is best and move on. We can learn the good and bad from these emerging patterns. We can determine where we can help and what to preserve or steer clear of.

Many of these women who fell into these nontraditional jobs grew up thinking they should have family in a traditional sense. However, now that they work like men and are often treated like men, it's hard to go away from work and switch gears.

Conversely, we noticed that although many of the family patterns were pieced together, these women usually didn't aspire to more traditional family forms. Single mothers, divorcees and gays didn't exhibit a longing or wistfulness for a husband or homelife prevalent in the general society.

Younger women, like Sylvia and Tanya, appeared more at ease with their lifestyles. They were raised amid a public discussion of changing roles and new possibilities for women. Their contemporaries include men who were a central part of that discussion. Since they married after they already had their nontraditional jobs, their partners have a better idea of what they were getting into. They didn't have to go through the subtle realignment of changing family roles like Pam or Lorie.

Our observations teach us that with the passage of time there has been progress in accepting more varied roles for women. Hopefully as this occurs more and more, some of the early difficulties borne by these pioneering women have or will disappear. And freedom of work choice for women will become a reality.

Lorie Swenson, Customer Service Technician, Telephone Company, Forty years old

Pretty and blonde with a about her, she rambled on with a naive enthusiasm that belies a strength of will. Married and the mother of a son, fourteen, and a daughter nine, years, old, she resents feeling like the mother of three when her husband behaves like a jealous child. The oldest of four children, she has three younger brothers. Her father worked for the city as a supervisor for waste treatment. Before becoming a homemaker, her mother worked for the telephone company. Twenty years ago she opted to go to work for the telephone company right out of high school, and she has never regretted that choice.

"I've been married almost twenty years. My husband fills orders in a warehouse for supermarkets. I make a little more money than he does. At first he was threatened by my job, because I was working with men.

"I experienced his jealously major league when I went to Des Moines, Iowa for three weeks of training, still coming home every weekend. He was stuck at home with the kids and had all that responsibility that I always took care of. I told him we had discussed the new job and training, so he knew it was coming. And I even had child care lined up.

"Over the years I've gotten so independent. My husband used to be the strong cocky one. We've changed roles. He says he feels he's supportive but he's not. We do get along. We do things together but I compare our relationship to other people's. I know it is not satisfying. I like him but many times I feel we've drifted apart. When we had kids I took a lot of the responsibility. He kept playing competitive softball. Plus he stopped for beer afterwards. I got a lot stronger and just went and did things without waiting for him. I gained confidence from friendships I developed at work and from accepting responsibility. I don't worry about it anymore.

"My dad used to take the boys up to the park and hit them fly balls, and I was right in there with them. I enjoyed that. Before graduation I took a test to be a phone operator. Both my mother and grandmother had been operators so it seemed natural. Medical benefits and decent stable pay drew me to the phone company. The year I turned eighteen, on September 11, I started with the phone company and moved out of my house on September 12.

"My parents gave me the option of going to school but if I flunked out I would have to pay my own way. I was immature and would have just partied so why go? I wanted to be independent. I wanted to earn money because I always wanted the stuff others kids had. That was twenty years ago and it turned out to be the right choice.

"The phone company was secure twenty years ago. Even ten years ago it was secure. But, in the last two years it is not as stable; now they are not going to take care of you to retirement.

"But, I don't foresee a buyout or the company going under. I have twenty-two years now and have worked hard. Only eight more years I'll have thirty years and I'm out of here. My daughter will be sixteen. I can be home more.

"About one year ago I got involved in Mary Kaye cosmetics. I come home in jeans and work boots and an hour later leave decked to the hilt. The summer now is really busy with the kids so I don't have time to attend meetings, but believe it or not, I go to Mary Kaye and get all this confidence. When I don't go I miss that fix—all the positives. I think it's all the hype and all the support. Believe it or not there is no back stabbing. I've met a lot of nice, warm, genuine women who help each other out and really cheer each other on.

"Now, I not only have one career but two. My goal is not to drive a pink Cadillac now—maybe in eight years. One year my tax guy said, 'I've never seen anyone make money at this.' That was really uncalled for. I let him intimidate me. What a DINK. Why did I put up with that? (By the way, the next year I switched to a different accountant.)

"I was a telephone operator for seven years. I had been interested in home interiors but college was required. I didn't know what else was available. The phone company had the benefits. I was so young and I didn't think long term. There was medical, I got half the phone bill paid and raises every six months. I was immature and just seeing the dollars was great. I think I made $78.00 a week. Back then for a person with no college it was considered a great job. I liked it, because I'm a talker.

"I had supervisors along the way who were not so nice but they just made you a better person. One group chief called me out and told me I was making too many mistakes because I was talking too much. You know how much I love to talk. I tried, but I might say something when there weren't any calls. Every time a light came on I heard this voice, 'You're talking too much.' I remember a time I had a strep throat and called in sick. The supervisor said, 'Well, you don't sound sick.' When you're nineteen that's traumatic. Now I wouldn't put up with that.

"After about two years I wanted a change. I was motivated by the money and better hours. A promotion got me away from weekends and nights. I put in papers for the transfer to repair clerk probably looking at a book listing all the jobs, and I then interviewed. Back then there was more movement in the company. As repair clerk I took repair calls for people with phones out of service and advised when we would be out.

"My trend is to stay two years and then do something else. Once again I needed a change from repair clerk so I moved to completion clerk. Then, I got into training for six months to be a customer service representative pushing sales. But, that wasn't up my alley. There was pressure for sales and to keep your numbers up. They wanted you to overcome customers objections. If an elderly person was on welfare, living alone in a one bedroom apartment, she didn't need three lines, touch tone and call waiting.

"I spent seven years as a Maintenance Administrator testing and dispatching for repairmen. I sat in front of a computer terminal. I liked the customer contact. I found problems in the central office or recalled customers for information or to arrange access. You talk a lot on the phone to repairmen. So when I went outside I did know a lot of the terminology. I knew how to read orders and cable information and everything fell into place.

"Three years ago, March 1989, money motivated me to 'go outside.' In the place where I was working they were putting up all those little temporary walls and that just drove me nuts. I probably would have gone outside years ago, but the weather really scared me even though I had played competitive softball, rain or shine, for years.

"Outside, being a Customer Service Technician was the biggest change. Almost everything I do is physical. It's not very glamorous and the winters in Minnesota can get into subzero temperatures. It's hard to dress and stay warm in those conditions. I was the only woman on an eight-man crew wondering if I could pull my weight. Usually you ride with someone in a truck training about three weeks. I rode with a guy a few days but all he showed me was how to sit in the truck, drink coffee and read the paper. After my three weeks of training in Des Moines, my boss felt I was ready to work alone and apply everything I had just learned. I wasn't going to tell on Dick and get him in trouble, but I told the boss I needed more training time before I started repair alone. I learned nothing from riding with Dick in those three weeks.

"When I was with them they were very nice but I wondered if they thought: 'What a dumb shit.' Sometimes I wonder if I do that to myself just making up their doubts. But once I gained my confidence by working up to four repair calls a day, I didn't care what they thought because in my eyes I was keeping up with the big boys. That only took a couple of months.

"Dispatching for so many years I knew how much work you were supposed to do in four or five days. I figured I'd worked up to that level and proved something to myself. I didn't like paging other guys for equipment and didn't want to bug the foreman.

"I remember one guy I worked with when we were up on a pole and his arms reached over and 'accidentally' touched my breasts. I never confronted him. Part of me thought maybe it was an accident and part of me thought it wasn't. I moved out of the way just in case. I wanted to make sure it didn't happen again.

"It's okay as long as they aren't making comments about me personally or my body. If language and joking gets too offensive I just walk away. I don't want the crew I'm with now to feel they have to change. They call the tool box a Butt Box—probably because you flip it on one end to sit on. I still hear dirty jokes even though I know they hold some stuff back. It shows they respect me. Sometimes they page me now for help or my opinion and that makes me feel good.

"Two years ago I was paired up with another woman working outside for the lottery doing work on a pole with aerial wires. On one nice sunny day a guy drives up and says, 'Right, it takes two ladies—help each other out ladies.' That made me mad. The job gets done, they also pair up men, but people think women have taken jobs away from men.

"I try not to whine. My salary is up to about $675 a week plus about $10 per hour overtime which I work about fifteen hours per week. More and more women have started to go outside.

"Women customers ask me questions. I give women confidence. I think most women think the job is strenuous and overwhelming. Recently a woman was so excited to see a repair woman she asked me how she could fix her phone jack. I told her to go home and try it, that I'd be there two hours. When I went back to my truck an Estee Lauder gift and note of thanks was sitting on my seat as thanks for the help. Things like that make me appreciate my job. The physical part is not for everyone. Sometimes I feel like, 'Oh, my gosh, this will take me forever.' Bitter cold days I rarely go outside anymore. I'm not usually on a poll—I've gotten spoiled. But no matter the weather or conditions, the orders get done; they have to. I'm not going to ask another person to finish something I started."

Tommie Lee, Automobile Repair Service Writer, Twenty-five years old

Tommie is the first female service writer at the Volvo dealership in Berkeley, California. A mature male customer told us he was incredulous that such a young, attractive woman really had the capacity to understand problems with car engines but despite his misgivings, she did. She tells us that she knew nothing about her field when she began but jumped at the opportunity. It paid more money than her more conventional job at the dealership .

"I guess what motivated me was greed because I said I would take whichever job pays the most money. The dealership was great about it. I worked there about nine months then moved to California. I had been working two jobs just to pay for an apartment. It was all work and no life. I'm single and have a boyfriend who has two kids we get every other weekend. I'll probably work on my own family in the next five years. When I started I was making about $20,000 a year. I was making more in San Francisco, but then I took a service manager position in Pleasanton. I didn't get along with the boss above me. He didn't like my hair or my uniform; it made me look like a postmaster he said. They had a problem with mice and didn't deal with it so I left. Now I make about $40,000 to $45,000, depending on the year.

"Sometimes women want a man to help them. They tell me they would rather talk to a man. I say: 'No problem' and I go and get a man. If they want to be narrow minded that is their problem. If we are real busy sometimes a man will come up and tell the woman I'm really good and experienced. Sometimes she accepts that and sometimes she whispers under her breath she'd rather talk to him. I'm more sympathetic than men if customers call in and are in an accident. I always ask, 'Oh, is anybody hurt?' The men just say, 'Okay give me the information.' I also tend to follow up a little more to see if customers are happy with the work.

"More than knowing the automotive business, you need to have good people skills. You really have to listen. That's the main thing. It takes time and then you get to know what questions to ask. You learn as you go along. I had a female who had been doing it thirteen years tain me. About 15 to 20 percent of service writers are women. I have been doing it for eight years. This is my fourth dealership. I started in Indiana at an Oldsmobile dealership as a receptionist. I got there because I was living with my boyfriend whose mother went into the hospital for a hysterectomy. She was working that job and asked me to go in for her while she was sick. I was doing a lot more than they expected, filing a lot of warranty claims. Just out of boredom I started reading the warranty claims and repair orders—just to see what the customer was stating and what the repairs were supposed to be. That way I got familiar with the terms. I then moved to Illinois and applied at a couple dealerships there for any job available. When one interviewed me they said, "We have different openings which do you want?" I wanted the one that paid the most, which was Service Writer, even though I had absolutely no mechanical background.

"I'm happy with what I do on the good days. Women bring gifts sometimes—around the holidays mostly. Guys don't try to flirt. I'm their boss. Customers don't hit on me or think I'm gay. I hire and fire. It's hard sometimes. It reflects on their pay check whether they did a good job or not. It's hard for me. I don't always have a lot of patience.

"I would advise others going into this work to be very patient. Listen and definitely keep an open mind about everything. The times customers aren't happy with the service, be patient, don't take things personally. They may be upset with their car, their day, something triggered them to let it out, but you can't let it get to you. Keep an open mind. Men aren't born with mechanical knowledge. Women can learn just as easily."

Lorie's family is a microcosm of the profound social change occurring in society. She and her husband made their marriage contract over twenty years ago when women had few options and most certainly never thought about these blue collar jobs. Their relationship, remarkably one of the "traditional families" we interview has bumped along with the social changes. Both Lorie and her family have had to adjust over the years to her nontraditional career. Unlike Lorie who began her job at a time when few women did physical labor, Tommie, just twenty-five, has been supported in her job choice and experienced social acceptance at the outset.

Most striking and similar, though, is the upbeat attitude that drives both women through bumps and rejections in work/life patterns as they resolve conflicts to sustain intimacy in their work life and home life.

FOURTEEN

THE GAY WORKING LIFE

"Being gay doesn't make it much worse except that we are lightening rods. We're women, lesbian, outspoken, lightening rods for economy."

Madeline, Splicer, Telephone Company

Because blue collar jobs have in the past been identified with a macho culture, the entrance of gay females in such positions often provokes negative reactions and strong backlash.

Nontraditional work can seem a haven for some of the gay persuasion. Dress, interests, self-supporting pay and evaluation of skills rather than politics are, for those gays, fairer standards than many in more traditional areas.

However, though not all women who work in the trades are, the question of being gay looms like a large question mark over the heads of all women in nontraditional jobs. Are they or aren't they? Are they all? Why else would women do this? Look at them.

Accusations of homosexuality are hurled like grenades bombing all women who enter the trades, regardless of their sexual preference. Serving as a stumbling block, this negative assumption weeds out many women who don't want to defend themselves or explain. We don't know the real statistics. Many women in these jobs feel that there are as many gays in their numbers as there are in the general population. Gays themselves feel there are more gays in blue collar jobs because nontraditional jobs attract nontraditional women.

Madeline, Splicer, Telephone Company, Thirty-nine years old

Madeline says she was once young and beautiful, but not anymore. She also confesses that it's a relief that men have stopped trying to hit on her. Though most people presume she's not gay, she's never tried to hide—she came out long before she took her job at the phone company fifteen years ago. Athletic, savvy and politically active, Madeline is proud of her work and her life.

"I'm a Jill of all trades. I've also been a conscious feminist, so the idea of nontraditional work was appealing. It was a political statement.

"I've been an out lesbian for a long time. It was never a big deal in Seattle. There it was okay to live and let live. Here in Oregon it becomes a big deal. Measure 9, the Anti-Gay Oregon Citizens Alliance, won in about seven counties. People are whipped up about homosexuality. Even though the state passed a law counteracting the anti-gay measures of the individual counties, and even though the state knows these anti-gay measures can't be enforced, in conservative people's minds the restriction has now become a question of democracy.

"In the last few years there's been more of a backlash than ever before—just general backlash against feminism—against women who speak up. If I was really sweet, didn't say a word and didn't object to anything everybody would be fine. A lot of women just say fine and go along with the guys. I have been a shop steward for fifteen years and a splicer for fifteen years, and I don't have to take it anymore. I don't have to listen to this shit anymore. Here the guys go fishing with management. The good old boys side with management over women and minorities in this garage. There's a mystique that white men are getting the short end but only two men have been fired in this garage and both are black. Guys stand around in the supply room and talk, but when you come in they stop. They flavor the whole atmosphere. People are afraid to take a side because if they do, the same thing that happens to us will happen to them. And they are sneaky. The ones that really hate us poured urine in the women's truck. We saw all of them pull into garage. We left and next morning there it is. They hate it because we're outspoken. If they make racial remarks we take them aside. For example, one guy was making remarks about fat women. I told him it was offensive. He said, 'But you're not fat.' He didn't realize most women feel fat.

"Some of us who have been working there so long are used to this grinding, sexist, right wing crap. The week before the 'Outside Looking In' conference, a strip-o-gram came to my garage for somebody's birthday. Since, I'm the Union representative, I was told some people were offended. I called second level and filed a grievance. After the conference some of the guys passed around a petition condemning me. They said the strip-o-gram was just in fun. One-hundred and fifty signed the petition. A lot of women signed the petition even though they didn't agree—just to get along. And, I wasn't even there—I was just responding to complaints. I knew exactly who started the petition, but I didn't mention it. The petition was sent to the president of my Union who backed me up 100 percent. Sometimes I feel like I'm hanging out there. It got so bad I felt like I didn't want to go to work because it seemed like everybody hated me.

"They passed out anti-gay literature during the voting for Measure 9 in Oregon. Being gay doesn't make it much worse except that we are lightening rods. We're women, lesbian, outspoken, lightening rods for the economy. We are the working class who pay all the taxes; we pay property tax and income tax. Rich people don't have to pay taxes. They have loopholes.

"My base pay is about $35,000 annually. We make $17.00 an hour, but most people work overtime and can get up to $60,000 to $70,000 a year. We do make such good money. A lot of people are scared the company is going to surplus us. We were surplused two years in a row so people are nervous. Their anger is a fact—maybe it's EEO kicking them out of the jobs or maybe I would have more seniority if it weren't for the women. Rush Limbaugh believes women should be in the home and because they are not, white men are getting the shaft. But, so many white men got jobs because their family worked for the phone company. On many jobs the guys are barely literate. It sure affects my morale. I don't want to be there.

"Every morning I get up and swim a half a mile just to get a release and if I didn't I wouldn't be there. I'm competitive. A guy in my pool and I try to see if we can beat each other. That gets out a lot of tension and I can come to work and feel pretty good. I only see people a half hour in the morning and a half hour at night and yet even passing someone by without them saying hello or hearing them stop talking does have an affect on me and my job. Recently a black man got fired when three white guys ratted on him. He had verbal arguments with four of them and he got fired. I'm doing the grievance. They feel the Union has been taken over by special interests—women and color. I say, 'In what way?' I ask, 'Have your salary or working conditions changed?' Most operators are women or colored working in the worst conditions. I've been denied certain opportunities—but not training, I make sure I get training. I mean opportunities for advancement, like when there is an opportunity to be in charge, I am the last to be asked. Being in charge is at the discretion of management. When there is a special project they never think of women. Guys are more accepting of non gay women. There is one gay woman, still in the closet, who avoids me because she doesn't want anything to happen or anyone to find out she is gay.

"The only advantage of being a women is that management was required to put women into the job. But I was the one who had to stay there. I did the work. When we started fifteen years ago there wasn't a women's john in the garage. When we asked they just laughed. We called EEO and got a bathroom in two weeks.

"Another advantage to being a woman on the job is you don't have to worry about being macho and getting into like ridiculous situations. If I need help, I'll call for help. I don't try to muscle it and then miss work for two weeks with a bad back. One manhole had toxic waste and these macho men and even one macho lesbian went down all day and got sick. Women are open. Being a woman, I didn't come in presuming I know everything. I didn't have to worry about looking like a fool, especially in the beginning.

"I'm proud I lasted as splicer this long. A lot of women who started with me dropped out. Finally, I've stuck to one thing for many years. I'm also really proud that I've outlasted some of these bastards. I've been here and they haven't scared me off. It's a nontraditional job to a certain extent. I'd like to see other women come into the job, but not the way it worked for Rosie the Riveter when after the war there was a big campaign to put women back into the home. I want it not to be a big deal. During the war there was camaraderie. There is certain camaraderie here—generally with people who work outside and other women. It's nice. I could be doing worse. I like getting filthy because girls are supposed to be so neat.

"I went to the University of Michigan and worked full time as a telephone answering service operator doing the night shift to put myself through school. I got a B.A. degree. Since I was on the loose I moved out West to Seattle as an operator because I had experience. I knew this woman through the feminist movement who worked as an installer, and she told me I should try outside. It sounded like a party. I was athletic and liked working with my hands. So, I put in for a lot of jobs. I had no idea what it was whatsoever. I went on a job visit with an obnoxious guy and woman who said to ignore him. They were both absolutely filthy and I said, 'Great, I'd like to be filthy.' I accepted the job in 1978. That was when NOW instigated a class action suit against AT&T. A consent decree said they had to have a certain number of women in there by the end of 1978. This was so unlike what girls are supposed to be. And what really appealed to me was the great amount of freedom of movement I could have. Also, I had to prove I could do that.

"My parents are real liberal. Dad is a veterinarian. Mother is a welfare worker. I'm the oldest of six kids. We were Catholic and enlightened. They encouraged each of us to do whatever. We lived out in the country in Bement, Illinois. We'd play army man. I worked for my dad on Saturdays from the time I was thirteen years old, cleaned cages and assisted in vet technology. He always said I could do whatever I wanted and never thought I would fail. They gave me a lot of responsibility and assumed I would succeed. They think it's great what I do now. They are very proud. My mom was frightened about me pole climbing. They always had a whole sense of justice—that everyone should be treated equally. They think people of color are interesting not horrible. Being different is not a problem. Where I came from it was acceptable being gay. I came out long before taking the splicing job.

"One of my support systems is the Union. I can call and say, 'Hey, this is going on. Give me some ideas.' I can go blow off steam. They know what I mean and who I'm talking about.

"The Tradeswomen Network is another big support. But, they don't help on specific problems. They give support to any woman who has lasted on a job for more than five months. During Measure 9, women in other trades—closeted gays—called me and asked, 'What do you think I should do?' In some cases they worked on jobs where their employer would fire them if they knew. Here we have a support system.

"My live-in partner is the other woman on the crew. Everybody knows we're together. They get our names mixed up and call me and mean Allie, my partner. She doesn't have as much hope as I do. I keep trying. She's been a support for me. We can count on each other. If I'm missing, I know one person who is looking for me. I feel safer. We try to look out for each other.

"I've been conscious of being a feminist since I was sixteen years old so the idea of nontraditional work was very appealing. Actually, it's a bit of a political statement. In the beginning I was very conscious of being a woman. People would stop and say, 'Wow! it's really great you're out there.' They still do, but now it doesn't give me the same sense of satisfaction. It's like 'You have no idea how easy this is.' It's not a challenge. I can do it in my sleep. It can get rough physically, and as I get older I find myself getting tired. But now I know all the tricks so I don't have to work as hard as I used to.

"There were women from all walks of life and all kinds of backgrounds climbing poles when I went to splicing and pole climbing school. It was like Amazon Heaven! I had a great time in school. It was wonderful. The instructors really liked me because I'm friendly and easy going. They were really encouraging. I tried not to be a confrontational feminist. I figured if you want to learn the job you have to kind of hang out with the guys. We made jokes all the time.

"It was an incredibly packed few weeks if you wanted to learn what they were going to teach us. And, in this particular place they were rough on the ones who couldn't get it. I felt like it was easy. I didn't understand women who couldn't get it. I was going to be a math major at Michigan so it's the technical stuff I like—the theoretical things about splicing and communications. Print reading was supposed to be hardest part of the class but engineering prints are easy for me to understand. Now I'm even critical of my mistakes because it should be easy for me. It's like a puzzle—how to get wires from point A to point C. The new technology now still is a challenge.

"I could go into fiber splicing. That would be a challenge. But, I have an idea I'm mortal. Do I want to be climbing a pole at age fifty and go into a manhole in the middle of winter when it's raining cats and dogs and freezing cold? The answer is no. So, I'm going to night school to become an accountant. And, I couldn't be going to night school if I didn't have this job. They pay for it. One thing about working outside, I couldn't go back inside and have a boss who was breathing down my neck. I couldn't deal with that. I really like to decide what I'm going to do today. I pretty much work alone. If I need help I can ask for help, I decide what I want to do, what route I'm going to take, when I'm going to break for coffee or lunch, how much I'm going to get done today and tomorrow. I like that. That's the best part of the job."

Penny Whistler, Electrician/ Staff Representative for IBEW Apprenticeship Program, Forty-five years old

With a calm, self assured, reflective demeanor, she represents her trade and profession by realistically informing other young women of the benefits and advantages of becoming an electrician. She chose the trades over teaching and has found satisfaction with that choice. As a gay person, who is also in blue collar work, she has sought to recruit other gay women through the *Lesbian News*, who might be interested in the trades.

"I think there are more gay women in the trades. Maybe more gay women are in the situation of having to take care of themselves, and any single woman taking care of herself is more motivated for a high paying job. Gay women are willing to take risks doing things nontraditionally because they are already nontraditional. It's okay to dress like this." She points to her jeans and shirt. "They think it's cool. Some women would never even think of dressing like this. I never advertise that I'm gay, but I don't shy away from it either. I don't offend anybody. I don't make a big deal about it. I'm okay with everybody and so consequently everybody is okay with me.

"When I was in the apprenticeship program, the subtle, antagonistic messages I received made me think, 'Why are you here? You don't really belong. You don't want to get dirty.' It was cruel. I realized later they treated a lot of apprentices that way. I saw a lot of racism, and that was very sad and hard to see—especially if you were African American. These women have to be some of the strongest. Many had children at home and had to work so they put up with it. Some of the women used to intimidate the men. They took an 'attitude' that scared the men.

"Out on the job site during lunch break men would want me to sit and talk to them. It bothered them when I would go off and isolate myself reading a book. I would tell them, 'It is my time, I'm not out here to keep you guys company.' I'm pretty likable. They liked me as a woman, but they didn't always like me as an electrician. According to them, I was bringing the trade down, I was taking their job. There was a lot of, 'Hi, babe.' I'd tell them to fuck off and they didn't like that. I said that to a journeyman when I was an apprentice. He caused a big stink, and since all the other guys teased him, he came up to me saying he wanted to clear it up. I told him, 'You're the one who is mouthing off. If you just shut up everyone will forget about it.' He finally relaxed and shut up.

"Most of the time, at the beginning, I was afraid to speak out and talk back, because I was afraid I would be kicked out of the apprenticeship program. So I put up with a lot of stuff I shouldn't have. I would internalize it which affected my self esteem and how I felt about my work. I would be so nervous sometimes I would drop my tools.

"And I was good, but I didn't believe it. Eventually I got more confident. I finally realized the risk of getting fired wasn't worth what it was doing to me. It wasn't my way to get fired. It took me to my fourth year to say, 'What's the worse thing that could happen to me if I talked back?' Die—which wasn't going to happen, so I started talking back. But it took me long while to do it and I'm a strong woman.

"Two or three times I got in somebody's face and said I wasn't putting up with this anymore. I had one guy who was an alcoholic—a foreman. I said, 'Give me my check.' When I spoke up, talked back, their attitude would change and they treated me differently. The whole atmosphere changed. This is after putting up with it for two months. Eventually the time got shorter and shorter. I never had a bad result from speaking up. Never!

"The apprenticeship program can ruin your home life. It can destroy relationships. Instead of getting up at 7:00 A.M. you get up at 5:00 A.M. I talk to apprentices now and say, 'If you just start doing something new, you have to talk to your partner and share or you're in deep doo.' You're neglecting your relationship which is a priority. I had to get up at 6:00 A.M. on Saturday and study for six hours learning code DC/AC theory, transformers, motor control and conduit bending. My partner also applied to the program; she didn't pass. It was difficult to talk about something exciting that happened on the job when there were some feelings of jealousy. So I couldn't come home and talk about the exciting things I did because she resented me. There was no support. A relationship is two lives and you have to work on each other's lives. You have to have a date one night a week where you don't take your work with you and go away at least one weekend. Somebody has to understand. I've been living with a woman now for about four years. It's taken me this long to find a healthy right relationship which I'll be in as long as I'm here. But you have to let your partner know how tired you are or that you need to study. I want the other person to understand I have to take care of myself.

"My former partner decided to relate outside the relationship and that was sad. This happened in my first year of the apprenticeship program. I did consider giving up the program, but I just saw it as such an opportunity. It was a challenge because it was so different. It was going to push me to do something I'd never done before. And the money was good. Today apprentices start at $9.00 an hour and at the end of five years you make $25.45 with an opportunity for overtime. You can earn $40,000 to $50,000 a year. As a teacher you can be offered a contract starting at $17,000.

"In the trades I was willing to deal with this. Every morning, before leaving for work, I wrote in my journal how good I was. I would do these affirmations and then go to work feeling I was really good. And I was. I did good work. I had self satisfaction. I was doing something very different and took pride in that. I didn't want to fail or quit. That was my self imposed burden. I saw where things could be different.

"We just had a woman (working with us) who had tattoos all over her arms. She was gently removed from a job in a bank building, because the contractor was worried it was offensive. I said the firing was okay as long as they would also remove a tattooed man. I haven't run into projections that I am or am not gay. I remember a man hitting on me only once. He would not take no for an answer. Finally I told him, 'I'm married with five kids and my husband will shoot your balls off if you don't back off.' He got the picture.

"Also, I've noticed that guys like it when I let my short hair grow a little longer. Guys treat me differently. When I get it cut they say: 'Oh, why?' or 'Oh, it looked nice.' But I'm not there to please.

"My background was white middle class. My dad sold insurance and my mom went back to college when I was in junior high to teach. I had a happy childhood although later I learned my dad was an alcoholic and there was some dysfunction. I learned values: common sense, a practical sense of survival and to take care of myself. I was the youngest with two older brothers. The oldest is a doctor and the second took over my dad's insurance business. I put myself through college. My parents didn't pay a dime. I was working thirty hours a week as a teacher's aide and had a job with the New York City Recreation Department.

"I didn't live my life thinking I wanted to be an electrician, but I couldn't get a job. I always knew I wanted to be a teacher. My mom was a teacher. By the time I was in eighth grade I had my whole career planned out. But as a substitute, I was making $35.00 a day, so I had to reevaluate my life and career. It was awful. I was so good—so dedicated. They wanted me to do all the after school programs without getting paid. If I said, 'No', they said, 'Well fine, if you don't like it I have fifty more behind you.' I didn't like the way they treated teachers, so I got a real estate license. I learned a lot about business. I made money, sold houses and taught a training meeting every week with the agents. Eventually I got bored.

"A friend of mine was painting houses. She was working for a woman contractor getting $6.00 an hour. I knew how to run a business so, lo and behold, I became a painting contractor. During that two and a half years I went to New York University on Career Days and spoke about being a painter. I met a woman electrician. She encouraged me to apply to the apprenticeship program. I investigated different nontraditional careers. The physical aspect of the job was intriguing. Then in 1981 I went to a career day put on by the federal government on construction.

"A year later, I was notified I was number four on the eligibility list for the Electrical Training Trust, a facility run by contractors and labor. It's a nonprofit training entity which governs the apprenticeship program with standards approved by the state. One week later I get a card telling me when to show up for orientation. You go through two orientations and go to work. You go to school two nights a week at one of five campuses scattered throughout New York City. You go five years with summers off.

"Today women are treated differently and better. There is an apprenticeship committee to help support women. It took me a year and a half just to get used to the tools. I had never worked with tools as a kid. But I enjoyed it. Everyday was different. It was creative. Someone said run conduct pipe from point A to point B and you had to figure out how to do that. There were all different kinds of installations for electrical work so everyday I had to learn something new. You didn't get bored. That was something I really liked about it. It was analytical. You troubleshoot. I learned a skill I will always have. No matter where I go, I can wire somebody's house. I have all these skills and I know it and I feel very good about myself.

"I looked at all the trades for three things: what paid the most, what I could do when I was fifty, and what was the most stimulating. I applied and passed the exam—mostly basic math, nothing to do with electrical.

"I am now working full-time in the Electrical Training Trust. I work on apprenticeship curriculum, Career Days, graduation and the day to day organization necessary to keep sixty classes going and I talk at high schools. In 1992 there were twenty women apprentices out of about 540. Now the total is thirty-five. Since I've been working in the office, our only paid ad was to the *Lesbian News* which was okay with my boss. I know lesbians are more willing to take a risk and I knew it was a magazine that women read. I've also put some ads in the free newspaper. Out of the thirty-five women I think about 40 percent are gay which is higher than the general population.

"I'm glad to be working in the staff job. I loved the work of electrician but I hated the environment—the dirt, the air, drywall and grinding tile dust had an adverse affect on my lungs. I'm health conscious. I still do electrical work but now I pay someone to crawl under a house or go into the attic because the dust and asbestos is incredible in my nose. I also got sick of proving myself. If a woman makes a mistake everyone knows it.

"Women are important to construction jobs. There is a noticeable effect on the job site, and the trades get along together much better, people are polite, there's not so much crude language and behavior and the morale is higher. When there are no women or few women there is heavy competition around the trades. Often women treat people better. Many men feel you make $25.00 an hour and they don't need to tell you you're doing a good job. Women know people need 'atta boys.'

"Women haven't even tapped into their abilities. These jobs are easy. A lot of women have skills; they are neat and particular. I can lay out the circuitry, but a man could visualize hanging the fixture and I just stand there going, 'Duh.' Men are more analytical—better with spatial relations.

"Career counselors? Who are they? Have they worked different jobs? I met a guy at a high school who just graduated from college and being a career counselor was his first job. I asked, 'What do you tell them? What do you know?' For women the nontraditional work is not part of their consciousness. Women worked in World War II taking men's jobs because the men were at war, but women were fired when the men came back. What does that tell you? Women are/were still taking men's jobs? It is still true today."

Jeanine Woodson, Sound Electrician, Thirty-four years old

Her very colorful language fits her style. She's black, gay and very bright with a flat top hair style that's shaved on the sides. Though she presents herself in a funky sort of way, she was very serious and perceptive about politics and about herself. Her daring and acceptance of herself and her openness about her gay lifestyle make her a unique woman.

"Now that I'm not drunk or not loaded, I'm painfully aware that (nontraditional work is) like going into a battlefield and having your psyche assaulted all day long. I internalize it and am walking around like a time bomb.

"I think there are more lesbians in the trades. It's someplace they can be themselves and do what they want. They don't have to put on dresses or adopt a mentality which is smiling and being emotionally available for men.

"I haven't met too many gay men in the trades. Lesbian baiting is another way to hold women out of good paying jobs. It scares off some women. White guys are more friendly to me than black men.

"I got in about eight years ago really just kind of on a lark. I was kind of bouncing around—not having any idea what I should do. I went to the Union and they told me what I needed. At that time you went to work for a shop doing dinky stuff waiting for an apprenticeship to open up. My nose was a bit out of joint because you were supposed to work two months and it took me six months. I lived in mid-Wilshire and traveled to Santa Fe Springs by bus because I didn't know how to drive. I had to drop my daughter off at 6:00 A.M. so, I was trying to find a way to make a living not just for me but a life for my kid also.

"My mom is a housemaker and my dad actually was an electrician. They are Jehovah Witnesses. We led the most sheltered lifestyle. We didn't associate with other kids, because we were standing on the street corner and knocking on doors. There were no celebrations on birthdays or Christmas. My parents were emotionally repressed. I guess they did the best they could. They adopted both of us, my sister is four years younger. We didn't get to do the things most kids take for granted. We couldn't talk on the phone or spend the night because we were under my mother's supervision all the time. We both went wild. My first drug of choice was sex. I guess it was my way of escaping. I still have a relationship with my parents. We talk, but it's not cozy.

"My seventeen year old daughter got herself a 'big sister,' because she felt like she needed a heterosexual female to relate to. We're both alike in that we're not really tuned into what we want to do. We'll figure it out. Raising her now is not bad. I've started to really appreciate her. She is like my one true friend. What irked me was when she was really dependent—she came to live with me when she was seven and I was twenty years old. I was relieved when my parents took her as a baby. I had no inkling I would ever have to be responsible for her. I paid my bills but wanted to party. I was like, 'Where's my next joint and six pack of beer?' I wasn't interested in being a full time parent.

"It was a fuzzy period, because I was drinking and using marijuana. Most of my life I spent being a classic underachiever. Finally I got the apprenticeship which was good, because I was just about to say, 'fuck it.' My first job in construction was at the big Hughes building in Marina Del Rey, California.

"I was the only woman on the crew, the only black and this non Union firm had just switched to Union, so the guys didn't know what to think. They were not used to women or blacks. Obviously, I was a little different than other girls. I was crazy and loud and queer. I could cuss real loud and these people were crude anyway. However, I could tell right away they were not use to queers. I was working with this young, little, white middle class Italian kid who always had plenty—complete opposite from me. He didn't think women belonged in the trades. But, he thought I was interesting, because he never met anyone like me. Then the religious types would try to convert me, 'Have you met Jesus?' 'No, I really wasn't looking for him.' They just couldn't get that I was acting like one of the guys.

"You can't show fear; they tune in on that right away. But the other end of the spectrum—that's not cool. They expect you to be a woman even if you're working at the trades. A lot of the time their idea of a women is a calendar girl—a Playboy centerfold. It was baptism by fire. There were two other women on the site—a tin knocker (sheet metal worker) and a heavy equipment operator.

"The work was okay—pulling cable for the telephone system. It was exciting for me because I had never done this work. They were impressed, but, I still didn't know diddly and nobody was going to tell you. One of the Union guys took me under his wing. I didn't pay much attention to the work. It was the atmosphere that interested me because it was so foreign from the office environment. Office guys have the same mentality, but they are quieter about it. The shit house graffiti gave you a good feel on where these guys were coming from.

"If I thought they were giving me a hard time, I'd fight it. The nature of apprenticeships is they give you a hard time and you are just supposed to take it. So, I was branded as an attitude problem. I don't think I was any more arrogant than any of the guys but coming from me it was viewed that way. Basically my personality goes against the grain. I'm not going to be terribly diplomatic. At this time I was starting to get some political sense. We were working on school sites and we saw dilapidated schools and tired teachers in the black areas.

"Also, the way I looked didn't help. I had a flat top and the rest of my hair shaved. I had been through all the other phases of black hair care: Gherry curl, which is long and drippy, chemically straightened and then curled; braids, perm. I finally just got tired of it. People said, 'No, that's too butch looking.' But, I said, 'No, I just want to cut it off.' Initially it was much more about convenience than a statement, but then my hair began to say, 'I'm not here to be a cupie doll.' Some men resented me. Kids asked me at a school if I was a man or a woman and I answered, 'I'm a dude with tits.' Finally, I got a car—this beat up old Dodge. I was unlike anybody people knew.

"Once I was working with an older guy who was about to retire. In the middle of the summer he asked me to go to his car for an extension cord. It's about 90 degrees and I walk up four or five floors in this parking lot about a mile away only to find he had parked his truck right next to where we were working. I was steamed. I felt like he sent me on a wild goose chase. I went off on him and started yelling and cussing. This wasn't even for a tool but for his music from the radio. What's the f—ing story? Well, the story got back to the apprentice committee. I didn't care if he did it maliciously, he wasted my time.

"I didn't pick my fights. I fought about everything. I felt uncomfortable and the only way I could ease my discomfort was to fight them back. Their take on it was I have an attitude problem telling me 'Sometimes you have to put up with it.' I was like 'Well whatever.'

"All through my apprenticeship I had a chip on my shoulder because I felt like the male apprentices were learning more. I was still in a fuzz and starting to lose interest in the trades because I didn't like the atmosphere. I wanted to finish something I started and wanted to stay around and give them a fight for a little longer. The apprenticeship was supposed to take four years, mine took five. I had a big meeting with them. I said, 'I go to school, get good grades. What's the story?' They told me the contractors didn't think I fit in. I thought I didn't have anything in common with them and didn't see why I had to kiss their ass. I'm just going to do my job. I don't need to know about your wife and kids because you don't want to know about my girlfriend. Union meetings are still a boys' club. I look at the trades and the military as the last bastion of white male supremacy. It's the last little thing they've got that is theirs.

"I persisted because the money is good. I can do this. I already paid my dues. I like the work itself. I would like it more if I really felt I knew what I was doing. It's my one marketable skill at thirty-four years old. But, I want something else. I am going to school at night. In the last two years I worked maybe a total of seven months so I want a short term program that I can finish that will make me money. I'm working on being a radiology technician. The math is killing me.

"My parents are around. My daughter has them and a lot of friends. I have friends. I'm on the board of the United Lesbians of African American Heritage (ULAAH), because I believe in what they are trying to do. They try to provide a voice and space in the community."

Most of the gay women we interviewed are enthusiastic about assisting other gays on an individual basis and also reaching out to the larger community for understanding and acceptance. While their styles are different, they all believe it best to get along and are reflective about how. Penny's style is more relaxed and easy going. She can get along with everybody and not make big issues. Madeline, shows the strains of tension as she juggles her obvious anger at being treated unfairly by filing grievances, promoting Union activities, accusing males of urine spills, swimming competitively and turning to a counselor in despair. These upsets mix with her pride in getting along during training, being good at engineering and ultimately hanging in there for fifteen years. Madeline is matter-of-fact about being gay. Being gay wasn't terribly upsetting to her liberal parents; so she felt comfortable about coming out long before starting work at the phone company.

It's not much worse working in a man's world as a homosexual female than as a heterosexual woman, Madeline feels. She doesn't feel specifically persecuted just because she is gay. Being any kind of woman or person of color on a blue collar job just aggravates men who are angry anyway about women taking their jobs.

Both Madeline and Penny now educate others about gay women in nontraditional jobs, counseling workmates and new recruits. Madeline attended tradeswomen's meetings for her own support and to help women who had more pressing problems than her own. Closeted gays contacted her for advice. To her, the very act of taking and keeping this job and her satisfaction at being a member of the counter culture and being a laborer were clear political statements that educated and gave proof of the positive possibilities of her work.

Jeanine's style is to be assertive, ready to fight and to defend. It's provocative. However, it's true and real. It's the ultimate in taking a stand supported visually in dress, mannerism, language and defended with deep intelligence and a philosophy that people are entitled to be who they are to find comfort and respect. Jeanine's style of education is to shock. This usually provokes a quick verbal response but reflection as well.

Penny's response to her male coworkers who ask her to join them for lunch is striking. She is dogged tired from work, getting a half hour to recoup and men want her to talk with them during lunch. She definitely asserts her seriousness about her job and not being a playmate when she says, "I'm not here to please you guys."

Penny was deliberate in her counseling to prospective apprentices. She feels that taking a job as an electrician requires thinking through what it's impact will be on relationships. Penny feels the relationship needs to be given priority attention. Recognizing that a couple is made up of two separate lives in which each person needs support and attention, she defined her own personal rules: spend at least one night a week on a date, leaving work out of it and spend at least one weekend a month away.

Penny, Madeline and Jeanine represent the growing number of "out" gays in the nontraditional professions. Since blue collar work has traditionally been a macho men's area, actively homosexual women represent the most dramatic difference in the new women coming into these jobs.

Our study shows that there seems to be a pattern. Many nontraditional women workers have nontraditional lifestyles. Which came first? The work or the life? We don't know which dictates the other like the famous chicken and the egg riddle. But, we do know that often lifestyle and work complement each other providing greater comfort in each area. It also suggests that women with unconventional lifestyles may find a better fit in nontraditional women's work rather than in more constricting traditional workstyles which are usually outgrowths of rigid family roles.

At least getting information about new options in traditional work/life patterns may be worth exploring.

PART VI

WHAT WE'VE LEARNED
FROM THESE WOMEN

"You better make sure you know what you're getting into."
Penny Whistler, Electrician

Information pulled from these stories suggest significant social shifts, which challenge us to expand our concept of humanity, human potential and traditional notions. Girls can do math and science. They can operate maxi sneakers and fire trucks. They are smart, strong and suited to work outdoors as well as doing traditional nurturing tasks. They can wear blue collars as well as white or pink. These trailblazing women are part of our own collective potential and we of theirs. These stories and struggles are powerful, because they are part of the sisterhood of women; they are our own.

Implicitly this nontraditional bravery questions other social myths and outdated constraints. It prods all of us to examine patterns locked rigidly in our individual and social lives.

FIFTEEN

LESSONS LEARNED

"I only encourage other women to do this if psychologically and mentally they can handle the pressure."

Sylvia, Undercover Narcotics Agent

Put Teeth into Compliance

According to the law, contractors and states must put forth a "good faith effort" to comply with the regulations. We say that good faith has become the lock on the door of opportunity for women. We want to eliminate "good faith effort" as a measurement of compliance so that we can turn good faith into good jobs.

History tells us that for years after World War II women were seriously under represented on construction jobs. Pushed to comply with voluntary affirmative action goals, employers complained they were unable to find trained women to do these jobs. Despite this though, women were actually trained and registered with the unions, these women often were denied employment. Furthermore, they excused their inaction by denying women were out there or even wanted these jobs. This was only partially true. For women, lack of positive information, inaccessible apprenticeship programs, frightening and rejecting interviews and flat out hiring and training discrimination were the discouraging factors. Men were the reluctant gatekeepers.

Two things happened in the 1970s to help open nontraditional jobs to women. Following the lead of the 1964 Civil Rights Bill, Executive Order 11246 set up specific goals and timetables for women in construction, requiring employers to commit to Affirmative Action. This order made contractors responsible for providing a harassment free work place and combating the isolation of women employees. This included actions requiring all contractors and subcontractors holding a Federal or federally assisted construction contract in excess of $10,000 to where possible, assign two or more women to each construction project and recruit women from female recruitment sources. The numerical goals were 3.1 percent by March 31, 1979, 5 percent by 1980 and 6.9 percent by 1981.

Secondly, apprenticeship programs, registered with the Bureau of Apprenticeship and Training, United States Department of Labor or any State Apprenticeship Council were instructed to set numerical goals based on women's participation in the local labor market and specified recruitment techniques that emphasized the importance of outreach, giving advance notice of opportunities to women's centers and publications. The information was to be distributed thirty days in advance of application date.

These goals have never been met.

The first success story of how these factors can come together was the building of the Oakland Federal Office Building between December 1990 and June 1993. This is a model for how to put teeth into compliance. Here the efforts of one vigilant compliance officer and the relentless, dogged pursuit of the San Francisco Women's Bureau culminated in women working 8.3 percent of the total hours of which 64 percent (51,000 hours) were worked by journeymen women in twenty-four different trades or jobs—well in excess of the national goal of 6.9 percent—at $20.00 to $30.00 an hour plus benefits. It was an historic first.

The general contractor agreed to set up an Affirmative Action Committee with representatives from all interested parties. Statistics on female and minority hours were made known in the public meetings of the Affirmative Action Committee. Subcontractors were brought in to tell how they intended to meet the goals. One man said he knew about the goals, but since they had never been enforced before, he hadn't done anything to find women workers. Some said they couldn't get "qualified" women.

In most cases "qualified" means having a high school diploma, attaining the age of eighteen and applying for an apprenticeship. Not much experience is required in the "mud trades," such as cement work or brick laying. One apprenticeship coordinator wrote a letter to the prime contractor indicating he had no women on his apprenticeship list and therefore would not be able to have women available when that job came up. Once this fact was made public, women started signing up in two separate offices which were open forty hours a week.

However, many apprenticeship programs operate so discreetly that women have no way of finding them and applying.

The overwhelming odds of achieving such a goal were defeated by nothing less than "hand to hand combat" as women reached out in every way they knew to inform, cajole, threaten, train and recruit the willing women out there who wanted to work these well paying jobs as we were told by Madeline Mixer, whose job is to agitate for compliance. The success of this project can be translated into the next Federal projects.

Propaganda Pays

Government and business went all out to recruit women into nontraditional jobs during World War II. They paid huge sums of money, got the best advertising talent, and initiated a massive media blitz, which glorified and revered the country's new hero—Rosie the Riveter. The campaign focused on women doing their patriotic duty. Rosie-cheeked Rosies in red bandannas and slacks, tools in hand were on the cover of *Saturday Evening Post*. Inside the magazine's fiction portrayed heroic, happy and healthy working women. And it worked. Women defied prior convention and entered these jobs in an unprecedented number.

Today pictures of nontraditional workers exist in tiny obscure trade magazines printed on cheap paper, produced on a shoe string and are usually circulated among the already converted. Only their own communities see these modern day women workers in dirty overalls. Only their families and the weary compliance officers at EEOC know what opportunities exist. Where are the pictures of these women in our national media, Hollywood, television or women's magazines? They are almost invisible.

What blue collar women need is attention, visibility and celebration. Job availability in this economy is worth celebrating. Good pay and benefits, fun and satisfaction are rewards that should be identified and promoted. Widespread public relations campaigns need to be initiated. Women's organizations, government and social agencies need to promote blue collar jobs. High school counselors need to train and to inform students of such positions. Front page color pictures on national magazines of modern day Rosies would do the trick. It all makes good sense because for society, energy rolls from positive images of successful women in nontraditional jobs.

Meetings and publications, orientation, and career days for nontraditional women should include testimonials from women who have entered the trades. Imagine the inspiration for women who can't support themselves or their family when she hears a women saying, "Here's how I did it. I used to be on welfare—now I own my vacation home in Hawaii." Organizations run by women in the trades need to hold up hope and let people know that there are women who have happily made it in these jobs.

Wonderful Free Opportunities DO Exist.

Although they are not well promoted or easy to find, such guides as the Directory of Nontraditional Training and Employment Programs Serving Women published by the Women's Bureau provide outstanding information on jobs. It outlines wonderful programs for women with and without qualifications and backgrounds that help in all arenas. It gives guidance in life skills as well as technical skills and self esteem.

Women Do These Jobs, Even in This Tight Economy

Today, women do many jobs which were formerly considered men only territory: firefighter, sanitation worker, plumber, urinal cleaner, undercover narcotics agent, ditch digger, utility worker, electrician, heavy truck driver, welder and on and on.

The numbers of women in registered apprenticeships has steadily risen from the 1970s according to the Bureau of Apprenticeship and Training, Employment and Training Administration and United States Department of Labor. The demand for women in nontraditional jobs is actually up in certain areas. For example, contractors working on Federally funded projects need to meet hiring goals; government contracts necessitate hiring women in various occupations; private employers attempting to meet EEOC goals want qualified women. Women who seek employment need to be savvy about looking for these special hiring opportunities. They can take advantage of new hiring rules to level the playing field and raise the numbers of women in these trades. Historically, society has been responsible for excluding this capable resource. Now, women can make this disadvantage work in their favor.

Women Can Do These Jobs

Women can use tools, work in a foundry, read a blueprint, dig a ditch, fix and climb, lift and repair and withstand. These jobs fit many women's aptitudes, backgrounds and preferences.

Some women have early experiences on farms, in shop classes, using tools and machines. However, even women with out backgrounds in these areas can learn to use these tools. Preapprentice training programs can wipe out any experiential disadvantage women have and put many women on an equal footing with their male coworkers. In the recent past, employers, recruiters, unions and compliance officers have begun to provide the catch up experience needed for women with inclination and ability who lacked only hands on experience. Women can do these jobs once they are taught to use the tools, properly trained and supported.

Women May Do These Jobs Differently From Men

Women sometimes need to adjust the work to their feminine physiques. Upper body strength or the size of female hands can mean scaling walls with the strength of their arms instead of their legs. Some women will have to learn the correct way to lift heavy weights or wield oversized tools. Other women are unfamiliar with certain cars, tools, guns and have to learn to use them correctly.

Emotionally many women we approached do their jobs differently from men. They are more open, disclosing, embracing and less typically "macho." Women told us they say "ouch" when it hurts, refuse to go into yards with threatening dogs, won't go down utility holes—more commonly known as "manholes"—with questionable or toxic air and refuse to lift more weight than they should when it means spending the next two weeks nursing bad backs. Some of the women police officers we interviewed, described themselves as conciliatory and calm. Some indicated that they are able to get their suspect with gentle coaxing rather than force. A common trait was that they seemed more sympathetic and less competitive.

Women Like These Jobs

They gathered satisfaction by hard physical exertion, being outdoors, freedom and seeing the physical manifestation of their labor as a wall goes up, a building is built, a bathtub installed and a drug addict is apprehended. As a whole, they do like paying the bills, supporting their family handsomely and freeing themselves from unhappy dependent family bonds.

Women Want These Jobs

Women have testified in Congress as well as in representative bodies in other countries, that no matter how hard they have to work, they like it. They like seeing what they've done. They like to take their children down to see their accomplishments.

Where else can you get on-the-job training with benefits, good compensation with only the benefit of a high school diploma? Women want jobs in fields that have comparable pay for comparable work in areas that can be satisfying and suited to their interests, aptitudes, and lifestyles. When these jobs are offered and women become aware of them, they sign up. If there were more advertising and apprentice programs, even more women would apply.

We Need More Women in These Jobs

Few Federal projects have met national goals for hiring women workers. Unions and contractors say the proof of women's lack of interest and ability is their small numbers on these jobs. However, our research shows that the numbers are rising and given opportunities, women will line up for these jobs. More women in these jobs prove that women want these jobs and can do them.

A critical mass of women will make job conditions for blue collar employment better. Experience shows isolated females have a difficult time. Savvy companies pair up women; savvy women find others. Women need women because in groups they strengthen their voice, become accepted and lessen the distraction and notoriety that one woman often provokes. They provide community, camaraderie and comfort, thus strengthening job performance.

We Need More Women Involved in the Hiring

Women understand female psyches and bodies as well as psychological, biological and familial (i.e., child care) needs. Often women are better at detecting appropriate and inappropriate female candidates. They have been there and have dealt with the issues. Their experience is critical to successful hiring and good retention. Men, who often exclusively do the hiring, can overlook the potential of females. To be maximally effective, companies, unions and counselors must include qualified women as recruiters.

Women Need Help with These Jobs

Women need training and tips in how to find these jobs, and how to do these jobs. In order to utilize their physical endowments they need to learn how to lift and shoot, use their backs, how to balance, print and carry. They need on-site child care and child care referrals. They need employers who comply with existing federal and state goals and regulations. In addition, they need further legislation and enforcement. Women need to be hired, developed and promoted. They need career advancements to supervisory positions. They need options and relief from years of backbreaking physical exertion, drying sun and general exposure as they age. They need respect for their choices and respect for their contributions.

Women need advice to toughen up, to ignore, to demand, to complain, to get support, to get outside relief. They need help in reminding themselves of the satisfaction they get from their work. They need social endorsement.

The glass ceiling is not limited to top management. It also applies to the invisible barriers that run across resistant horizontal walls that bar women from any open opportunity.

In order that more women know about and have the opportunities to gain blue collar jobs, interested women need better record keeping and monitoring of access, promotions and appraisals. They need money for research to collect data about the true numbers of women already trained and working and the number that want to work. They need planning rather than serendipity to get and maintain these jobs.

As well as groups of women to support them, prospective workers need individual support to reinforce shattered self images and conflicting role models. Socially they need assistance from government, business and academia.

Women Are Fortified By Information and Training

Information provides standards and criteria for measurement and assessment. If women who want these jobs are afforded this information and given access to training programs, they can be as proficient as any man. This preparation can erase fear and insecurity and provide a base for action and reaction. However, when they do succeed, many of the women profiled in this book revealed their own tremendous struggles to get these necessary components. Betty, the policewoman, isn't scared in a shoot-out because of excellent preparation at the police academy. One telephone technician and a service writer weren't intimidated by men's jobs, because they worked as dispatchers and became familiar with terminology and standards.

We Need Support Groups for Women

Despite the fact that most of the women profiled have succeeded almost every portrait reveals the person's need for support from other women in similar positions. Support can change a lonely battle and feelings of isolation into a celebrated cause. Trudi Ferguson, one of the authors, originally became interested in studying more women in blue collar jobs when she was hired as a consultant for women in the phone company who had to handle success alone. They were ready to quit until they found renewal and exhilaration in discovering other women who had solved similar problems. But, there is good news and bad news about support.

The good news is: some support is there. Women find it in friends, family, relationships, work mates, workshops, children and parents. Sometimes love and acceptance is offered by others who help pump these trailblazing women back up and send them out again into new tough work arena. A few outside organizations provide aid, motivational sessions and provide sources to lodge complaints, specific advise, reinforcement, a sense of relative perspective, camaraderie and information about jobs and lifestyle. Madeline turned to the union for activism and friendship. She went to a therapist who advised her to seek more friends and interests outside of work. Laurie went to a hypnotist to raise her self esteem.

The bad news is: there is not enough support—especially in the immediate accessible work environment. Much more needs to be done by government, corporations, unions and the media.

One successful example is "Women at Work," a support network and job referral organization for women in the trades and nontraditional work. They hold monthly meetings and provide:

- Companionship and support for women who are isolated and often lonely, because they are the only or one of the few women on the job site.
- Information as to where to meet women who actually work in the trades.
- Motivational speakers who address special topics.
- Training for the women officers in the group in leadership, organizational skills, etc.
- Specific skills in dealing with conflict, sexual harassment and communication, and training the female body in adaptive lifting, digging and drilling.

Outside Danger in the Gatherings Themselves

"Outside Looking In" and a woman from the Los Angeles Department of Water and Power complained of organizational repercussions to these all female gatherings. Women who attended were criticized, because they got time off work to attend women only support groups. Consequently care has to be given to make support groups open to men or have comparable groups for men. An alternative is for women to gather outside of work hours; so they don't bear additional resentment. However, organizations have resources and authority to convene such important groups. Not to do so will have a decisive negative impact. In the case of women who have few support mechanisms it will impact morale, absenteeism and productivity. It will impact the bottom line.

Trudi Ferguson, Ph.D., Organization Development Consultant/Author

One of the groups observed while gathering research for this book was at a Women at Work trade meeting. It was held in the Los Angeles Department of Water and Power Building conference room. "Upon entering I saw twenty-eight women of Anglo, Black, Asian and Hispanic descent seated in a circle. They wore mostly jeans and rough shirts and most wore little make-up. Individually I met one grandmother holding her tiny granddaughter, several operating engineers, a few electrical service representatives, an electrical assembler, some warehouse and tool room operators and a mechanical helper. The administrator from Trade Tech was recruiting for projects with Federal Employment and Training funds and advising women how to get into environmental fields.

"The group was led by two women from Department of Water and Power. Job pamphlets were strewn around The leaders presented material about job openings and talked about application strategies and opportunities. Women from the audience shared their experiences. They advised where to get good trade reading matter, which book stores or libraries carried study materials to bone up on tests involving arithmetic, spatial relations and skill areas. Some of the jobs had adequate training sessions, with good child care. For some jobs, like mechanical helper, experience was needed; others only required the ability to read and write. At the meeting, they showed a video about the availability of nontraditional jobs at DWP. Unfortunately, according to the leader only one percent of these jobs are currently held by women. The video included a motivational speech by a journeyman electrician. Her dream to own her own home was made possible only by springing free from her original position of secretary to enter nontraditional work. She ended by saying she just put a down payment on a lot in Kauai.

"As the meeting went on, other speakers were introduced. An International Brotherhood of Electrical Workers (IBEW) representative spoke about apprenticeships.

"Two women in the audience announced they were attending from a local radio station profiling women in nontraditional jobs.

"The feeling generated at the meeting was one of camaraderie. Interests and goals were shared. Women who had not been able to get needed information shared their concerns, discussed their problems and opportunities and got useful advice in a forum through which they could feel their needs addressed and met. Seeing their comfort and relief was an important sign that women, even when they are ambitious and committed, must find the facilities which publicize the real facts about the employment many so desperately need and want."

SIXTEEN

ADVICE

The organization, "Women At Work," realizes that women considering nontraditional jobs need counseling. They have designated a trained person to advise prospective women trades employees. We asked her to share her expert advice with our readers:

"The biggest pro is the tremendous earning power of the women who work in the nontraditional professions. Also, it's great for building things and getting a sense of accomplishment. For women who have an aptitude for working with tools it's a wonderful thing.

"The biggest con is the discrimination. There is a wide range of problems women have to put up with, from dirty jokes to rape. Women have to figure out how to handle it on an individual basis. Some just ignore it. Some take action. Some get involved in the Union and take it to court. You have to somehow show you're tough enough to do the job and hang in there. You have to know when to choose your battles. You can't get offended by every little thing.

"It will get better 1) when there are more women and 2) when people at the top take action and are serious about it."

The women we profiled in this book also have offered words of sage advice gathered through their own varied experiences:

Kathleen (plumber)—*Young women going into the trades need to have their eyes open to the actual harshness of the physical labor. Just because they are women, men are not that supportive. Men aren't going to run over and give them a hand. Even now guys don't want you there. Women have to take the attitude—I'm here. You're constantly tested. Even the youngest of the young don't think you know anything.*

Tanya (lifeguard)—*It takes a special kind of person. You have to be flexible and able to get along in a situation that is definitely male dominated.*

Mary (welder)—*Still, I get upset. It is a real hassle with only five or six women out of 3000 doing this work. I was talking to high school girls. I don't like to do that but I thought it was important because I love the job. It's not that the women do not want to go out there but it is too hard to get work. Before women get into trades in large numbers, changes need to be made. First we need really strong compliance people. Hopefully President Clinton will get some help. The laws are on the books, but nobody is enforcing them.*

Valerie (oil rig worker)—*I'd tell aspiring women: 'Go for it, but it's no Sunday School picnic.' You have to know your onions. I had to study manuals from top to bottom. They are not going to give you the information. When it comes to the football huddle you have to sit your butt right in there.*

Pam (cable splicer)—*I never noticed problems with what I do. I finally get the chance to play in the mud. There is more freedom outside. It is a different atmosphere than inside. Inside a lot of women are petty. When I go in I say that's why I left. It's backstabbing and petty arguments. You have to dress a certain way. Outside people work together to achieve a common goal. I enjoy it.*

Wendy (alignment)—*If a person is really determined enough, regardless of race, creed and color, you can do anything—if you put your mind to it.*

Betty (police)—*Women are an asset to the organization because diversity is an asset. I'm not bound in the tradition of the way police work is done because I'm nontraditional in the first place being a woman.*

Silvia (pressroom)—*This is a great job for a single mother foreign born who can work nights and take care of her child during the day, without a college education and earn a good salary.*

Linda (welder/artist)—*There's got to be just as many women out there with mechanical ability who just haven't been able to tap into that. What helps is access to information and classes to introduce more women into it. There has to be as many women with ability. Budget cuts don't help. There's a preconception because women are brought up to be afraid of sharp tools, machinery and fire. Women are thorough, patient. For one, take time and be careful with measuring and don't just rush through it.*

Sylvia (narcotics agent)—*I only encourage other women to do this if psychologically and mentally they can handle the pressure. It's a great job for some women. You have to be strong minded. You can't be thin-skinned. You're dealing with other policemen everyday who have the idea that this is a man's job.*

Cheri (mover)—*I worked as hard or harder than the guys there. I was raised believing that when you get paid a dollar you work 110 percent. As a woman I can go into a man's job and give 110 percent while guys stand around giving only 50 to 75 percent. It's a job ethic.*

Lorie (customer service tech)—*The physical part is not for everyone.*

Tommie (auto repair service writer)—*I would advise others going into this work to be very patient. Listen. Definitely keep an open mind about everything. The times customers aren't happy with the service, be patient, don't take things personally. They may be upset with their car, their day, something triggered them to let it out, but you can't let it get to you. Keep an open mind. Men aren't born with mechanical knowledge. Women can learn just as easily.*

Madeline (splicer)—*Right now for women to do nontraditional jobs, the most important ingredient is tenacity. If a woman comes into the job and doesn't think she knows it all, she will actually learn it. It gets tiresome when people expect women not to know anything.*

Penny (electrician)—*You better make sure you know what you are getting into. Visit a job sight and find out what it's like to work physically eight hours a day. I hate to see people go through the psychological aspect of defeat and quitting. It is so exhausting. I lifted weights for a year before going into the apprenticeship program. There were times at lunch I didn't even eat. I'd go to sleep. It's so physical. You don't have to take the work with you, but you can lose the balance with too much physical exhaustion.*

Jeanine (sound electrician)—*A lot of girls don't even think of this work as an option. If you have any sensibilities you are going to get offended on a daily basis. If jobs that were traditionally women's were valued as much as men's work, women wouldn't have to go into these jobs. But, in order to make that much money women have to work outside. I have as much right to this job as anybody. I have a family. I make $19.00 an hour which isn't chump change.*

PART VII

HOW TO FIND AND KEEP NONTRADITIONAL JOBS

"Nothing I can tell you verbally can really prepare you for the reality of what you are getting into."
Susan Suafai, Apprenticeship Coordinator

Finding a nontraditional job takes tough, persistent detective work. Nowhere is there one, single, clear guide to these job opportunities. Worse, the possibility, the simple physical picture, of women in hard hats, is not in our consciousness. Nor is this vision in the consciousness of the job trainers, counselors, funding organizations and law makers.

Fortunately there are places: utilities, unions, apprenticeship programs, tradeswomen's associations, task forces, newsletters, government agencies, nonprofit organizations, demonstration centers, colleges and universities, vocational schools and training centers; people: employers, contractors, experienced tradeswomen, apprenticeship coordinators, company CEO's, human resource managers, EEO coordinators, students, faculty, bureaucrats and laws that support the movement of women into these nontraditional jobs.

This section provides a comprehensive guide to finding and keeping these jobs. It includes a listing of the resources and examples of apprenticeship experiences from individual, programmatic, organizational and governmental perspectives of the issues and hurdles involved. This guide will assist women into these jobs. Even in this slow economy women have these unique options. Because they have lagged so far behind, women now have some distinct advantages. With curiosity, determination and this guide, they may find jobs where they are welcomed and actually courted. However, the key to finding them is to be creative when you search.

SEVENTEEN

THE STEPS
TO GETTING INVOLVED

"Good recruitment ideas have taken years to develop."
Melinda Nichols, Apprenticeship Program Manager,
Seattle City Lights

To make this movement of women into nontraditional jobs successful, both the prospective employee and the prospective employer must get involved. Here are steps both sides must take.

How to Find a Nontraditional Job—The Employee's Guide

♦ Think hard about whether you really want this job. Do you mind getting dirty, wearing jeans, working outside? Can you handle hard physical work? Envision negative reactions from male colleagues, wives, possibly your own family and friends. Will these negative attitudes defeat you? How will you handle such reactions?

- Do a self assessment. What kind of job are you interested in? Do you like to do detailed intricate work? Would you consider digging ditches?
- Go to your Regional Women's Bureau and other knowledgeable centers. Their resources and connections will provide information about past, present and future possibilities. They know people who can help. They know places that are training and hiring. Get referrals to local tradeswomen's networks.
- Follow-up on those referrals. Attend a tradewomen's monthly meeting.
- Get copies of tradeswomen's magazines.
- Seek out and talk with women in the trades and/or in the particular company in which you might be interested.
- Go to a trade college and look through the catalogue to see what kinds of courses are offered.
- Take a class in a trade you are considering. Try out things. It will give you more information and indicate to a prospective employer you are serious enough to work.
- Consider the State and Federal Bureau of Apprenticeship and Training and Standards. They generally maintain lists of openings in apprenticeship programs and can often council you individually as to opportunities and problems.
- Ask around about career days often held by educational institutions. These are an opportunity to meet women from a variety of trades and professions who can offer job guidance.
- Go to job placement centers and consider job counseling with specialists aware of expanded opportunities for women in nontraditional fields.
- Find out about particular training or pretraining programs in your area. These may be available through private industry councils, grants or private employers.

- Ask about government construction projects in the area that mandate hiring a percentage of women in construction.
- Find out who is hiring. Go there.
- Consider taking an entry level position with a company where you'd like to work. You can work up.
- Consider local police, fire-fighting and maritime offices. They have fewer women on their staffs and are making efforts to recruit more.
- Bone up on your skills. Take courses in algebra, math and physics.
- Work out. Get in good physical shape. Lift weights and build your upper body strength.
- Work on life skills, self esteem, time/stress management, financial planning, assertiveness.
- Consult bibliographies, videos and other references on women's experiences in nontraditional work.
- Get support. Talk through job changes with your mate, family or friends. What kinds of support will you want and need? What will a new job mean to your relationships?
- Think through in advance your style of reaction to snide comments and discrimination. Role play effective ways of defining your limits.
- Have realistic expectations of union assistance, colleague cooperation and work site conditions to reduce eventual disillusionment.
- Create and maintain support networks to ease the burden and carry you through difficulties.
- Get a mentor, friend or guide to help.
- Have a positive mind set. Women have advantages even in this bad economy. Many government projects need women to keep their numbers up. Take advantage. Go where you are needed.
- Go to them. They won't come to you. Take charge!

How to Hire and Keep Nontraditional Women— the Employer's Guide

- Re-examine myths about women not wanting or being available to do this work.
- Hire or consult an experienced tradeswoman.
- Conduct a heavy internal and external outreach and recruitment program. Use all potential sources including all media: radio, television, newspapers (both traditional and nontraditional,) public service announcements, educational institutions, government agencies, correctional facilities, military out placement, unions and women's and community organizations.
- Contact government agencies like the Women's Bureau, Bureau of Apprenticeship and Training, state Division of Apprenticeship Standards and unemployment offices for information and planning help.
- Become familiar with women's groups with experience in running programs.
- Benchmark with other companies that either voluntarily or through court mandate have instituted outreach, training and retention programs. Invite speakers and consultants.
- Consult pioneer women in nontraditional jobs both within and outside of your organization. Lift them up and make them visible. Invite them to speak and educate internally. Have brown bag lunches. Let them chair informal panel discussions and monthly support groups. Seek their advice on problems, lessons learned and successes.
- Conduct orientation and assessment sessions to aquaint women to the realities of nontraditional work.
- Establish preapprenticeship or apprenticeship training that includes life skills and physical conditioning.
- Do gender/diversity training so women and men have a safe place to express concerns, re-educate one another, and address their successes and failures.

- Provide sexual harassment training to management and employees so that the problems will be minimized.
- Establish a task force to monitor these issues on an on-going basis. Make one person responsible for monitoring, investigating, and reporting these issues.
- Provide support groups for women in nontraditional jobs where they can meet and share with other women. This might include monthly meetings.
- Have one person responsible for site walkthroughs as each problem is identified.
- Appoint a buddy for each nontraditional woman hired.
- Provide counseling to alleviate problems.
- Try to hire a "critical mass" of women in nontraditional jobs, so they are not isolated.
- Compile and distribute a reading list for management and employees to familiarize them with the recruitment, training and retention of nontradtional women.
- Keep statistical and anecdotal records of your company's efforts to learn patterns and avoid repeated mistakes.
- Maintain a tradeswoman database.
- Celebrate successes and share data with employees.
- Monitor special nontraditional initiatives and reevaluate.
- Conduct exit interviews to determine why women leave and what their experiences have been.
- Target training programs to encourage women into new nontraditional areas in which the female labor pool is deficient. Work with educational institutions and existing labor pools such as iron workers.
- Set up special projects that encourage women, for example: special "women at work" T-shirts, bulletin boards with information for to nontraditional women.
- Address the child care issue by providing on-site care or referral assistance.
- Provide transportation guidance.

EIGHTEEN

THE ISSUES

*"I loved the idea when I was a journeyman I could quit a job I
didn't like and go back to the union hall and get another job."*
                                   Vivian Price, Electrical Apprentice

How to think about women for these jobs, how to get these jobs and
how to keep these job are the issues that women and organizations
have to steer through to successfully achieve national employment
targets. Case studies exemplifying awareness, recruitment, training,
retention, the laws and apprenticeship offer practical advice.

Awareness

Most women don't know these jobs exist. The Wider Opportunity
for Women in Washington, D.C. conducted multiple surveys to
identify key barriers to women in nontraditional work. Repeatedly,
lack of information about these jobs surfaced as a key obstacle. Not
only do women not know what possibilities and opportunities await
them, but people in responsible leadership and hiring positions are

equally ignorant. The problem is: we don't think in terms of women working in these jobs.

Raising the possibility to women, counselors, unions and employers that women can do these jobs is the first step in increasing their numbers. The media and community leadership teams that include unions, community based organizations, government agencies, and the private sector must develop outreach programs. Newsletters and videos can portray positive images of successful women in nontraditional work. Employers and unions must talk about their own positive experiences with women in these jobs.

Nonbias in Recruitment and Assessment

Gatekeepers believe that women don't want these jobs and that women are not available. We must educate them and pierce these myths. Perhaps they'll learn by statistics, for instance, the numbers of tradeswomen employed on such construction projects as the Los Angeles Century Freeway and on projects by Stein & Company show women represent over 10 percent of the workforce. These statistics tell us women are there and willing. These successes need publicity.

In addition, we need to make great efforts to ensure nonbias in assessment since most assessment is based on past experience. For example, most women don't have paid or even non paid past experience in the trades. Women haven't, for the most part, grown up wielding a hammer or tools. But their lack of experience doesn't mean women would not be good at these jobs.

One of the early programs, Women in Apprenticeship, aimed at getting women employed as apprentices in San Francisco. Funded by the United States Department of Labor in 1974, it was part of a national program to recruit women apprentices. Beginning with an extensive information campaign, they reached large numbers of women through radio and television announcements and articles in community and major newspapers in the area. They recruited through existing programs and talks at women's groups. It turned out to be an opportune time because some women had wanted to get into programs for years but didn't know how. So many women responded that the orientations, which were originally done on a one on one basis, proved too time consuming and they had to resort to mass orientations. This program, since copied and expanded, serves as the basis of recruitment efforts even today.

Training

Women's successful mastery of these jobs depends on specific psychological preparation and skill training. Women have to be prepared to handle sexual harassment. They need to review their math skills, since a lot of these jobs require math. Also, women need help in learning about physical training. Many jobs require heavy physical labor and women are not always conditioned in upper body strength. The training often is simple. Women need remedial help in measuring things, using scales that include balances, judging how much sheet metal is required by a trapezoid shape, knowing which way things turns, gauging pressure or how to bend conduits. A typical week of training consists of:

Monday	Career Orientation	1 hour
	Math Review	2 hours
	Blueprint Reading	1 hour
	Fitness	2 hours
Tuesday	Job Site Tours	2 hours
	Spatial Reasoning	1 hour
	Math Review	1 hour
	Tool Use and Identification	2 hours
Wednesday	Tradeswomen's Panel	2 hours
	Mechanical Reasoning	1 hour
	Work Ethics	1 hour
	Fitness	2 hours
Thursday	Work Related Laboratory	2 hours
	Sexual Harassment Issues	2 hours
	Assertiveness Training	2 hours
Friday	Work Related Quiz	1 hour
	Math Quiz	1 hour
	Vocational Guidance	2 hours
	Fitness	2 hours

Retention

Once the women are hired and trained the trick is to retain them by setting up a hospitable environment. Otherwise they will leave. Most employers don't think about the issues of men's resistance to their women colleagues, sexual harassment and privacy. Employers must scrutinize the work sites to reduce hostility, eliminate sexually explicit material and create private facilities— or, at least put locks on the coed bathroom doors. They must provide training for men and women to help ease the adjustment. Also, they must establish support groups so the women have a place to air and share. Mentors, buddies, gender workshops, company-sponsored support groups and task forces help.

Apprenticeship

"In the days of Ben Franklin, who learned the printer's trade as an apprentice, apprenticeships were the main way for someone to enter a skilled occupation. Today, of course, many different paths can lead a young person to a career. But for many occupations, apprenticeship is still one of the best ways to enter a skilled trade or profession."

—Occupational Outlook Quarterly/Winter 1991/1992

Apprenticeship is one of the best ways for women to enter nontraditional jobs. Apprenticeship gives women options, because their skills are portable. They can use the same skills in different locations and with different employers. Becoming a journeyman provides a ready made and respected reference. It certifies experience and qualifications. Since employers and unions join together to design the specific length and structure of apprentice training in the particular trade, the journeyman's career path is automatically mapped out. In coordination with government, minimum standards are established to ensure quality control in the craft. While it is a central path nevertheless we should remember only about 15 to 20 percent of construction jobs are union. Women in apprenticeship represented 7 percent in 1989 compared with 3.1 percent in 1978, according to Factos on Working Women Department of Labor Women's Bureau No 90-5 January 1991.

The apprenticeship program usually takes a minimum of 2000 hours on the job training by qualified journeymen. Every six months the apprentice takes a test and gets a 5 percent step increase to the next level. Finally, at the end of the program they take a journeyman's test and if they pass they are issued journeymans cards. These programs take from three to seven years. The certificate awarded at the completion of the apprenticeship is recognized throughout the particular industry as assurance that the individual is qualified in all work processes of that craft.

Apprenticeships also require 144 hours of related classroom instruction to supplement the basic on-the-job training. This may occur one night per week or one week at a time twice a year. It depends on the craft.

The National Apprenticeship Act of 1937 (The Fitzgerald Act) authorized the Secretary of Labor to work with state apprenticeship agencies, the Department of Education, and representatives of labor and management to protect the welfare of apprentices. This act also promotes the establishment of apprenticeship programs. Apprenticeship programs are commonly registered with the Federal Government or a federally approved state apprenticeship agency. Currently twenty-seven states, the District of Columbia, Puerto Rico and the Virgin Islands have apprenticeship agencies. In other states, the Department of Labor's Bureau of Apprenticeship and Training (BAT) oversees apprenticeship functions.

Of course there are rules and regulations—especially about absences. Apprentices, annoyed with the paperwork, must keep their hours in a blue book. But, the number of absences can be important. The contractor can let you go with cause if you have too many absenses. Even if you don't know the rules until you mess up, it's still too late.

In the past there was no requirement for teaching credentials and many good craftsmen were made into lousy apprenticeship teachers. In about the last ten years apprenticeship classes started requiring teacher's credentials.

Interestingly the largest number of women apprentices enter between ages twenty-five to twenty-nine, but almost half begin an apprenticeship after the age of thirty. Nontraditional jobs are a tough sell for young women coming right out of high school, because they're not glamorous. Women seem to turn to trades more in their mid or late 20s, after having other work experiences. Then they are often attracted by the pay. There has been a dramatic increase in the number of women apprentices from 1980 to 1990. Nationally the number of women apprentices is about 5 to 6 percent. California's percentage of women is higher (about 10 percent in September 1993), but California includes industries aside from construction (such as correctional officer apprentices) in those figures. For example, in December 1992 women in construction in California represented 5.49 percent.

A big problem for the construction industry is keeping the numbers of qualified women. Often qualified women, after completing the apprenticeship program, find construction hard and opt for a job within a system like a school district. This happened to plumber, Kathleen Tracy, profiled in Chapter 1 and Yolanda Valdez profiled at the end of this chapter. They find the hours, stability and work slightly less demanding and the environment more hospitable. Construction is one of the hardest areas to recruit and retain women, because it is so rough physically and psychologically. Trades, such as ironworkers and roofers, also have fewer women because they are dangerous, hot and dirty. More active recruitment will increase the number of women in these fields too.

It is true that women drop out in higher numbers than men in the first year of the apprenticeship program. Usually a woman is not prepared for the reality of the work and the work life. She has no idea of what she is getting into. One apprenticeship coordinator says, "It doesn't matter how descriptive you are. Nothing I can tell you verbally can really prepare you for the reality of what you are getting into." It's literally labor. You can't describe it if you haven't been through it. Often the women who make it through the first year stick with it. There is actually a higher percentage of women than men who finish. These women are the ones who are really committed. They see the advantages.

Women can become an apprentice by:
- Getting a "hunting license." They get contractors to sign an endorsement letter for them.
- Testing for the "list trades." This is similar to civil service testing for qualification into certain trades. Women need to apply to take the test. Then once they take the test and pass, they are ranked and called in order. The list trades include electricians, sprinkler fitters and plumbers.

Other basic requirements include being of legal working age and having a high school diploma or the equivalent. Some trades, like electricians, require high school algebra with a C grade or better. Minimum requirements vary from trade to trade.

Now there are more women in the trades and in the classrooms than there were in the 1960s, 70s and 80s. For example, no women were on the lists in 1978. Today, since there are more women in the trades, there is a stronger support system. The State Division of Apprenticeship Standards keeps numbers of women in the various trades. Federally, the Bureau of Apprenticeship and Training of the United States Department of Labor sets national standards and coordinates with the state.

Laws

Women workers are regulated by the complex web of federal, state and local laws including Title VII of the Civil Rights Bill, Fair Employment and Housing. Two crucial regulations apply to women in construction work. One is a consent decree, signed in 1978 that stipulated:

- ◆ All contractors and subcontractors on federal or federally-assisted construction projects must take specific affirmative action steps to employ women for 6.9 percent of the hours worked in each trade. This regulation is enforced by the Office of Federal Contract Compliance Programs of the United States Department of Labor.

- ◆ Apprenticeship programs, registered with the Bureau of Apprenticeship and Training, United States Department of Labor or any state apprenticeship council were instructed to set a goal for women at 50 percent of the program sponsor's labor market area. This works out to approximately 20 percent of apprentices indentured in any given year.

The second is the Job Training and Partnership Act aimed primarily at job training of low income women passed by the federal govenment in 1982. A certain percentage of this money goes to training women with a portion of that dedicated to training women in nontraditional jobs.

More recently women, lobbyists and legislatures have been pushing to include information, training and laws about better paying, nontraditional jobs.

The Nontraditional Employment for Women (NEW), passed in 1991, amends the Job Training and Partnership Act. It promotes capacity building for women in nontraditional jobs and teaches the system how to work with women. The Women's Bureau supports this effort by funneling over $1.5 million in grants to special projects. In 1993 six grants were dispersed to demonstration centers designed to assist with recruitment training and retention of nontraditional women. Specifically the purpose of the act is to:

- Encourage efforts by government at all levels to provide wider range of opportunities for women under the Job Training Partnership Act;
- Because over 7,000,000 families in the United States live in poverty and over half of those families are single parent households headed by women;
- Women stand to improve their economic security and independence through the training and other services offered under JTPA;
- Employment in traditionally male occupations leads to higher wages, improved job security, and better long-range opportunities than employment in traditionally female-dominated fields;
- The long term economic security of women is served by increasing nontraditional employment opportunities for women.

This act is to facilitate coordination between JTPA and Vocational and Applied Technology Education Act to maximize the effectiveness of resources available for training and placing women in nontraditional employment.

The Women's Bureau and the Employment and Training Administration (ETA) jointly support this effort to develop exemplary programs to train and place women in nontraditional jobs. The 1993 projects include two-year college degrees in Texas and Washington; blue-collar electro-mechanical skill training in Louisiana; prevocational and apprentice-type training in Washington and

Maryland; and various forms of eductional material, outreach workshops and capacity building.

Another federal law, School to Work, under the Employment and Training Administration, Office of Work-Based Learning passed in 1993. It gives planning grants to states to encourage businesses to develop ways to integrate people into job categories through school training. This provides opportunities for schools to coordinate with businesses in providing specific on-the-job training. It takes the concept of apprenticeship into other nontraditional areas and affords women opportunities to explore work in new, more lucrative areas—maybe less physically demanding—through school programs.

The fact is as much as 75 percent of American's young people do not achieve a college degree, according to the Department of Labor, and many of them are not equipped with basic academic and occupations skills needed in an increasingly complex labor market. Many of the best old manufacturing jobs are gone. Therefore, many high school graduates don't find stable, career-track jobs for years. Employers are reluctant to take a chance on inexperienced high school graduates. There are obstacles to these programs, which include reluctance of traditional players, employers and unions. Also schools are not set up for work based learning. Demonstration centers must include structure work-site learning, integrated school and work-based curricula, work-site mentors and post-secondary connections.

Using the School to Work program requires awareness on the part of prospective women workers and cooperation from the businesses. One recent example in California is an international shipper that works with Long Beach Polytechnical high school and community college students for two years for part time on-the-job training. Here employers are involved in curriculum development; classrooms reflect demands of the workplace and specific on the job performance requirements; tests measure job specific criteria such as performance quality, production rates, safety, customer satisfactions and manufacturer's specifications; lessons are expressed as "Work Orders" reflecting those used in industry and actual work site material, manuals, installtion instructions, safety materials, forms, tools, etc. are part of routine lesson context.

The purpose of this program is to motivate students to stay in school while learning about the work in which they may eventually be involved. It also provides a link to apprenticeship. Although the program has not realized much nontraditional placement yet, it represents hopeful, new, nontraditional job opportunities for men and women.

One post-high school level program is the Apprenticeship and Nontraditional Employment for Women (ANEW) in Renton, Washington—a training program for low-income women in construction and electrical/mechanical trades. The training is five months long with classes eight hours per day in math, blueprint reading and drawing, mechanical and electrical theory and practice, basic carpentry and construction techniques, practice skills on shop projects and introduction to pipe, concrete and welding. Strength and endurace is increased by doing aerobics, working out with weights and by doing at least one hour of hard physical work each day. Additionally, a five month course at Renton Vocational Technical Institute addresses life and personal issues.

Many particularly innovative programs were the result of legal action brought by women against companies that were noncompliant with existing laws. Ironically great inroads can and have been made when federal funds are involved. The court orders also afford a kind of flexibility to move around other limiting procedural requirements. They give violating companies an easier way to tap into untrained or untested women without violating the usual testing qualifications or seniority listings more easily than companies who are voluntarily trying to increase the number of women without such court orders.

Women in Apprenticeship and Nontraditional Occupations Act, passed on October 27, 1992, provides funds through the Department of Labor to inform employers of technical assistance available to employers in preparing the workplace for women in apprenticeable and other nontraditional occupations. Specifically, it includes outreach to employers and labor unions; orientations for women, unions and employers; preapprentice programs; a computerized database of available tradeswomen; liaisons between women employers and unions and exit interviews with women to evaluate their on-the-job experience.

Changing Legislation for Police Officers

As new regulations are being put in place, like NEW Act, old regulations are being questioned in the interest of expanding women's opportunities in nontraditional areas. For example, a recent controversy arose over the requirement for women police applicants to scale a five foot wall in order to qualify for acceptance into the department, when the Los Angeles City Council questioned whether the wall was a sexual barrier against women, rather than a true job related test.

"The wall, with its emphasis on upper body strength, is one of the biggest reasons that women are turned away from the department," stated a *Los Angeles Times* front page article on April 11, 1994.

About one third of the women who take the test can't pull themselves up over the wall because it requires so much upper body strength. Whereas only 5 percent of the men applicants can't pass the barrier. Currently women represent only about 15 percent of the police force. So, what can the Los Angles City Council do to meet its goal of increasing the police force to 43 percent female officers?

Many police departments around the country have eliminated this test, arguing that scaling a five foot wall has nothing to do with being a good police officer. Is scaling that wall ever called on again in the doing of the actual police work? Some say scaling a wall has nothing to do with problem solving, mediation and community policing—skill areas increasingly more emphasized today. The wall requirement only serves to bar women who bring a greater sensitivity and a different, much needed police perspective.

Although this proviso is being examined, Los Angeles Police Chief, Willie Williams, argues that although we all want to move toward greater problem solving, police work still involves crime fighting as well. He was quoted in a *Los Angles Times* article on April 5, 1994: "The role of police is expanding instead of shifting. Police work will always involve physical abilities." He further believes scaling a wall is a very real job related skill which might be used to pursue criminal suspects, find missing children, etc. Just as other job related skills like normal vision might discriminate against certain people, physical skills that are truly job related may have the unintended and unwanted consequences of discriminating against women. Nevertheless they, according to Williams are necessary and real.

Williams also argues that applicants can retake the entrance test. As a matter of fact the LAPD provides special training classes to help any applicant—male or female—pass the test. Also, in an effort to accommodate women into the police force the height requirement of the wall has already been lowered from five feet eight inches to five feet. Furthermore, LAPD statistics show that women improve their pass rate on the second attempt to almost the same rate as men.

Results of the various studies of climbing walls on police duty are controversial. A state study on job related tasks for police indicated "climbing is a critical activity that occurs with extremely high frequency. Sixty-nine percent of all climbing involved fences or walls and of those climbed, two thirds involved solid, six foot walls." But another study from a law enforcement trade magazine did not substantiate the need to climb or jump or drag in the manner measured by the physical entrance tests.

Other test requirements being examined are dragging a dead weight and hanging on a bar. Both the City Council and the Los Angeles Police Department are considering whether these types of requirements should be changed in favor of more general physical fitness requirements.

This debate illustrates the change in social thinking and the acceptance of the desirability of increasing the number of women in the police profession.

Yolanda Valdez, Painter, Forty-five years old

Yolanda is Mexican American. She's 5 feet 2 inches and weighs 125 pounds. She started in apprenticeship at age thirty-seven. From the beginning she has been independent. She raised her twin daughters by herself without a husband.

Her determination to work hard and go to school for years, to stick with it when others drop out, to find and take advantage of hard working opportunities in preapprenticeship training and to put that training to work for her is impressive. She has always been able to persist and keep that goal in mind even after earlier unsatisfying work experiences. Now she concentrates on the benefits and appreciates what she has done for herself without anybody holding her hand or breathing down her neck. She has seized the opportunities and understands why she should be proud and grateful.

"I got into the painting trades in 1985. Prior to that I worked in aerospace at Rockwell International Space Division where they are notorious for layoffs. After five years I got laid off. I went to graphic arts school at the East Los Angeles Occupational Center. I can't remember how I got into that, it was so far back. I think I got a flyer about graphic arts. I said to myself at the time, 'Gee, I should go check that out.' I found out they had a computer type setting class which fit because I had previous experience with that at Rockwell. I signed up and went at night.

"I started working for design studios and publications, but it was too confining. I was always in a little room with my computer and stacks and stacks of paperwork. I thought to myself, 'Hey, I'd like to make more money than this. There has got to be something else.' After six years I was only making $11.00 per hour. I had always been a 'do it yourselfer' and liked doing painting and hand work. I had heard unions wouldn't let women in, or if they did it was rare. That discouraged me from even trying. A friend told me about a preapprentice program for women. I signed up in May 1985 at the Chicano Service Action Center for carpentry. They taught me how to use power tools, hand tools, how to read a tape measure and gave me classroom instruction. It was a six-week program. It wasn't a very good program. The instructor wasn't dedicated and one half the time he wouldn't show up and we've just be sitting there. One woman in this program mentioned the Century Freeway Program and gave me information on who to contact and how to apply. I checked it out and got accepted. I had a little experience from the Chicano program and was able to convince them I was capable. They screen you to see if you are capable. Preapprentices worked on homes along the bought-out freeway starting from Norwalk to LAX. It was a really organized program. They gave you basic hand tools, saws, tape measures, crow bars, cat's paw, a 20-ounce hammer and a nice tool box with a tool belt. You were required to wear work boots and dress like you were in construction. It was rebuilding neglected homes. It lasted eight weeks, from August to September 1985. Every week was something different to work on—roofing, framing, flooring, but it didn't include electrical or plumbing. A lot was crammed at you in eight weeks—it was hands on. It was a really a nice program. I passed everything. They had job developers who worked with the participants and they asked contractors if they would pick up some apprentices. The job developers asked me what I wanted to do. I said I liked painting. I like decorating and thought it would be a good thing to get into.

"The job developer got me a job with the Painters Union at the lowest level first period apprenticeship. You work your way up nine levels starting at about $5.00 per hour and for every 800 hours of on-the-job work you get a pay increase. You have to work up nine levels to get $21.00 per hour. The apprenticeship takes about four to five years. I got mine in four and one-half years, granted by the Joint Apprenticeship Committee Los Angeles County Area Painting/Drying Finishing Industry.

"I went through my apprenticeship working for different contractors. It was real hard emotionally. The men just don't accept us. When I got in, the first contractor was pretty nice but had me doing all the shit work—covering everything with drops, sanding, spackling, cleaning up, cleaning paint brushes, masking, asking me to go get him this, and watching the spray rigs. Journeymen just wanted to come in and start working. As an apprentice there is a lot of sexual harassment. Just certain individuals felt women were taking their jobs and they had families with kids and needed money more. There were the jerks who were just going to make you miserable—they were miserable themselves. There was men's locker room talk. I'd have to tell them, 'Hey! I don't like that language.' Some men felt women were not strong enough and said things like, 'It's not a nice job for women. It's dirty and hard.' I tell them I like it. I do like it. I get a lot of enjoyment out of the before and after effect.

"I only saw maybe six women on jobs the whole time. I was allowed to go to apprenticeship school after I worked as an apprentice for about three months. You have to take the list of classes they suggest. Usually its ladders and scaffolding at the apprenticeship school with two to three instructors. They used to have night classes two times a week but after I started they changed so that every quarter you have to take off work a whole week to go to classes and employers would not pay our salary. Then you would have to sign up for unemployment for one week. There were sixteen classes required, including basic drywall, blueprint reading, spray painting, paper hanging and wood hanging, in both the classroom and the lab. The school is like a big warehouse with labs where you did a lot of hands on projects. Apprenticeship requires 2,100 hours of work experience. Also, you had to take first aid and be certified. There was no physical conditioning, but women were encouraged to lift hand weights to build upper body strength for carrying four foot to forty foot ladders, and 2-by-4s. I had to set up forty foot extension ladders. I didn't think I was going to be able to do it. I had to set up scaffolding, work on scissor lifts on wheels, cherry pickers or condor lifts and swing stage for the side of buildings like window cleaners use, carrying five gallon buckets of paint. There is a lot involved in painting. People are ignorant of all the different types of painting. People say, 'Gee, any four year old can to do it.' Different types of painting require different types of work.

"What kept me going was I really wanted that journey level certificate. I wanted to get in civil service because it paid well and offered security. Working with unions you usually had three months off a year. November to March was real slow unless you were in real good with a particular contractor. I knew the apprentice certificate would open doors.

"I worked on the downtown library for years and Kaiser Hospital. Union work is big work—not mini malls or houses. I worked at ULCER medical center which I enjoyed. I also worked at Wayside Honor Rancho Los Angeles Jail. Peter J. Pitches was brand new construction. That's the dirtiest. It's all dirt. You have to share an outhouse and they smell. It's disgusting. New construction is not my favorite but it lasts a lot longer. Dust is blowing and there is dirt mud and it's yucky, but it pays the most. Construction is always top pay. I've worked at Santa Anita Race Track after they closed the place. There is a maintenance contract, but journeymen only earn $18.00 per hour because it is maintenance. Repainting older buildings means less money.

"Now I work for the state prison Department of Corrections paid by the state of California. I'm not union anymore. I earn $3,400 per month. I work everyday with job security and protection against sexual harassment. Unions have no EEO committees and no support. You are all alone out there with all those men. It can be really lonely unless you are really strong and you can put men in their place. Working with the state, men know they can't get out of line. They are afraid to mess with the women and harassment is not as blatant. Men know harassment will hit them in the pocketbook. Also on union jobs men would make comments about my body or call me a dyke. Some men love to humiliate women. If you don't give into them you are called either a whore or dyke.

"But, I stuck the apprenticeship out. A lot of apprentices are young high school dropouts with not more than a ninth grade education. A lot were illegal immigrants who didn't speak English. Instructors weren't effective. They just come in and say, 'Okay, here's your book, start reading and I'll give you a test.' They'd have a paper with the answers and the guys would pass it around. But, I always read my books and took my test. I was going to learn something even though I was in class with bunch of goof-offs. It was like continuation school with a bunch of idiots—drug addicts on coke or alcohol. It's hard to get in. But when they need apprentices, they would take in a bunch of guys. It's who you know—a neighbor or uncle—if you're a guy. Union and contractors lie and say women don't apply, but when you go in to apply they say, 'We are not hiring right now.'

"I got into the apprenticeship from the job developer. The Union had an agreement with the Century Freeway. It was a political thing. Maybe once a year I met a woman but of the few that were there most didn't complete the program. I didn't have anybody for support. The first five years I was all alone. I'd talk to my friends when I came home.

"There were few requirements. You just have to pay union dues. If you don't go to class you can get suspended or warned. They are strict about time and you had to be there when class started. If you missed class one day you had to come back when the course started all over again. After I got my card I stayed at journey level for two years. But once I was at journey level it was harder to get work. I was warned. Contractors don't want to pay high journey level wages. Contractors take advantage of apprentices and hire them when they are cheap. They'd rather keep the old boys. I had to resort to work maintenance rather than construction which was less money. The $21.00 per hour jobs were reserved for 'the boys.' I worked maintenance at Santa Anita for six months in between other painting jobs referred out of union hall. Once I completed the apprentice school I found out it doesn't help you. I like interior work in offices. It's cleaner. But they sent me to rough outside jobs. The nice jobs are saved for their favorites. I worked most all the time until 1991. Then I was off for four months because of the recession and Persian Gulf. It affected all the building trades.

"Finally I got a tip; they needed a female painter at the men's prison in Tahacipi. I had just bought my house in Pomona and I said,

'I'm not moving.' But the Union agent urged me to consider the job because it was with the state and I could get my foot in the door. I filled out an application and sent my resume. Within a week I had an interview and got hired. Employers know union workers have to go to school and are trained well. I went up there and rented an apartment and lived up there ten months. Both my daughters were independent and it was just me to consider. After my six months probation, I put in for a lateral transfer to Chino for the California Institution for Men—where I am now. I like it. It's twenty minutes from my house. I supervise a crew of in-mates. I don't really do the work myself. I can paint if I want to.

"One of my daughters joined the Navy, and the other is working. They're both married. I have no guy. I'm single. I was thirty-seven years old when I got into the apprenticeship, but I was able to keep up with everybody. I'm not a big women. The work is hard but I'm happy with the money and security. I've improved my way of living. Now I'm able to buy a house and car. I just bought another new car. I'm financially independent. Now I can do a lot of things I couldn't do for years like travel and go out of town. I never married. I had my twin girls at nineteen. I always lived with just me and my girls. I'm not the type to depend on anyone. But, one thing I have really benefited from is the tradeswoman's network. It has been a great support.

"Everybody I know is real proud of me and the work I do. At first my dad was like, 'What do you want to be a painter for?' He was from that era. My mom had worked at Douglas with her sister on aircraft during the war like Rosie-the-Riveter but she never talked about it. Sometimes I'd hear her and my aunt talk about it.

"I was a late starting with the trades. My two girls were in high school. I just thought, *Now is a good time for me to make a career change.*"

Yolanda Valdez's story epitomizes how one can take avantage of the possiblitities that exist within the system.

There are many more opportunities. The problem for a lot of women is finding out about them.

NINETEEN

SOME RECENT EXAMPLES

"I learned women are out there willing and able to take utility craft jobs—in big numbers. Just because a woman is small and dainty doesn't mean she won't be interested. Office work can strain the brain. It can be difficult to work in an enclosed environment with a lot of people around you all day."

Vivian Minotin, Human Resources,
Department of Water and Power

City Utility—Los Angeles Department of Water and Power

The special preapprenticeship program to assist nontraditional women into utility craft jobs at the Department of Water and Power in Los Angeles has not received much publicity. It is a political hot potato because it is falsely viewed by some as discriminatory against men. Management also has reservations about publicizing this program because it may look like an admission of company wrongdoing. Normally, companies don't launch such a comprehensive program unless they have a court judgment against them. Finally, women themselves who have trained and benefited by the program haven't been placed in jobs. Their sense of frustration is growing.

What is true is this program began with a single male manager who noticed there were no women applying for the electrician distribution mechanic (people who climb up poles) trainee position. This was in 1991 when DWP only had one percent women in any type of nontraditional position. This man was sensitive to the situation because he had a daughter working in the company although not in a nontraditional position. He started asking why women weren't doing this type of work, and the response from the field managers was the usual—women can't do this type of work. Suspicious, he started researching other companies and found that women held 30 percent of the blue collar positions at Seattle City Lights. After finding out women can and do, do the work, he then rallied for support from other managers to get something going.

Through this one manager's efforts, the DWP began a program to recruit more women by 1993. It was open to the entire community, so, not surprisingly, most of the participants turned out not to be DWP employees.

Vivian Minotin, Human Resources, established the Utility Craft Pretraining Program which ultimately trained 222 women from both within the DWP and the community at large to qualifiy for nontraditional jobs at the DWP. Over 300 male and female volunteers were recruited from craft and noncraft positions to work on ten committees that ultimately recommended six different classes to train women: basic math, basic electricity, basis physics, reading comprehension, tool identification and strength conditioning. A series of twenty-five accelerated and highly interactive classes met three times a week at night or on weekends. They even provided child care.

Initially the program was designed to give participants knowledge, skills and tools to make them more competitive and prepare them for entry level tests open to the public. But, because of Los Angeles budget constraints, openings were restricted to city employees. In January 1994, the Los Angeles City Council decided that the women in the preapprenticeship training program were also eligible. That was a major victory. The program, thought of as an empowerment program rather than specifically for job training, was designed to develop a more diverse candidate pool for utility craft jobs and to give women a leg up on the open testing.

Unfortunately, only one exam has been given since the program began. Remarkably most of the women scored in the 80s in the test—scores ranged from 70 percent to 99 percent; however, no one has been offered work yet. That one test, for electrical mechanic trainees, was going to offer twenty positions and the highest woman ranked was thirteen. To tide them over, many of the women who took the test have developed support groups and study groups to help them improve their score when the test is given again— hopefully only a year later.

In conjunction with normal DWP recruitment, they recruited for this program mainly by word of mouth and at regional occupation centers, military discharge centers, trade groups, interest lists taken from city fire and police departments and high schools. Prospective candidates from a list of over 2000 were told that the first 300 to respond would be invited to orientation to ensure only the most motivated and interested would show up. Out of the 300 responding in the first week, 50 percent came to orientation and 99 percent of those women signed up for the program with a dropout rate of 3 to 15 percent.

Candidates participated by physically trying jobs and walking through the departments so they would be fully aware of what they were getting into. They also took an assessment pretest that gave instructors information about the level of the students. The entire program is self screened. People aren't thrown out for absenteeism. The DWP figures if participants can pass the test even if they don't come to the classes, they are still aided in the process. The DWP goal is to help women prepare for the entrance exams and jobs.

Although this preapprenticeship training program was done without a court mandate, a court order would have enabled them to hire and do things outside normal methods. Companies mandated by the court to equalize opportunities for women can create parallel lists split on gender lines and then select two or three women to one man. That's how some companies end up with one-third of their field force women.

Still, the strength of this DWP program is that 222 women received free training that could help them move into better paying nontraditional jobs. They are now empowered to work at DWP or any number of other places. The difficulty is raising hope and expectations. These 222 women have worked hard to position themselves for new work and as yet due mainly to the economy, they haven't been able to take advantage of that training. About half are appreciative and about half are frustrated and angry.

Contractors

Susan Suafai currently works as Affirmative Action Coordinator for a general contractor, Huber, Hunt and Nichols, in San Francisco. Her job is to recruit women in the trades for their construction jobs. Media spots, newspaper articles and radio announcements have been her most effective tools. The articles generally explain what the apprenticeship programs are, that they are run through the union, how much money can be earned and the concept of learning while you earn. They also describe specific examples of women in the trades. Radio announcements briefly state, "We are recruiting women for apprenticeship programs." They also give a telephone number, the starting wage of over $6 and the wages of $20 to $25 per hour in three to five years.

In this job Susan works directly with community based organizations that recruit women for nontraditional work. There are seven or eight such organizations with some addressing specific ethnic minorities.

Huber, as contractor for the federally-funded San Francisco library is required to meet certain Affirmative Action goals. Subcontractors also are required to sign an agreement to meet minority and women employment goals. Generally subcontractors are receptive to these requirements since most have done work for the City before and most have had women on their crews. However, when they state they've used women but don't have any there, Susan asks, "Why didn't you bring her along?" If they don't have women, Susan identifies women for them to hire. In fact, some trades, such as ironworkers, don't have enough women. Reinforcing ironworkers are hard to find because "rebar" is such grueling work. What makes the San Francisco project work is that the Project Manager will go to the highest degree—such as withholding payment—to make it work. "I have dangled that threat more than once," Susan says, and the Project Manager will back her. In San Francisco there is a pool of women in these trades. In some areas you have to look harder to find them. From Susan's experience, if women get beyond the first year of apprenticeship, usually they are committed for the long haul.

Training Grants

Electrician, Lynn Shaw, profiled in Chapter 9, has managed grant money flowing from the Job Training and Partnership Act. Currently, she is directing a program funded by a grant to train Latino women for nontraditional jobs—the Somos Humanas Undias Business and Education Institute.

To recruit the trainees she advertises in the *Pennysaver* and gets the word out verbally, using the possiblity of good jobs for women as the bait. She then must certify that the respondents meet the financial criteria to participate in the training. Yet, she turns no one away. Those who don't qualify can attend as observers. The class, held in a community center or church, includes sections on women in labor history, sexual harassment, and technical skills training. It also offers child car and free passes to weight rooms because so many jobs require physical training and upper body strength. Shaw then takes the women *en mass* to apply for the apprenticeship programs to mitigate the intimidation they usually feel—as single women—when violating the male world and challenging the myths that this is only men's work. She helps to reduce the women's fears and educate the men who control this application process by demonstrating that, contrary to popular belief, women do want these jobs. After all, here are twenty of them. It then makes it hard for the apprenticeship coordinator to defend his exclusive male numbers and to say women don't apply for the jobs. It's a great experience, she says.

However, Lynn is concerned that many of the grants given to promote women in nontraditional work end up with well meaning people who have no prior experience with the needs, problems, possibilities or past history. "Too often," she says," they have to start from scratch."

Privately Funded Nonprofit Organizations

Kristin Watkins of the Wider Opportunity for Women, a lobbying group funded by private Ford Foundation and Irvine Foundation money, directs efforts to train women for productive employment. A portion of this money and effort is devoted exclusively to train women in nontraditional jobs and increase women's chances of becoming self sufficient.

Wider Opportunity for Women offers another example of seed money put through private industry councils. It goes into communities in several demonstration centers. Leadership teams, composed of representatives from the private sector, unions, community based organizations and various government agencies, survey key sectors in the community to discover three key barriers and three key strategies for employing women in nontraditional jobs. Barriers always include lack of information and the need to increase outreach—such as—videos of women doing this work, employers and unions talking about positive experiences they've had with women doing this work, brochures and public service announcements.

In October 1992 the Women in Apprenticeship and Nontraditional Act was funded. It authorized the Department of Labor to give money to women's organizations to help employers and unions to integrate training and employment opportunities. Also included were efforts to support nonbiased assessment, training and retention help.

Nationally, the Department of Labor funds the Women's Bureau which has regional offices that give small grants for such things as newsletters, advocacy, compliance, resource referral, special projects, surveys and statistical compilation, talks at high schools, and networking. It has also promoted the play, "Journey Worker Jones," a history of women doing nontraditional work.

On a national level, the Bureau of Apprenticeship and Training within the Department of Labor sets national apprenticeship standards. Similarly, on the state level, the Division of Apprenticeship oversees standards. It also has a Women's Advisory Committee.

Many organizations representing women operate on a local level. For example, the Los Angeles Unified School District (LAUSD) has a tradeswomen's task force that is actively and carefully monitoring LAUSD's progress in implementing the adopted goals. In 1993, LAUSD hired less than one percent women in all trades. Yet, the goal remains at 6.9 percent and 21.5 percent for apprenticeships. Although the school district uses over $100 million in building funds they still hire almost no women. Shaw says the one contractor who met their goal was the one contractor they targeted for picketing last year. The January 1994 Northridge earthquake has necessitated the rebuilding of sixty-two schools. The task force is looking closely at using women for these projects.

Federal/State Construction—Century Freeway

The Los Angeles Century Freeway was an enormous construction project funded by federal and state money and thus subject to federal and state employment standards—more specifically—fair targets for female workers. A law suit was brought against the State of California and those constructing the federal highway for noncompliance with goals for women (10 percent) and minority workers (60 percent) on this construction program. Women at the time represented about .0388 percent of the workforce. As a result of a consent degree the Women's Employment Program was established in 1988. Susan Suafai was hired by the court to serve as the coordinator for the Women's Employment Program.

The program was set up specifically to recruit women to work in construction of the Century Freeway. Susan worked it from September 6 ,1988 to May 31, 1993. In 1988 women were employed in the trades but not in numbers the court wanted. Since the construction of the freeway displaced people and jobs in that community, part of the dictate of the court was to establish quotas for hiring people displaced from the area. The geographical recruitment area was eventually broadened for women because so few women were available within that limited area. Susan's staff of five who were all paid by the court, worked in the field directly with contractors to identify women in the trades or with skills. They started with heavy outreach through the media and at correctional centers where there were lots of women who had been trained in blue collar work such plumbing, gardening and the military. They also held job fairs and recruited heavily by advertizing in a South Central paper, *The Wave*, and got 700 calls. Then it became a matter of screening. The majority of applicants were definitely low income.

To assist in job readiness the project started with paid preemployment training—an eight-week program for men and twelve weeks for women, teaching such things as getting up early, math skills, carpentry, building a tool box and nonunion or trade job information on how to apply. The program contributed to the eventual success in employing many of the freeway construction workers. It was especially benefitial to women who had no experience with work in the trades or with work in general. The general contractor, Caltrans, also helped by demanding enforcement and recommending monetary sanctions if a subcontractor was deficient in using women and minorities. As a result, they exceeded 9 percent employment of women.

The effort of the program is directed at contract compliance. The question is how to enforce goals to get the demand for these female workers which will keep up the supply. It is cyclical. If contractors don't try to meet goals—in other words, create the demand for women—employees in the trades, and the supply of women in the trades will fizzle. It was hard at first because qualified women couldn't be found. But the Project cajoled saying men were not born with hammers in their hands. Contractors had to provide the opportunity to start. Often women would be sabotaged by putting a brand new apprentice up walking on a fifty foot beam or men urinating off bridges with women working below, or making trained female carpenters do laborer's work so they don't learn on the job. The Project persisted in demanding decent opportunities for women to practice skills required by the trade.

In the Century Freeway Project, four sub contractors were subjected to $10,000 sanctions for lack of good faith in things above or hiring women for a day or two and then letting them go. The awarding agency in this case Caltrans withheld money from the General Contractor who then withheld the money from the violating subs. In the last three years with the preapprentice program the Century Freeway has exceeded goals hiring 8.5 to 12.6 percent women workers with iron workers, pipe fitters, outside electrical workers, pile drivers, operating engineers, surveyors; all trades in freeway construction. They had a housewife who had never had a job before win an award as a bricklayer in national competition. She doesn't look like the construction type while wearing her glasses. But, a body builder who works out at Gold's gym, who they thought would be one of the real success stories, didn't last two hours. So you can't draw conclusions about who will make it. They even have a woman foreman in the hardest back breaking trade, reinforcing iron. She comes from a long line of workers in this trade.

Now they have a long waiting list for women to get into the paid preapprentice program. If ever there is a shortage in trades like the bricklayers, the project will do the recruiting and arrange training through community colleges such as the Los Angeles TradeTechnical College. A project representative says, "We can get the women in these jobs—the problem is enforcement. Apprentices stick it out when they have a genuine interest and a desire to work outdoors."

Community College Training

The Los Angeles Trade Tech is a regular community college that offers more than ninety-one vocational certificate programs and includes much training in nontraditional work. Eve Madigan, Sexual Harassment Coordinator and Director of Career Counseling, has provided career counseling and monitored sex stereotyping through repeated grants. She has worked vigilantly for years to audit female populations in these nontraditional classes and feels strongly that women need advocacy. If enrollment of women in nontraditional classes (she defines nontraditional as having less than 20 percent female in a male population and visa versa) dips from four to three, she is on the spot to try to find out what has happened and resolve problems. Eve gets women to network with other women. They have a brown bag lunch once a month to share their universal problems—the problems for women working as auto mechanics are the same as the problems for women working as carpenters. Counselors from Trade Tech get together with others from other college programs that cater to nontraditional work in an effort to find common experiences and strategies. Though they have a small budget, they work consistently and well.

Madigan says in the past fifteen years women have made no progress. If anything, she feels they are losing ground. The economy, certainly, has had an effect. As the economy gets worse, employers are more likely to hire people who can play a number of roles. It is harder to keep women in apprenticeship and vocational programs because they always have to perform better than the men. It's just not okay for a woman to be average. Also, she is discouraged by the biased assessment that any woman who works in a nontraditional job must be gay. Unfortunately, success depends on the consciousness of people in the program, rather than the women's inherent interest, skill, tenacity and intelligence.

Stein & Company's Success Story

Chicago based Stein & Company is a multifaceted real estate and construction firm that has repeatedly broken records in hiring nontraditional women. They routinely have more than 10 percent women working on their construction projects.

In 1989 they began work on the Ralph Metcalfe Federal Building. This work included a commitment to the federal goals on hiring women and minorities—that is, basically hiring 6.9 percent women. In an effort to reach that goal, Stein President, Julia Stasch, established the Female Employment Initiative (FEI).

The goal of FEI was to make the work site hospitable to women through supporting workers concerns and monitoring and reporting on job-site conditions. Specifically, the program, in partnership with contractors, building trade unions and community associations, consisted of:

+ Two monthly site walkthroughs looking for such things as lack of bathroom privacy and graffiti
+ Weekly meetings with foremen
+ Collecting women's employment statistics
+ Compiling a database on the number of years experience, skills, addresses and phone numbers of the women in the trades
+ Maintaining bulletin boards that posted community programs of interest to tradeswomen
+ Conducting exit interviews
+ Establishing a buddy system where each skilled trade was assigned to an FEI member
+ Directing efforts to supply women in deficient trades
+ Conducting sexual harassment workshops attended by employees, superintendents and foremen
+ Producing an in house video explaining FEI to all workers
+ Conducting an orientation in community based groups and schools
+ Inviting women interested in the trades to tour the job site—and even distribting FEI t-shirts to the tourists

Contractors often would defend themselves saying certain trades, such as brick layers, had women on the union lists who wouldn't come when called or came dressed inappropriately or who got through the training only to give up once on the jobsite. To reduce this actuality, FEI accepted a larger responsibility—that of aiding the community and the union by orienting women on union apprenticeship lists, touring construction sites and helping women prepare during the eighteen-month to two-year wait for apprenticeship positions to open up.

President Stasch got her job at Stein & Company, because she knew its chairman, Richie Stein. She had been a school teacher but was willing to hire on as a secretary and take the chance of working her way up in the company. Needless to say her gamble paid off. She saw the good of the FEI program from both a social and business point of view and was able to sell the concept to her colleagues and subcontractors.

Current program administrators testify it was her determination as a woman president that led to the program's success at Stein. The program resulted in record numbers of over eighty-five nontraditional tradeswomen out of 500 employees working in the trades at Stein. Stasch's success has not gone unnoticed. She has gone on to become Deputy Administrator for General Services in the Clinton Administration.

Another Stein project was the United Center Stadium Building. This project, in an area with typically high unemployment, had community residents who saw employement opportunities there. So, Stein & Company took twenty-five residents on two weeks of exploration that included labor training centers and exposed them to clean up, safety and concrete placement. The Company got agreement from contractors to hire from this group and placed about half of them.

One smart move in the beginning of this program helped ensure its success. The CEO hired Stephanie, a tried and true veteran in working with women in the trades, as FEI director. Stephanie's previous job was with Chicago Women in the Trades although her experience as a tradeswomen's advocate began years before when she worked rehabilitating buildings and buying and selling small properties and getting to know tradeswomen in the process. Stephanie represented the voice of change. She was a woman well connected in the community who knew tradeswomen, how to recruit and how to keep them. As a result, Stein & Company exceeded their female hiring employing goals with over 10 percent women in nontraditional work.

Stein & Company reported lessons learned:

- ✦ As more women worked on site attitudes took an up-swing.
- ✦ Union recruitment was never mentioned by the women employees but workers credited recruitment through media and other females or family members. The power of the media cannot be underestimated.
- ✦ The number of women with preapprentice training increased significantly.
- ✦ There are misconceptions among some women about what the unions will and will not do or can and cannot do for their members. Higher expectations from union/business agents often leads to disillusionment within the trade industries.
- ✦ The project's owner/developer has the greatest leverage and must take the lead position in the program.
- ✦ The owner/developer must develop a model for a training program for any trade where female membership is very low.

Because of repeated inquiries and requests, Stein & Company has provided an excellent report and step by step guidebook on their successful program.

Melinda Nichols, Apprenticeship and Technical Training Manager, Seattle City Lights

Melinda represents a public utility that has 30 percent women in trades.

"Prior to about 1988, Seattle City Lights had twenty-eight women in line worker programs and only two came out the other end. It was extremely hard trade work, climbing poles up to 125 feet and around live wire. In the mid 1980s there was an altercation between a female apprentice and a line worker who tried to make her attach to a safety line and come down his way. By the time all was said and done there was some incredibly bad press. One cartoon had a bunch of guys on a pole built tree house way up that had a sign saying 'No girls allowed.' Partly because this was a public utility, there was extreme pressure from the Mayor who wanted the mess cleaned up. The company made a lot of resources available and the CEO was held accountable. They hired an experienced tradeswoman and activist who had taught under the Apprenticeship and Nontraditional Employment for Women program which had trained women longer than any other program in the United States.

"They developed a preapprenticeship program. They hired a Ph.D. psychologist to prepare the women mentally and a consultant in physiology to help with the physical training. The physical requirements of the job were looked at and they validated standards. Seattle City Lights recruited like crazy. They got 1,200 candidates for twelve jobs. Melanie did more specific recruitment, analyzing women applicants, asking what they do and what they like to do. She went to places where you find aggressive, strong, risk taking women, like soccer tournaments, rugby tournaments, softball and basketball games, and recruited one on one.

"We robbed other trades. Because we are a stable company, we were able to recruit away from other trade jobs. I've got feelers out all over the place. We recruited from other places such as the fire department, police, rock climbing clubs and health clubs. We sent out brochures, offered training sessions and held clinics through high school physical education prorams. We strategized a lot. Good recruitment ideas have taken years to develop.

"Once recruited, we bring women into a preapprenticeship program. We find that increasingly necessary because not all women have qualifications and history. We researched and taught them how to exercise and how to be strong enough to get through climbing school. They needed to know how to survive leaning out, turning on a pole, thirty feet up in the air. It's harder than the phone company because it's higher and you are dealing with 22600 volts of electricity. Heavy cross arms (4 by 4s at the tops of poles holding wires and insulators) have to be lifted or held in laps while women worry about energized wire around them.

"Once Seattle City Lights put in the preapprenticeship program, they came out on the other end four years later with 20 to 30 percent female employment in the trades in all the jobs including meters, carpenters, construction electrician and cable splicer. They graduated three line workers last year. They lose about 25 percent of the women in the pretraining but they used to lose them all.

"To reinforce the program they have done a lot of diversity training. Integration of women is a daily part of life here. It is reinforced organizationally by things such as awards. Increasing women in trades is not something you can do two days per year. For example, the climbing instructor won an award which was part of our reinforcement and respect program. We promote women. Our current CEO is a black female. That makes a lot of difference. This all started in 1987. We followed women around with camcorders. I was really moved by it because what the women do is so amazing.

"It's hard to get a profile of women who do that. But I know it's harder for women if they have children. People question whether you will live. It's so physically demanding and scary."

Vivian Price, Electrical Journeyman, Ph.D. Candidate, Teacher at Los Angeles Trade Technical College, Member IBEW Local 11, Elected Chair of District II of Local 11

Vivian's story offers insight into some significant patterns of female apprenticeships. She started working at a nontraditional job when she was older and had less attractive work experiences as her frame of reference. Her determination was based on difficult past jobs and the hope of a certified portable skill.

"I was thirty-five years old when I entered the apprenticeship program. Prior to that I had worked many places. I knew I no longer wanted to work for one company. I had worked in Long Beach for two years, as an industrial electrician in a maintenance local. My job was dirty, smelly, carcinogenic, with constant harassment which wore me down. That one place was with the same guys, same bullshit, same bosses, constant harassment. I finally decided I don't want to be here in thirty years. Even though, after a few years, some of the guys started to accept me, I didn't feel there was ever going to be an openness to women at the refinery.

"It helped I was older and had difficult work experiences, so I saw the advantages of the apprenticeship.

"I was highly motivated by the idea that if I went through an apprenticeship I would have the skills and I could work when and where I wanted to, relatively speaking. One thing that helped was a support system of friends. I could tell my problems to them and find solutions.

"I applied to the Electrical Construction Union and got accepted and reported to the hall where they gave me papers to report to a job at the airport. I went to school two nights a week for four years.

"I was determined, because I had been in male dominated jobs and worked with tools in a refinery. I loved the idea that when I was a journeyman I could quit a job I didn't like and go back to the union hall and get another job. This is a luxury you can earn, going through the construction apprenticeship."

United States Army

The United States Army, with its well defined hierarchy, alleged meritocracy and commitment to federal equal opportunity regulations, offers us another example of women's success in nontraditional roles. How do the dual impulses of such an old traditionally male establishment fused with federally mandated and regulated equal access play out to afford women freedom to land where their interest dictates?

Ninety-one percent of all the specifically military Army career fields are open to women. 65 percent of all Army positions (which would include ground combat) are open. The only positions not open to women are direct combat such as infantry and artillery. Currently women comprise 12.6 percent of the active Army, 7.7 percent of the Army national guard and 21 percent of the Army reserve.

In 1942, the Women's Army Auxiliary Corps began official entrance of women into the Army. Historically, the largest category of women has been in the medical services as nurses, doctors and medical technicians. However, over the past ten years, there has been an increase in women from 52 to 65 percent in open military positions, such as military police, engineers, road builders, heavy equipment operators and signal unit communications workers. By April 1993 combat aviation was finally open to women—primarily affecting women officers.

Major Linda Ritchie says women have done well in the Army. They re-enlist at higher rates than men and their success rate in getting promotions and special school assignments has been consistently excellent.

She attributes this success to the fact that the criteria are "right out there." It is clear to everyone what they must do to achieve. They don't need to rely on hidden agendas, politics and buddies—so often the case in the private sector.

Margaret Ferguson, one of the first WAVES entering the Navy during World War II, Seventy-two years old

Margaret Ferguson gives us a glimpse of what it was like in 1943, as one of the first groups of women who entered the armed services in jobs heretofore the exclusive domain of men. She had youth and a sense of patriotic duty to bolster her courage.

"The truth of the matter is that I don't think anyone knew what to do with us. It was all kind of made up as we went along.

"I had a sense that this was pioneering. We were patriotic and cared about our country and we had an obligation, like the men had an obligation. We were pioneers because women had never done this before. I knew it was important. Otherwise, they wouldn't be guarding us like they were. I knew I was making a contribution.

"To get from Sugar Camp to where we worked in Dayton, we had to march down the hill. You can imagine how the townspeople reacted to seeing a group of women marching down the hill. They had 75,000 airmen at Wright and Patterson airfields and only about thirty WAVES marching down the hill. They thought we were 'adorable.' They would invite us to dinner and holidays or pick us up. We didn't have to walk back; they would give us rides and cart us back. They welcomed us. Who ever saw women doing this? It made you feel like a celebrity. I feel very proud still. Today women do this all the time, but in those days women didn't. It was adventuresome to be that age and go across the country on your own. I felt like I was doing my duty. I think it's hard to understand today because now women are so free, but in those days it was really unusual for women to be doing this.

"I enlisted because all the boys were going away and I had a boyfriend who was drafted. I didn't want to be at home with all the boys gone. When everybody had gone to war, there was no reason to stay home. Being in the Navy seemed like a big adventure. I had never been away from home before. I didn't know anybody else specifically going into the Navy. But it was a very patriotic period. You wanted to do something to help the country. WAVES had been going for only about six months. I just went to the naval office to enlist. A first batch of WAVES had been trained in the Midwest about six months earlier. I was in the second batch. Of course I chose the Navy, everybody knew the Navy was more selective. One reason was because it was smaller. The Army, thought to be a bunch of peasants, took everybody. The Navy had regulations—you had to take tests and be interviewed. Because I was in an intelligence unit I had to be investigated. They talked with neighbors I didn't even know, in Baltimore, the town where I was born.

"I went on a train from Los Angeles to New York with fifty other women. I didn't know any of them. I went all by myself. I was very adventuresome in those days, more so than now. You were totally protected. It turned out to be lonely and I was homesick from time to time. But I never regretted my decision. I missed my father and brother and my boyfriend. I only saw him once during the war. It was a very maturing experience, because you were really on your own and had to prove yourself. You had to do the work and get along with people.

"We went from New York to Washington to Dayton, Ohio. There was a small group of women stationed in Dayton stationed working at National Cash Register at their summer training facility at Sugar Camp. We stayed in the cabins while they built dorms for the winter.

"I can't tell what I did; it was top secret. I literally signed an oath when I left the Navy that I would never divulge what I did. To give you an example of how secret it was we had two gay women in our group and someone saw them. They sent agents from the Office of Naval Intelligence and discharged them. (We were guarded by Marines. This is how secret it was.) The secret agents felt they would be blackmailed by the gay women about the work; they were that concerned about what we were doing. We were furious because we didn't really feel they were gay. Later the Commander took all the women into an auditorium and said, 'I'm going to tell you what these women were doing,' and he did. We were up in arms that they were being falsely accused.

"We had this group of women officers in charge of the us and they administered our housing, etc. In the summer more women came in. There were about 350 women working in a big crew in the summer, but only about thirty to fifty in the winter. Our work room was locked and it had to be unlocked even to go to the bathroom.

"In basic training in New York we lived in apartment houses in the Bronx. We were taught instruction in the Navy. We learned to march. We were taught how to salute. They talked to us about different kinds of ships. I remember nothing except thinking, 'Why are they teaching us all this stuff about ships?' when women weren't allowed on the ships. They weren't even allowed out of the United

Sates. I didn't resent that. I think having women in combat would be hard. Women have all kinds of physical problems. In the military you should be able to go anywhere, anytime, to go into trenches. Suppose you are in a ship out in the middle of an ocean. Is the Navy supposed to supply tampax? I don't think the Navy should ever be in a position where women could compromise emergency activity and I think they could.

"The women I worked with were very interesting. One became pregnant which was against Navy regulations. Had anyone found out, she would have been dismissed. However, she didn't tell anyone she was pregnant. She gave birth to the baby and nobody had realized she was pregnant. The Navy was responsible for that baby until it was eighteen because it was born to a WAVE while she was their responsibility. They had to support that child like the father, and I assume they did. She was a poor girl and had no way of supporting herself. That's why she didn't tell. It was a big deal for her to work in the guard shack for the WAVES.

"Women were from all over the United States. They were young without a heck of a lot of experience in life. My closest friend was from Whittier, California. I remember Pat Rose was from Brooklyn and she was an Irish-Jew. She was sort of wonderful, with a Brooklyn accent and a great sense of humor.

"In Dayton we could stay out until 8 P.M. and then we had to be back at the base. Marines guarded where we worked. Weekends we could get permission to go out in the evenings. I didn't go on dates. Two women who had the most dates and went out with men all the time were married and had husbands overseas. We thought that was unpatriotic. They ended up marrying the men they dated and wrote their husbands Dear John letters. Everyone thought it was terrible. There was very little leave time. Once I came home for seven days and toward the end of the war I got two weeks. We were paid about $37.00 per month.

"At the base we did physical conditioning, because we had an executive officer who was a gung ho health nut. She would take us out on the lawn and make us do calisthenics and we all complained about it. I don't think any of us could do push-ups.

"What I really learned was how to take orders. I had never done that in my life. The orders were like: what time to get up, what time to go to bed, what time to eat the food they put out for you, what to wear. Everything in your life was regulated. You had to be in uniform all the time.

"We went through basic training bootcamp. The tradition was for the trainers to be mean. At first they barked marching orders at us. But on Saturdays we were free to go into the city. Our trainer met up with one of the Navy women on the subway and struck up a conversation and that day and night they had some kind of nice time. After that he dated her and he became gentle and sweet and we had no other trouble. At first during training we marched in civilian clothes because we didn't have uniforms. I remember we marched by this reservoir with the wind blowing across the water. The women from California had just brought their regular clothes. We were freezing.

"My father thought of all the things I ever did in my life, the most wonderful was to be in the Navy. I didn't ask him before I joined I just came home and told him I enlisted. He was thrilled. However, others resented us because husbands and mothers felt women in the services took jobs at home and freed up men to go overseas into danger.

"I got a Presidential citation for the work we did, because the government felt it was that important to the victory of the armed forces. Everybody thought it was wonderful I was a WAVE and I was a celebrity in my circle."

Gail George, Army Communications, Thirty-two years old

After leaving the military Gail worked as an industrial pipe fitter with her dad and two brothers. She was so used to being one of the guys that she had a hard time adjusting to civilian life. "When I came back I wasn't used to working with all women." Now, she lives in Homestead, Florida and works in veterinary medicine.

"My first duty station, I was the only woman in my platoon out of thirty-five. I knew what to expect, because I grew up around guys. Never flirt; no sexual jokes. A lot of guys from different backgrounds, all they think is a women is good for only one thing. You had to start from the ground up, to show them you knew how to do things. It's all in the way you handle yourself. Some women felt you had to kiss up to make it easier. They missed out on a few things—being able to work with a man on an equal basis. Those women accepted themselves as lesser. But they didn't realize they didn't have to lower themselves to get by.

"It was either college or whatever. I wasn't into college. It wasn't enough of a challenge for me. I wanted to do something different. I had to find out about myself. Book knowledge was easy—it is written down. I wanted a challenge and to see if I was capable. I just went into a recruiter one day. I didn't tell my parents anything about it. The next day I took my parents out to dinner and told them. My dad was proud, but my mom wanted me to go to college. I signed up for delayed entry which means you go in a year later. I went out to California and lived with my sister, Sally, for a year. That was time I took getting my guts together, getting commitment. I had always had a fantasy kind of a romantic vision of a solider. Well, I wanted to see if I'm capable. Here I am ninety-six pounds. I wanted to know if could I survive. Nobody egged me on; I just went and did it.

"I was nineteen when I went into basic training at Fort Leonardwood, Missouri. I spent eight weeks there when they were conducting a test which involved training women with men—it gives you more ambition to try harder. It was the first time they had done it. (Now they separate training; we were the last.) They kept us separated for everything else, like living quarters, communicating and spending time together. Unfortunately, many of the people who signed up for the Army were running away from something—like you go to the Army to avoid jail. The Army was tough and you have to learn to adapt and survive all together. In college, you just worry about what you are going to wear. We learned physical agility, road marches, how to handle weapons, common soldier skills, everything to pass basic training. We did have different requirements, according to weight. I always said pound for pound I could match anybody. I had never done anything physical in my life. I had played softball and basketball but, come on. In basic training you were moving from the time you got up in the morning to the time you go to bed. The mental stress was hard, too, because they are molding you. You are taught to react. Mental duress was the hardest, because they are constantly hounding you, trying to separate you from the life you knew, trying to teach you. We learned communication, installing, communication system repairing. We took tests for skills and ability and I was assigned to communications. If I had been assigned to some kind of secretarial job I would have asked to be retested. I hate working indoors. This was much more fulfilling.

"I had a tactical job description, working with infantry. When I first got there I thought, 'Wow, it's all men.' They were very stand-offish. Every night one of the guys from the platoon would be standing at the door asking me out. You have to keep away from that, and keep everything on a professional basis. You have to watch what you do, because the first impression lasts. I made the decision I can either be a real asshole about it or deal with the commitment I made. If you go into a place and just watch how everybody acts, you can use that as an advantage. The military is so tight, and there are so many little politics, but, if you carry yourself in the right way, you succeed. This is what I decided to do and made the best of it.

"You have to have a sense of humor. Things happen that are unbelievable. You wouldn't have to deal with it in a civilian world. They always controlled what you wear, when you get up. If you feel like not getting up, you have to. I found out all I had to do is be early. When asked to do a job a lot of people say, 'I don't know if my squad can get this done.' I figured this out. You just say you can get it done and then go and figure out how to do it. They don't care how it is done as long as you do it. Boy, I used to think women whined a lot. You should see how the men whine. I just handed out tampons and asked the guys if they were on the rag. But it's psychological warfare. It's all in how you carry yourself.

"A lot of women are so used to it one way. Their brothers advanced or got the best education. They would think, I'm just a girl, so they don't try to advance themselves. I spent a lot of time showing my roommates how to advance themselves. As Neanderthal as men may be, women still stick themselves in that same hole. They think they're not going to go any further; so they try to please that trainer by flirting or smiling. A lot of women can't stand on their own two feet. I've always been around guys. I'm the youngest of two brothers and two sisters. I had a lot of freedom growing up.

"I worked right on the front lines during the war in Saudi Arabia. I had been sent to Germany when my unit in Maryland was shut down. I was in the soldier's boards competing for the highest recognition to reflect on my all male company. We did weapon firing, wore uniforms, knew Army regulations. I became solider of the year—first woman in USAER (European Theater). I was a communication specialist. If they go to war they can't get orders on who to fire on without me. They pick numbers. They don't care if you are a man or woman. They cover that up. My ambition was to become Sergeant Major of the Army. For that you have to be in a war, but since I had gone to Saudi Arabia, I could have been that. They weren't upholding the standards I was representing, though. Once I had enough knowledge about regulations, I was given more access to everything. I was disappointed they weren't following regulations. So I didn't re-enlist. A lot of leaving was just bad politics.

"I spent three years in tactical communications. Most of the time I was the only woman. During this time I did share rooms with women in different jobs, like running supply secretarial. Men were always jealous and felt women didn't belong there. You get an attitude from the men, because you don't let them in your pants. I had a few confrontations that were close to rape. In Germany, coming home from a function, one guy tried to have his way with me. I filed a complaint on him. I had no proof, but I thought, *I'm not going to take your crap.* They believed me, only because of my standing in that unit—I was one of the super soldiers. If I had been just one of the girls, they wouldn't have believed me.

"It was absolutely fun to have so much knowledge. These men actually listened to me. They had that faith in my ability. I had control of a lot of things. I volunteered for everything, seeing that the more information you had, the more doorways opened. People felt, *This woman knows what she is doing.* It frustrates me that everybody has capability but most people don't try to use it."

Nobody knows for sure the best way to include women in the work scheme; trial and error has become our teacher. Women's own past job frustrations inspire them to try new avenues. From the failures we can see what pitfalls to avoid and from the successes we can learn what works. Only then can we cushion the paths for the next line of women.

Recent examples show it can be done. We take heart in the successes of brave and innovative companies that experiment in their efforts to make a place for nontraditional women. Individuals open their hearts to us by describing their own difficult struggles to push through the glass walls. We learn by both their success and failure. The road is jerky. Ironically, a lot of progress gets made from situations when terrible injustices result in court orders.

Conclusions

On reviewing the history and lives of these women a few common themes emerged. There are women at work in non-traditional jobs all across the country. The strongest areas are supported by tradeswomen's organizations. Drawn from a national geography and social consciousness supported by federal legislation, they are found at meetings in big urban areas like New York and Boston in the Northeast, Ohio and Illinois in the Midwest, Washington and California on the West Coast. Concentrated in greater numbers in big urban areas, nontraditional women work at federal buildings as well as large construction projects. However, they are not necessarily represented by any greater percentage of the population. Today's farms are also dotted with nontraditional women installing wires above and underground, and fighting fires.

Small clusters of blue collar women appear in the South; however, the South has fewer strong tradeswomen's associations and fewer demonstration programs to support and promote women. We theorized that old Southern Cultural bias about women and appropriate feminine images are probably still present.

Although it has been argued that macho unions restrict women from entering nontraditional jobs, the unions also train, apprentice, certify, regulate, counsel and refer. However, unions have a tougher time in the southern right-to-work states and thus deny women one potential avenue of entrance into these jobs.

As a group, blue collar women represent a phenomena cutting across cultural and ethnic backgrounds. They mirror America's ethnic diversity. For example, among those we interviewed were: Hispanic painters and police; Black oil rig workers, auto mechanics, sanitation workers and ditch diggers; Asian electricians; Indian truck drivers and white plumbers, firefighters, auto service writers. Their's is a diversity greater than is found in the ranks of successful managerial women and certainly worth tracking in the future.

Age appears to be a factor. Women entering these trades are older and experienced in the vicissitudes of low paying unskilled unsuitable work. Thus, the high percentage of women in their late twenties and early thirties, previously from traditional jobs, are just starting to taste what the nontraditional world has to offer. Blue collar work is not seen as glamorous, especially to young women coming out of high school. High school graduates do not leap at the chance to take nontraditional jobs in their search to finding ways to launch their lives. However, the reality of the lack of other opportunities tempers their dreams and centers the women's attention on the good pay and benefits, freedom and the opportunity to learn a skill. Nontraditional work becomes more appealing as the women mature and have increasing responsibilities. They seem to grow into these jobs.

There is not one nontraditional woman with a single defining physical characteristic. They come in all sizes, shapes and hues, with and without education and with different sexual affinities.

Yet, their personality profiles reveal some ubiquitous similarities. Their background includes skills or experiences that are transferable to nontraditional work—such as growing up on a farm around heavy machinery, wrestling brothers, learning to fix things or living as a single woman in substandard housing. Most never stop to think about how the things they did growing up and in the normal course of their lives translate into job preparation and training.

We often see dysfunctional backgrounds: alcoholism, parental divorce, tough marriages and early pregnancies make them different from any women in the mainstream. Plus the inability to earn enough funds for themselves and/or their families to live on creates strong needs.

It's a rough life they choose. Physically and psychologically these women are beaten and battered, pushed and strained. They have mental bruises along with the scars left by the physical assault their bodies take. It takes a toll. They either come from toughness or develop a rough exterior quickly on the job.

The roughness sets them apart. As a group they are idiosyncratic. They are odd. Different. Counter culture. They are a tiny percentage of working women in the world' roughest, male-oriented terrain.

Yet, they are remarkably unself-conscious. Unaware that they are odd or different, they willingly tell us their life stories. Many are not conscious of the enormous shock their roles send to the whole social system. All know to some degree the struggle they are up against but few know the change they represent for society. They hear snide comments of customers, from coworkers who don't want to partner with them, from jealous wives and disapproving mothers. Often we noted a sadness in the distance they felt from the norm.

SOME RECENT EXAMPLES · 238

That they take society's rough jobs and crawl around on their bellies in the dirt is not lost on them. These subtle messages make them tougher. But they continue to earn their money and live their lives. It is this relative lack of self-consciousness that allows them to continue working and living these nontraditional patterns.

Not only is their work nontraditional, so are their many lives. While the traditional American family of a working father, domestic mother and two children gradually fades into distant memory, nontraditional women have symbolically leapt over a precipice six feet wide with sheer canyons on each edge. Many do not live in traditional families but as gay couples, unwed parents, single women and sole bread winners in numerous nontraditional arrangements.

As a whole, most of these women were unconventional even as children. Their background forms the foundation for their nontraditional work and present lives. On the one hand, many didn't have niceties and security of the traditional intact families. On the other, they were not and are not tied down by restraining convention of those traditional patterns.

We note that these nontraditional jobs often offer one of the only reasonable hopes for an alternative life, for nontraditional women who are by nature, interest, inclination or circumstances, cast out of the mainstream. Yet as more nontraditional women enter these jobs, they want more like minded women on the job with them.

The major motive for working these jobs is *money*! The financial gains for most women working nontraditional jobs are enormous. We also learned that most of the women like their work. Many of the successful ones have a sense of gratitude for employment that allows them new opportunities, that trains them, pays well and matches their interests and abilities.

Finally, we sensed a growing pride in them because of their mastery of their skills, the hazards and the problems of their occupations. They have had the ability to withstand, endure and ultimately prevail in rugged terrain. They have been pioneering trailblazers succeeding in living their lives more profitably and creatively, because they didn't accept the "men only" stereotype of blue collar work.

RESOURCES

Books

Baker, Laura. *Wanted: Women in War Industry.* New York: EP Dutton and Co, Inc., 1943.

Barandall, Rosalyn, Gordon, Linda & Reverb, Susan ed. *America's Working Women: A Documentary History 1600-to the Present.* Vintage. 1976.

Clawson, Augusta. *Shipyard Diary of a Woman Welder.* New York: Penguin Books.

Doro, Sue. *Heart, Home & Hard Hats.* Minneapolis: Midwest Villages and Voices, 1986.

Doro, Sue. *Blue Collar Goodbyes.* Freedom, CA: Paper-Mache Press, 1993.

Drake, Constance. *Time for a Change: A Women's Guide to Nontradtional Occupations.* Technical Educational Resource Centers. September, 1981.

Fabulous Century : 1940–50. Time Life Books, Inc. : Alexandria VA, 1969.

Fox, Frank. *Madison Avenue Goes to War: The Strange Military Career of American Advertising 1941-1945*. Provo, Utah: Brigham Young University Press, 1975.

Honey, Maureen. *Creating Rosie the Riveter: Class, Gender, and Propaganda During World War II*. Amherst: The University of Massachusetts Press, 1984.

Lederer, Muriel. *Blue Collar Jobs for Women : A Complete Guide to Getting Skilled and Getting a Higher Paying Job in the Trades*. New York: E.P. Dutton, 1979.

Linderstein, Mary. *Blue Collar Women: Pioneers on the Male Frontier*. Garden City, NY: Walshok Anchor Press, 1981.

Marcus, Greil. *Lipstick Traces: A Secret History of the 20th Century*. Cambridge: Harvard University Press, 1989.

Martin, Molly. *Hard-Hatted Women: Stories of Struggle and Success in the Trades*. Seattle: The Seal Press, 1988.

Michaelson, Maureen R. *Women and Work: Photographs & Personal Writings*. Kedding, MA: New Sage Press, 1986.

"National Women's History Project." *Women's History Network News*, October 1991. Issue #32.

Pinkstaff, Marlene Arthur; Wilkinson, Anna Bell. *Women at Work: Overcoming Obstacles*. Addison Wesley Co. 1979.

Ricci, Larry. *High Paying Blue Collar Jobs for Women*. New York: Ballantine Books, 1981.

Sealander, Judith. *As Minority Becomes Majority: Federal Reaction to the Phenomenon of Women in the Work Force, 1020-1963*. London: Greenwood Press, 1983

Stein & Company. *Case History on Female Employment Initiative*. Chicago.

Wetherby, Terry, Ed. *Conversations: Working Women Talk about Doing a Man's Job.* Milbrae, CA: Les Femmes, 1977.

Leaflets

Employment and Training Administration. Bureau of Apprenticeship and Training. Apprenticeship information, 1990.

Employment and Training Administration. Bureau of Apprenticeship and Training. Apprenticeship: Past and Present, 1987.

Employment and Training Administration. Bureau of Apprenticeship and Training. National Apprenticeship Program, 1987

Employment and Training Administration. Bureau of Apprenticeship and Training. Setting Up An Apprenticeship Program, 1989.

Employment and Training Administration. Bureau of Apprenticeship and Training. Women in Traditionally Male Jobs: The Experience of Ten Public Utility Companies, R&D Monograph 65, 1978.

U.S. Department of Labor, Women's Bureau. The Coal Employment Project: How Women Can Make Breakthroughs Into Nontraditional Industries. Washington D.C., 1985.

U.S Department of Labor, Women's Bureau. Directory of Non-Traditional Training and Employment Programs Serving Women. Washington D.C., 1991.

U.S. Department of Labor, Women's Bureau. Women in Nontraditional Careers (WINC): Curriculum Guide. Washington D.C., 1984.

U.S. Department of Labor, Women's Bureau. Women in the Skilled Trades. Washington D.C., 1990.

U.S. Department of Labor, Women's Bureau. A Working Woman's Guide to Her Job Rights. Washington D.C., 1992.

Magazine Articles

Edwards, Don. "Rosie the Riveter Might Not Get a Job Today." *Newsday*, May 4, 1988.

Hardy, Zoe Tracy. "What Did You Do in the War, Grandma?" A Flashback to August, 1945. Ms. August 1985, p. 1, 4-5.

Magazines/Newsletters

Dollars and Sense Journal

Tradeswomen Magazine.
 P.O. Box 40664 San Francisco, CA 94140
(415) 821-7334

Equal Means Magazine
Bay Area July 1993 MS Foundation

Sojourner Magazine
42 Seaverns Avenue
Jamaica Plain, MA 01230
(617) 524-0415

Videos

Antalocy, Stephanie. Trade Secrets: Blue Collar Women Speak Out. 1985. 23 minutes.

Citron, Michelle. *What You Take for Granted.* 1983. 75 minutes.

Gonasci, Sharon & Velasco, Dorothy. *Railroad Women.* 1988. 30 minutes.

Mon Valley Media. *Women of Steel.* 1984. 28 minutes.

Sources

Apprenticeship & Non-traditional Employment for Women (ANEW)

P.O. Box 2490
Renton, WA 98056
206- 235-2212
A five month training program in basic skills in nontraditional trades
for women. General all around background in carpentry, electrical,
mechanical, plumbing, sheet metal, hand and power tools, tool
identification, physical conditioning, employment issues, resumes,
job interviews, employment counseling. Funded by Seattle-King
County Private Industry Council.

Building Trades Apprenticeship Preparation Program
1074 E. La Cadena Drive
Riverside, CA 92501
714-686-6700 William Rogers
Provides trade orientation, career counseling, academic tutoring and
oral interview techniques to prepare individuals to successfully
compete for apprenticeship jobs in the construction industry.

Bureau of Apprenticeship and Training Regional Offices
Federal Building, Room 715
71 Stevenson Street
San Francisco, CA 94105
415- 744-6580
David Turner, Director
Promotes and develops apprenticeship programs. Sets training
standards, registers, monitors, and recognizes apprenticeships.
Assists industry in setting up skill training programs, primarily for
blue collar jobs. Makes information available. Keeps statistics on
apprentices in programs, (occupations, minorities, sex, age,
education). About 70 percent of apprentices included in national
data. Twenty-seven states have their own apprentice laws.

Bureau of Apprenticeship and Training
U.S. Department of Labor Room N-4649
200 Constitution Avenue
Washington D.C. 20210
202- 219-5921
Headquarters to provide guidance to the field, working with national
concerns, coordinating activities with Department of Labor,

recognizing new apprenticable occupations, coordinating with Department of Defense.

Boston Tradeswomen Network
P.O. Box 255
Dorchester, MA 02122
617- 288-3710
A support group for women in the trades.

California Department of Fair Employment & Housing
322 West 1st Street
Suite 2126
Los Angeles, CA 90012-3112
213- 897-1997
Takes complaints of employment discrimination and attempts to mediate resolution. Only 1 percent end in court.

California Division of Apprenticeship Standards
107 S. Broadway
Los Angeles, CA
213- 897-1385
A good resource for finding out which apprenticeships are currently accepting applications.

Center for Working Life
600 Grand Avenue
Oakland, CA 94610
510- 893-7343
Nonprofit organization which provides a variety of worker-based services, facilitates support groups and provides individual counseling for women who work in nontraditonal jobs.

Century Freeway Women's Employment Program
700 North Bullis Road, Room 12
Compton, CA 90221
310- 639-9181
Actively promotes the placement of women in apprenticeship jobs related to highway work, such as carpenter, cement mason, operating engineer and ironworker.

East Bay Painters - Joint Apprenticeship Program
600 Robel Avenue
Pinole, CA 94564
510- 724-3200
415- 647-8330
916- 393-2742
Enrolls for a four-year apprenticeship program in the painting
   industry (Tradeswomen applicants are invited to apply).

Electric Women
1836 Nipomo Avenue
Long Beach, CA 90815
A trade magazine for women eletricians.

Gender Equity Program
33 Gough Street
San Francisco, Ca 94103
415- 241-2308
Offers counseling and workshops to promote access to vocational
   training. Designed to help individuals find employment in fields
   that are nontraditional for their gender.

also at:
Smith Research Center Rm 126
2805 East Tenth Street
Bloomington, IN 47405
812-855-8104
Provides resources and technical assistance to counselors, teachers and
   students in area vocational schools and postsecondary institutions,
   to promote nontraditional occupational choices.   A mentor
   program, it matches up students with nontraditionally employed
   adults to foster encouragement and support for career decisions.

International Brotherhood of Electrical Workers (IBEW) Women's
   Group
2223A Ocean
Long Beach, CA 90803
310-438-9493

Vivian Price
Note: Contact Vivian for programs such as Summer Institute of
   Union Women. Support group and political/civic organization.
   IBEW Local 11 meets monthly in downtown L.A.

Jefferson Parish Vocational-Technical School
5200 Blair Drive
Metairie, LA 70001
318-736-7077
Occupational training including auto body repair, carpentry, welding,
   electrical, computer electronics, air conditioning and refrigeration.

Job Corps Regional Offices
James Matthews - Regional Director
U.S. Department of Labor - Job Corps
71 Stevenson Street
San Francisco, CA 94105
415-744-6658
A training organization for young adults between 16 to 24 to receive
   their GED or vocational training. Applicants must be poverty
   level.

Kansas City Tradeswomen
4115 Blue Parkway
Kansas City, MO 64130
816-831-2719
A support group for tradeswomen.

Los Alamos National Laboratory - IIRD-1
Los Alamos, NM 87545
505-667-8730 Employee Relations
Resources on sexual harassment in the workplace. Videotapes,
   handbooks.

National Association of Women in Constuction NAWIC
327 South Adams
Fort Worth, TX 76104
817-877-5551

Resources for continuing education, legislative awareness, employment referral, networking. Publishes a membership directory and organizes annual conventions.

National Tradeswomen Network (NTN) Kai Douglass
Tradeswomen Inc.
P.O. Box 40664
San Francisco, CA 94140
415- 821-7334

A tradeswomen-based network of organizations and individuals committed to increasing the numbers of women entering and working in nontradtional blue-collar occupations.

The National Women's History Project
7738 Bell Road
Windsor, CA 95492
707- 838-6000
707- 838-0478

Provides resources and information on women's history and political/economic concerns.

New Women's Law Center
11 South Main Street
Seattle, WA 98104
206- 682-9552

Nonprofit law organization to advance the legal rights of women through impact (high visibility) litigation, legislation, free information and legal referral, seminars and workshop in organizations and high schools/education. Runs a family law clinic.

New York Tradeswomen
P.O. Box 870
Peck Slip
New York, NY 10272
212- 227-2981

A support group for women in the trades providing meetings, discussion, newsletter.

Nontraditional Employment for Women (NEW)

243 West 20th Street
New York, NY 10011
212- 627-6252

This organization runs two programs to aid women in nontraditional jobs. Blue Collar Prep is a 10 week training program in carpentry, eletricity, health, construction terminology, blue print reading, job readiness, women and work issues. Upon program completion there is job placement. Requirements include high school diploma or GED and drivers license. If applicants don't qualify they may take Edge which is a 6 month program to prepare for GED.

Northern California Surveyors Joint Apprenticeship Committee
8105 Capwell Drive
Oakland, CA 94621
510-635-3255

Train apprentices for occupation of field survey.

Occupational/Skills Centers
Operated by local school districts or community colleges. Offers wide range of classes open to all at no cost or minimal charges. Offer on sliding fee scale.

Office of Federal Contract Compliance Programs,
Employment Standards Adminstration
U.S. Department of Labor
Washington D.C. 20210.
202-219-9471.

Enforces federal construction goals monitored in compliance reviews. Check to see if contractor has met availability goals for women in minority and evaluate good faith efforts to determine if contractors are doing all they can to recruit, hire and train women and minorities. Individuals can bring individual complaints with regional offices if they feel discriminated against.

Oil, Chemical and Atomic Workers International (OCAW) Union
Local 1-547
Women's Committee
4637 Manhattan Beach Blvd.
P.O. Box 66

Lawndale, CA 90260
310- 645-1311 Sylvia Zapata
Support group.

Operating Engineers Women's Support Group
335 Haddon Road
Oakland, CA 94606
510- 835-2511 Beth
510- 636-1134 Carla
Support group for women engineers.

Preparation, Recruitment, Employment Program, Inc. (PREP, Inc.)
1095 Market Street - Suite 712
San Francisco, CA 94103
415- 864-3255 Carole Brown-Lewis
Recruits, prepares and places women in nontraditional employment.
  Offers testing, guidance, labor market information and preparation
  for placement in occupations.

Sacramento Tradeswomen
Donna Lopez
1551 36th Sstreet
Sacramento, CA 95816
916- 456-5555
Support group for tradeswomen.

Seattle City Light
1015 3rd Street
Seattle, WA 98104
206-625-3000
Seattle electrical company pioneering and hiring a high percentage of
  nontraditional women.

Seal Press
P.O. Box 13
Seattle, WA 98111
206-283-7844
Feminist publishers of women authors.

Southern California Tradeswomen Network
78 North Marengo Ave.
Pasadena, CA 91101
818-796-6870
Support group for tradeswomen providing workshops, referrals,
newsletters.

State Departments of Labor and Industry
U.S. Department of Labor, Women's Bureau.
200 Constitution Ave. N.W. S3002.
Washington D.C. 20210
202-219-6611.
Provides research and representation for women's employment issues.
Provides guidance to regional offices.

State Divisions of Apprenticeship Standards.
See state directories for listings.

Stein & Company
227 West Monroe Street
Suite 3400
Chicago, Ill. 60606
312-372-4240
Construction company that has voluntarily exceeded limits in hiring
women in nontraditional jobs and pioneered a program to increase
nontraditional women.

Tradeswomen Inc.
P.O. Box 40664B
San Francisco, CA 94140
510-649-6260
Provides peer and advocacy support for women in blue-collar and
nontraditional occupations; serves as resource and referral agency to
community about issues affecting women in trades. Provides
information on apprenticeships, gender and racial discrimination,
sexual harassment, training and employment opportunities,
self-employed tradeswomen referrals, legal and governmental
referrals and technical assistance to individuals and agencies.

Tradeswomen Research and Education Project
9 Rockview Street
Jamaica Plain, MA 02130
617- 522-3749 Susan Eisenberg
Women in the workplace: oral history, policy, poetry.

U.S. Department of Labor Women's Bureau
Madeline Mixer, Regional Administrator
71 Stevenson Street, Suite 927
San Francisco, CA 94105
415-744-6679
Monitors working conditions of women, studies trends or needs, distributes fact sheet and provides information.

Vocational Equity Program
9600 Sims Drive
El Paso, TX 79925-7225
915-595-5714
Vocational equity specialists make presentations on nontraditional high wage jobs to students in secondary classrooms. Specialists work to prepare quality work force for the State. Publishes newsletter to promote sex equity in vocational education and runs sex equity and single parents in vocation education/conference.

Wider Opportunities for Women (WOW)
1325 G Street NW
Washington, DC 20005
202-737-5764
National women's organization focusing on women's employment and training. A national network of individuals and organizations which receive a newsletter, updates on policy related to women and employment, eligiblity for projects aimed at increasing nontraditional employment and training and literacy for women.

Wildland Fire Fighter Apprenticeship Program
1760 Creekside Oaks Drive, Suite 150
Sacramento, CA 95833
916-648-3000 Diane Miller
Teaches fire fighting skills during an 18 month apprenticeship.

Women and Manual Trades
254 Featherstone Street
London, England EC1Y8RT
Write for a conference booklet containing a description of projects and
    abstracts of papers presented at a 1993 conference on the
    Employment and Creation for Women in the Building Trades
    Across Europe.

Women at Work
78 North Marengo Avenue
Pasadena, CA 91101
818-796-6870 Gina Friarman-Hunt, Betty Ann Jansson.
Provides career information and job resources for all fields; career
    counseling, occupational testing, evening workshops and special
    programs in a variety of fields, including nontraditional areas. Also
    has a Southern California Trades support group that meets at DWP.
    Support resource: Wednesday drop-in counseling.

Women Building the Bronx
Karen R. Brown
The MOSAIC Center
1257 Ogden Avenue
Bronx, NY 10452
212-590-1010
A new initiative training female students in construction and building
    maintenance and prepares them for positions in these fields.

Women in Skilled Trades
3362 22nd Street
Oakland, CA 94612
510- 891-9393
Training in carpentry, sheet metal, welding, electrical, basic machining
    and pipe trades.

Women in the Trades
1044 Mississippi Blvd.
Memphis, TN 38126
901-942-4653

A support group for women in the trades.

Women in Trades and Technology
3925 Sunset Drive
Jackson, MS 39042
601-366-1405
Training for women in trades and technology through Hinds
    Community College.

Women in Trades Fair
P.O. Box 837
Seattle, WA 98111-0837
The fair brings together working women, advocates, apprenticeship
    programs, employers and educators to answer questions and offer
    support and mentorship to women. They are held in Oregon and
    Washington in April and May of each year.

Women's Business Network, Inc. (WBN)
510- 482-8583
Nonprofit organization dedicated to the economic empowerment of
    all women. Committed to helping women reach their economic
    goals, providing business opportunities for women of all cultures
    and experiences and building a low interest loan fund to help
    women start and expand their businesses.

Women's Employment Services and Training (WEST)
2306 J Street, Suite 200
Sacramento, CA 95816
916- 441-4207 Nancy Baril
Provides training to women by placing them with private sector
    businesses to receive paid on-the-job training. Trainees become
    full-time, regular employees when training is completed; WEST
    reimburses the employer up to 50 percent of wages paid during
    training.

Women's Maritime Association
1619 Pike Place #12
Box 743
Seattle, WA 98101

206-441-5678

Support network for maritime women from stewards to skippers. Engages in lobbying to seek solutions to safety, healthy, discrimination etc.

Women's Project
2224 Main Street
Little Rock, AR 72206
501-3725113

Works with other organizations to develop a nontraditional training program for young women between ages 18 and 25; provides support information and training job placement to women released from Department of Corrections.

Women's Training and Support Center/ En Trade
P.O. Box 6506
Albany, CA 94706
510-649-6260

Provides training and support for women wanting to learn trades. Offers a 16 week job training program and short one week classes, some in conjunction with Habitat for Humanity, to allow women to "get their feet wet" and see if they want this type of work. Offers one day empowerment classes on such things as home repair.